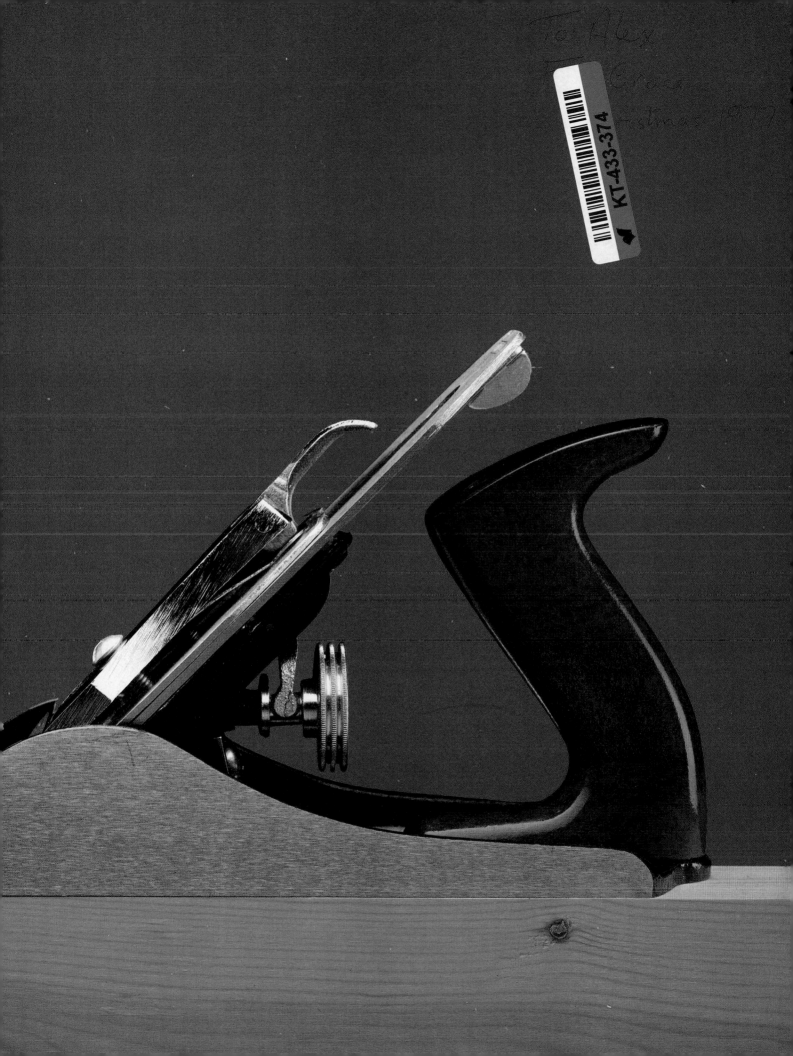

The All Colour
D.I.Y. BOO

Contributors & editors include
Harry Butler, Ron Grace
& Geoffrey Burdett

Sundial

Contents

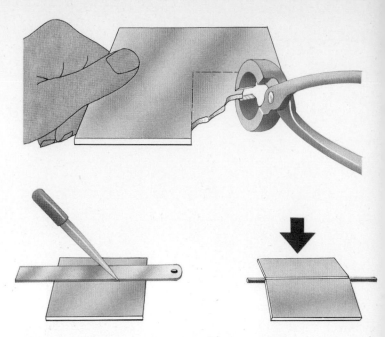

Structure

Services to the Home

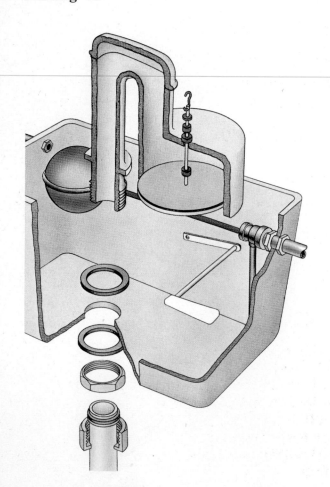

Illustrators

Allard Design:
Terry Allan
Lyn Brooks
Roger Courthold
pages 42–53, 82–111, 136–165
Bill Easter
pages 54–79
Osborne/Marks
pages 80–81
Michael Robinson
pages 28–41
Ralph Stobart
pages 10–27, 112–135

Title spread photographed by
John Rigby

First published in 1977 by
Sundial Books Limited,
59 Grosvenor Street,
London W.1.

© 1977 Hennerwood Publications Limited

ISBN 0 904230 21 X

Printed in Great Britain by Jarrold & Sons Limited

Woodworking

Decorating

Editor **Ron Grace**

Contributors
Geoff Burdett
Harry Butler
Roger DuBern
Ernest Hall
Alf Martensson
John McGowan
Ron Page

Introduction

As an enthusiastic do-it-yourselfer, willing to tackle any job in or around the house, I am probably more aware than most of the need for accurate and practical information about the various projects being attempted.

Not only is the cost of having a job done extremely high, but people need to be creative. And in doing so, they nearly always make a first class job because time is not important and they have to live with the end product for some time to come. So I have tried to cover a wide variety of subjects, each described in such a way as to give the absolute beginner sound basic information, yet progressing deeply enough to give those already knowledgeable a wider understanding.

For advice about problems, do-it-yourself magazines have comprehensive services and there are a number of specialist trade organisations who can help. Do not forget to contact your local council as you have to get their approval before carrying out structural work; however they are usually very helpful whatever you plan to do. The following chapters have been written by experts in the various fields and carefully planned and prepared to give you the maximum information in simple terms.

True do-it-yourselfers take care, advice, time and trouble to find out the right way to do a job.

Good luck,

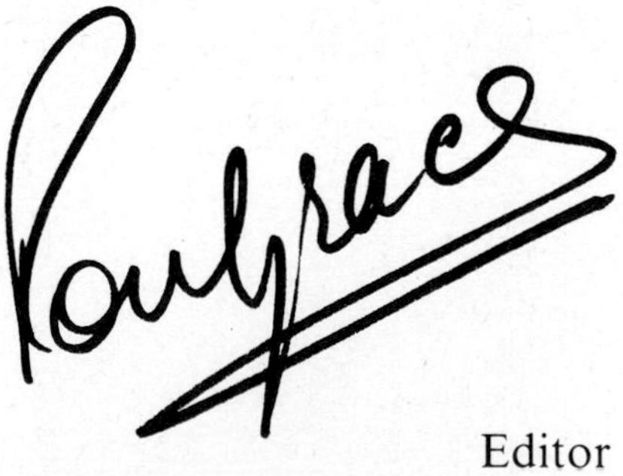

Editor

Please Don't Ignore This Page . . . It Is Not Worth Taking Risks

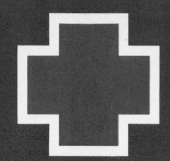

Safety First

Too often people take notice of safety warnings only after they have had an accident, so it cannot be stressed too strongly at this point that before you start to do anything at all you should stop and think about the tools, materials and chemicals you may be going to use, the heights and weights involved, and look ahead to the consequences of your actions.

Always read instructions supplied and read the vital safety measures necessary for particular jobs. They are outlined below, and throughout each chapter precautions and safety advice are included where relevant with every step. All electrical work in particular must be carried out with great care and in a competent manner. It is wise to learn about the general working principles of any subject before starting a particular job, so do not let yourself be distracted by new projects and repairs away from these words of advice—they are culled from my many years of experience both as a do-it-yourself journalist and a practical exponent of the art.

R.G.

- Always switch off and pull out the electric plug of an appliance before starting to do anything else.

- Check that you really have isolated any electrical equipment you are working on by testing with a neon test screwdriver.

- Never remove or interfere with the normal operation of safety guards on power tools.

- Disconnect tools from the electrical supply by pulling out the plugs before changing blades or bits.

- Keep cutting tools sharp; blunt tools frustrate the user and encourage incorrect techniques.

- Always keep fingers behind the cutting edge of a power tool; never allow any part of the body to be along the line of the cut.

- When working with power tools, clamp work securely, particularly metal workpieces.

- Wear the proper clothing. Never wear loose clothes, especially ties.

- Make sure ladders are secure before you climb.

- When working on a roof, use a proper roof ladder.

- On corrugated asbestos roofs, walk on a stout plank.

- Use proper equipment for access to high walls.

- Wear stout shoes when working on a ladder.

- When using floor tiling adhesives—or any flammable types—ensure that there is adequate ventilation and that there are no naked lights.

- Avoid inhaling chemical fumes, particularly when treating dry rot.

- When doing dusty work, wear a breathing mask.

- When working with asbestos products, read the safety hints published by the Asbestos Information Committee, in London.

- Glass fibre can irritate; wear protective clothing.

- When using a wire brush, hand or power, wear goggles to protect the eyes.

- Wear thick gloves when handling broken glass.

- Take extra care when using a blowlamp, especially in lofts and around eaves where birds' nests are often built.

- Don't put anything other than drinks in drink bottles. Children especially, often cannot tell the difference.

9

Structure
Roof structure and repairs

A damp patch on the ceiling is often the first sign of a leaking roof. Trace the fault before serious ceiling damage is caused by examining the roof from inside the loft. This inspection will enable you to pinpoint the source of the leak. Water will often trickle down the underside of a rafter causing a stain some distance from the original point of water entry.

Some roof troubles such as damage to slates or tiles can be spotted from ground level.

Getting to the roof

Choose a timber or alloy ladder that will extend at least two rungs above the eaves. A triple extension ladder will be easier to put up than the double extension type. For work over about 9m, a rope-operated ladder will be easier to erect. If the house has plastic gutters, a ladder stay will be required to hold the ladder away from the eaves because the gutter will allow the ladder to slip.

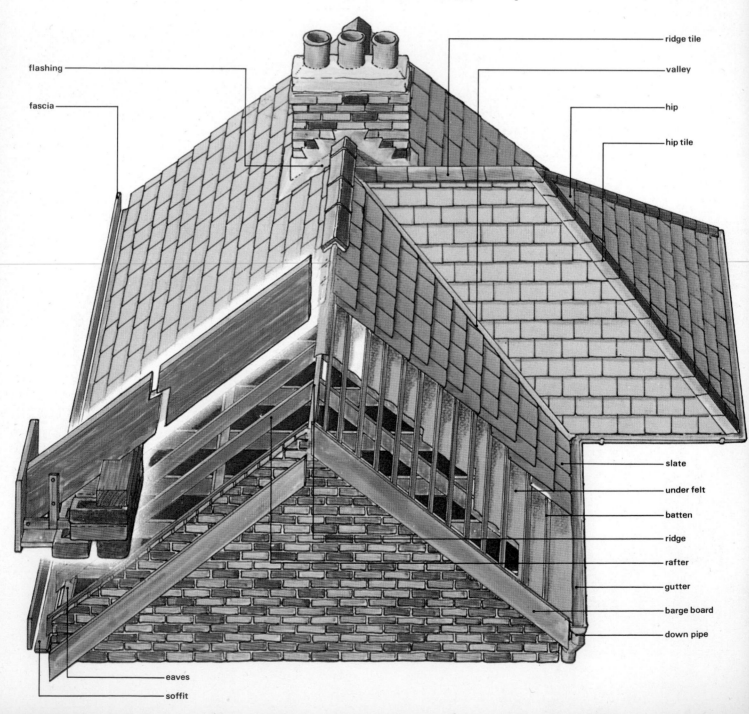

flashing

fascia

ridge tile

valley

hip

hip tile

slate

under felt

batten

ridge

rafter

gutter

barge board

down pipe

eaves

soffit

The distance from the foot of the ladder to the wall should be a quarter of the ladder height. For safety's sake secure the bottom of the ladder so it cannot slip or sink by adding pegs in soft ground or heavy weights against the foot of the ladder on hard ground.

Get someone to steady the ladder while you secure the top. It is best to lash the ladder to a stout screw eye fixed to the fascia.

Towers with working platforms up to about 12m can be hired. Over a height of 6m the tower must be securely tied to the house. As a general safety precaution against strong winds it is best to do this in any case. Check the manufacturer's recommended safe working height at the time of purchasing or hiring a tower. Many towers have outriggers to stabilise the base, so make sure there is room for these before obtaining the tower.

Roof coverings

Opposite: typical slate covered roof with a hipped extension. Below: this roof is covered with plain tiles which are laid in a similar manner to slates. All slates are nailed as, in this example, are the nibless tiles

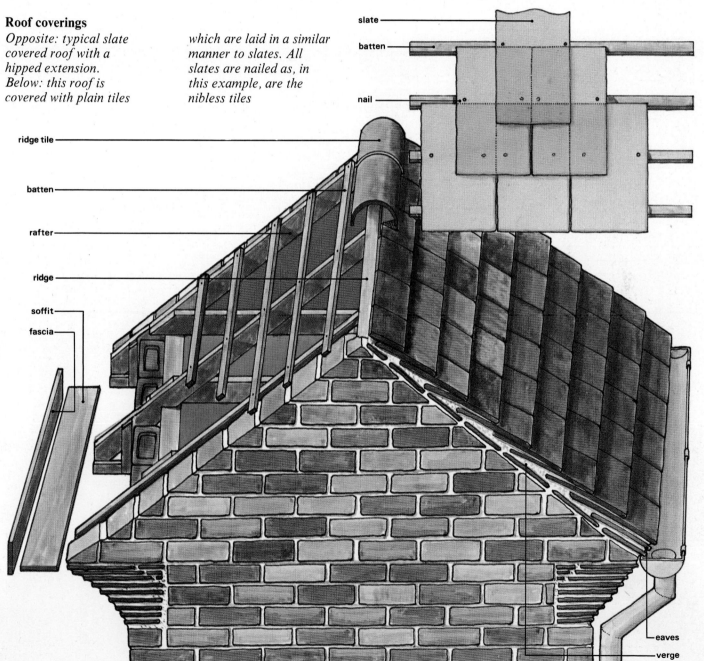

11

Proprietary roof ladder with tubular ridge hook

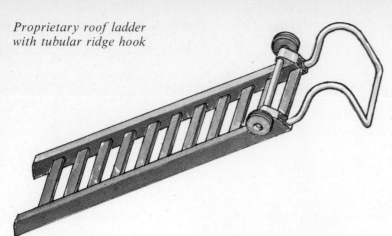

Home-made roof ladder with ridge hook of shelf brackets

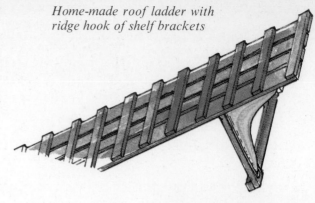

Slipping slate

Right: with the loose slate removed, a metal strip is fixed with the nail between two slates. Below: the slate is slipped into place over the metal strip. Below right: with the slate in its correct position the end of the strip is bent up and over to support the slate

Damaged slate

Right: to remove the damaged slate, a ripper is used to cut the holding nails. Below: the ripper hooked around a nail, a sharp tug will cut it. Below right: with both nails cut, the defective slate can be slipped out and a new one fitted using the hook technique

Larger damage

Right: the defective slates removed, the first new slate is positioned and fixed, starting at the bottom. Below: more slates are added, still working upwards. Below right: the final row cannot be nailed because they are slid into place. Metal strips are used to hold them

Extensive deterioration

To save stripping the whole roof a three-coat plus reinforcing treatment can be used to waterproof a roof which is in bad condition

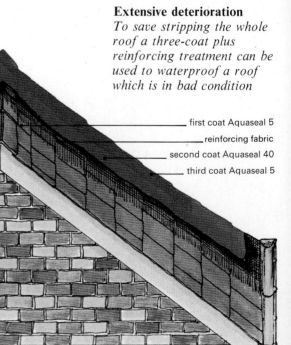

first coat Aquaseal 5
reinforcing fabric
second coat Aquaseal 40
third coat Aquaseal 5

Damaged tiles are removed with a bricklaying trowel

Once the nibs have been freed the tile slides out

One course of tiles in four is nailed to the battens

Lift the tile above and slide the new one in place

Half-round ridge tile

Inset: single-lap concrete tile

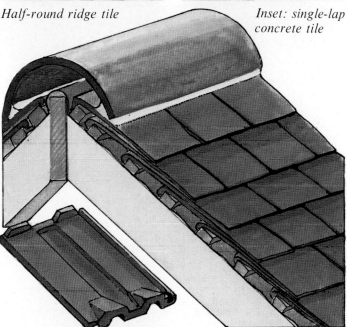

A loose vee-shape ridge tile is lifted clear

The old sand/cement mortar is cleaned off with a trowel

Careful use of hammer and cold chisel cleans the tiles

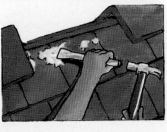

A bed of 3 to 1 mortar is buttered on to the tiles

Working on the roof

It is essential to have a roof ladder to span from the gutter to the ridge. In many cases chimney repairs can be carried out from a roof ladder, but with taller chimneys you will probably have to erect scaffolding on the roof to make a platform from which to work. Spread the load over as wide an area of roof as possible by erecting the scaffolding on lengths of stout timber. Loop the scaffolding right around the chimney so it cannot slip.

Repairs to slates

Slates usually slip because the nails that hold them in place have corroded. Loose slates can be secured with a clip made from a strip of lead, aluminium or copper about 25mm wide and 230mm long, or use a piece of heavy gauge copper wire the same length. Nail the clip to the batten or timber roof lining through the gap between the pair of slates below using a galvanised clout nail. Ease the slate under the row above and push it up into position keeping it flat. Bend the projecting end of the clip up and over to hold the slate in place.

Cracked slates can be repaired with bituminous mastic reinforced with a strip of aluminium foil, thin roofing felt or canvas.

New slates can be obtained from builders' merchants who also stock less expensive imitation slates. It is usually more economical to buy secondhand slates from demolition contractors, roofing merchants and many builders' merchants.

Slates are available in many sizes. New slates can be cut down to size by gently chopping with the edge of a trowel. Old slates may be brittle and break easily. If nail holes are required they can be easily made using a masonry drill.

Remove damaged slates with a slater's ripper which can be bought or hired. This has a long, flat blade with a sharp hook at one end. Slip the blade beneath the damaged slate and around each fixing nail in turn and pull the handle so the blade cuts through each nail.

If many slates have slipped it is best to strip them all and refix them with rustproof nails. At the same time check the battens for rot and cover the whole roof with bituminous underslating felt laid across the rafters from the eaves upwards. Use an insulating felt which has a glass fibre or mineral wool quilt bonded to the inside face. Refix battens at the same spacing as before to hold the felt in place. Finally renail the slates with large head galvanised clout nails. The slates should not be nailed tightly as this can cause them to crack. Remember that the top course of slates must be fixed with clips.

Alternatively treat the roof with three coats of liquid bitumen proofing with rot-proof reinforcing sandwiched between the first two coats. Lift flashings to continue treatment under them. Refix loose slates and repair cracked ones with bituminous mastic before applying treatment.

The ridge tile is bedded down with the trowel handle

Finally the joints are neatly pointed with mortar

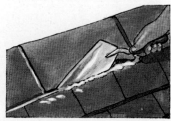

The deep hollows at ridges are filled with tile pieces

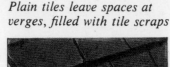

There are also spaces at the eaves, similarly filled

Plain tiles leave spaces at verges, filled with tile scraps

This membrane treatment is useful when slates are in such poor condition that it is not worth renailing them and it avoids the expense of relaying with concrete tiles. The membrane treatment can also be used for waterproofing asphalt, asbestos/cement, concrete, corrugated iron, lead, zinc and roofing felt roofs which are in very poor condition. It is not suitable over tiles or timber roofs.

Repairs to tiles

Plain tiles common on older houses usually have two nibs or projections which hook over battens spaced about 100mm apart. Every fourth course should be secured with nails. Sometimes nibless tiles are used and held only with nails.

To remove broken and crumbling tiles, lift the edges of adjoining tiles with a trowel and hold the tiles up with wedges. Use the trowel to lift the nibs of the broken tile over the batten. If there is felt under the tiles be careful not to damage it. If the broken tile is held with nails try to lever them out with a trowel or a slate ripper. Fix the new tile in place by pushing up until the nibs slip over the batten.

If a large area is being repaired, fit the tiles from the eaves upwards nailing the tiles as necessary. The last tile wedges into

Underfelt should be led into the gutter for drainage. Extra insulation can be fixed between the rafters

Leaks at a roof valley can sometimes be repaired with bituminous mastic reinforced with foil or felt

When beyond patching, the slates have to be removed

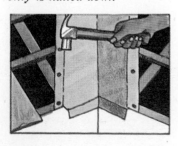

Thoroughly clean the valley ready to apply new material

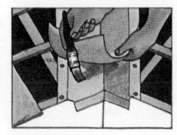

Measure and fit the sheet zinc over the valley

Trim the overlap at the eaves, leaving a turnover

With felt, the first layer only is nailed down

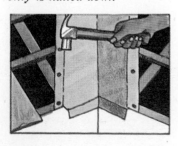

The next layer is stuck down with felt adhesive

The third and final layer is also stuck down

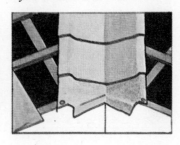

The slates are replaced in their original positions

place, although if it is a nailed, nibless type you will have to secure it with a wire or glass fibre paste.

When a nibless tiled roof causes problems through corrosion of the nails it is better to strip all the tiles and renail them. Take the opportunity to fix bituminous underfelt beneath the battens as with slate roofs.

Single lap concrete tiles used to roof new houses are sometimes dislodged by wind, but these are usually easy to slip back into place. When fixing large areas, all single lap tiles should be secured with 50mm rust-proof nails. Single lap concrete tiles are cheaper and lighter than plain tiles or slates and they are often used in replacement roofing work as they are also economical in battening. An old roof that has settled unevenly but is structurally sound should not be re-covered with single lap tiles. Plain tiles or small slates should be used as these will follow the contour of the roof closely.

Repairing the ridge

The ridge and usually the hips of both tiled and slate roofs are sealed with half-round or vee-shape tiles bedded in mortar. Sometimes the joints between adjacent tiles crack allowing water to enter. A small leak can often be sealed with bituminous mastic. Alternatively it may be possible to repoint the joints, but usually it is better to remove all the ridge tiles, chip away the old mortar and bed the tiles afresh. A suitable mortar mix for pointing or bedding ridge tiles is one part cement, one part hydrated lime, and five parts sharp, washed sand. Use a three to one, sand to cement mix to bed the hard blue ridge tiles of slate roofs.

With curved pantiles there is often a large gap to seal between the hollows of the pantiles and the base of the ridge tiles. To close this gap push flat pieces of tile in at these places. The same method is used to seal the gaps where the pantiles join the eaves and to seal the ends of the ridge tiles.

Sealing verges

Dampness in a gable wall is often caused by cracked or missing mortar along the verge. Cure by repointing with the 1:1:5 mortar mix specified for repointing ridge tiles. Fine cracks can be sealed with bituminous mastic.

Stopping rain penetration

Although a roof is in good condition, in older houses rain and snow may blow in under the slates or tiles. The roof can be stripped so that felt can be laid under the battens, but a simpler remedy is to fix bituminous underfelt in strips between the rafters in the loft thereby insulating and waterproofing in one operation. The felt should run from the ridge to the eaves, where the end of the felt is taken into the gutter. Remove the gutter and fascia board to fix the felt. Nail laths over the underfelt to hold the felt to the rafters at each side.

Repair leaking valleys and flashings

Cracks in valleys or flashing are easy to repair by applying bituminous mastic to a thickness of 1.5mm so that it overlaps adjoining surfaces by approximately 50mm on either side. Reinforce each repair with metal foil or thin roofing felt. Bed the edges well into the mastic, then cover with a further 1.5mm thick protective coating of bituminous mastic.

To make sure that no small cracks have been missed, coat the entire valley or flashing with a brush coat of liquid bitumen proofing available in brick red, white, ivy green and slate grey finishes.

If examination of the flashing shows that water leaks are caused by mortar missing where the flashing is turned into

Lean-to flashing

Remove the old flashing and brush the brickwork down

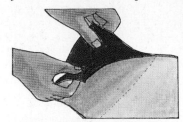

Peel the release backing from the adhesive strip

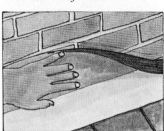

Apply the strip to the wall and roof tiles

Use a wallpaper seam roller to get good contact

Metal or special plastic flashing is bedded in a mortar joint about 100 to 150mm above the roof abutment

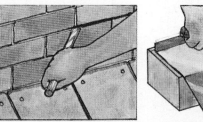

After removing the old flashing, rake out the joint

The new flashing is made by forming over a wood batten

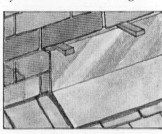

The lip is held in the joint by wood or metal wedges

With the flashing snugly fitted the joint is pointed

15

the brickwork, this can be cured by repointing with fresh mortar.

If the valley is beyond repair a new one must be fitted. Tiles or slates must be removed on each side, the old metal must be removed and the wood underlining checked for soundness and protruding nail heads. As lead and copper are very expensive it is probably best to reline the valley with sheets of 14 or 16 gauge zinc. Alternatively use three layers of roofing felt. Nail the first layer in place and glue the second and third layers down with roofing felt adhesive.

Replacing flashing

It can be a tricky job to replace a stepped flashing beside a chimney stack, or where a sloping roof joins a brick wall, so it is usually best to call in expert help for these repairs. It is quite easy, however, to replace a straight, horizontal flashing where a roof butts on to a brick wall. The simplest method is to use self-adhesive aluminium flashing strip. A similar type of flashing with a grey plastic backing resembling lead is also available in widths up to 900mm. It is necessary only to remove the old flashing, wire brush to remove dirt and dust, pull off the backing paper from the flashing and press it into place. With a pad of cloth, firm or roll down with a small wallpaper seam roller. For extra strong adhesion, especially where a surface is slightly dusty, the manufacturers sell primer for treating the surfaces to be covered.

Traditional flashing is made of zinc or lead, or felt which is less durable than the metal sheets. Cut the sheet to the required width and fold half up against the brickwork. Turn the upper edge to form a 25mm wide flange. Insert this into a raked out brick joint and wedge in place with scraps of zinc or lead. Gently hammer down the lower half of the flashing to match the slope of the roof, damp down the brickwork and point the joint with mortar.

Sometimes where a cement fillet is used instead of a flexible flashing it cracks away from the wall due to movement of the roof. Usually it is better to replace with a new flashing, but if the fillet is otherwise sound the gap can be sealed with bituminous mastic applied by trowel or other flexible sealing compound applied from a tube or a special caulking gun.

Chimney stack troubles

To locate the source of a leak in a chimney stack check the flashings and then check that the mortar between the bricks is not crumbling away. If it is, the mortar should be raked out and the brickwork repointed.

Then check the cementwork or flaunching around the chimney pots. At the same time check the pots themselves for cracks. Flaunching that is not too badly cracked can often be temporarily repaired with bituminous mastic, but for a lasting repair new flaunching is required. The flaunching will also have to be replaced if a chimney pot is cracked.

First cover the fireplaces in the rooms below, then remove the old flaunching with hammer and cold chisel. Be careful when handling undamaged pots as they are brittle and heavier than they look. If the pots have to be replaced, buy square base pots which fit exactly into the square flues.

Make sure the exposed brickwork is well raked out and dampened before applying the new flaunching. The mortar should consist of one part cement to three parts sharp, washed sand. Curve the mortar to throw water away from the pots and apply 60mm thick against the pots to slope down to about 13mm round the edge.

If the chimneys are no longer used, the stack can be sealed to make it weatherproof, but an airbrick must be fitted close to the top of the stack to allow air to circulate in the flue. A simple way to seal a stack is to remove the old pots and flaunching and then bed paving slabs over the top of the stack so their sides overhang the chimney stack by about 25mm all round. Another method is to bed a slate over the flue and cover the entire surface with new flaunching.

Roof board repairs

Rafter ends are sealed with fascia boards to which gutters are fixed. The underside gap between the wall and the fascia is sealed with a soffit board. On the gable end of a roof, barge boards are often fitted just below the tile edges to protect the roof timbers that rest in the gable wall.

Chimney damage

Here are some of the problems likely to be encountered and below, how to cap off an unused stack with paving slabs

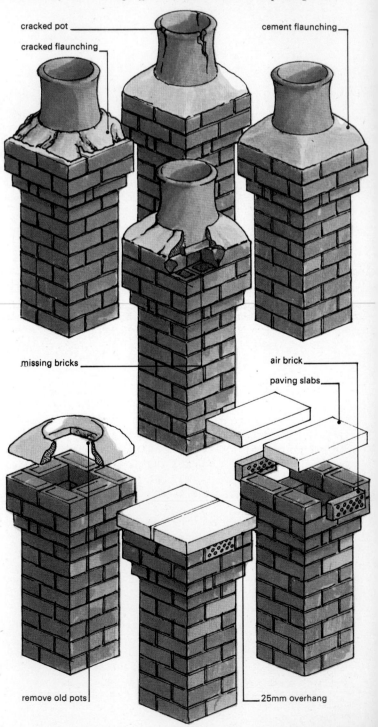

cracked pot

cracked flaunching

cement flaunching

missing bricks

air brick

paving slabs

remove old pots

25mm overhang

Barge boards that have been neglected need replacing

First remove fixings and lever the old board free

Fascia boards also suffer from the effects of weather

Remove fascia and soffit then repair rafter ends

Cut and fit suitable replacement timber

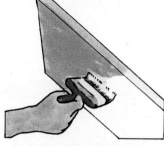

Before refixing, treat parts with three coats of paint

Mark and cut the soffit to fit snugly to the wall

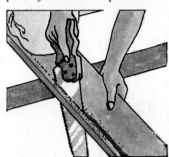

Cut the soffit board and paint for weather protection

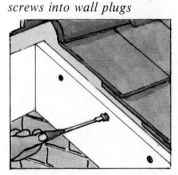

Fix the boards back using screws into wall plugs

Protection is completed by repointing verge tiles

Refit the soffit then prepare the fascia

Fit the fascia ready to receive the gutters

If not properly protected by frequent painting, barge boards may decay and need to be replaced. It can be very difficult and dangerous to attempt this work from a ladder, so use a scaffold tower.

Barge boards tend to be made of very heavy pieces of timber so take extra care when removing them. Use the old barge board as a pattern so the new board can be cut to the correct angle at the ridge or make a cardboard templet of the angle before removing the old board. After cutting the new barge board to size, make sure it is well preserved and painted before nailing in place. Make sure no slates or tiles have become loosened along the verge; if so, repoint with fresh mortar.

Fascias and soffits are fairly easy to replace. First remove the gutter. Then prise the fascia away from the rafter ends and if necessary pull the soffit away from its bearers. As a safety precaution, when about half the fascia or soffit has been freed, tie it to the scaffold tower as it may unexpectedly break free.

When the boards have been removed, examine the rafter ends for rotting. It may be possible to bolt a new rafter alongside one with a rotten end rather than replacing it. As a precaution, treat all timbers with wood preservative.

Examine the old fascias and soffits and rescue the sound parts to keep the amount of new timber required to a minimum. By making 45° circular saw cuts to coincide with the centre lines of rafters, neat joints can be made. After cutting to size, treat soffits and fascias with wood preservative. If there is a serious gap adjacent to the wall when the soffit is held in position, ensure a good fit by marking a cutting line on the face of the soffit by holding a pencil against a scrap of wood which is slid along the wall.

Use galvanised nails and fix the soffits first and then the fascia. Make sure the fascia is tucked well under the overhang of tiles or slates and that any underfelt protrudes to where the gutter will be refixed.

Corrugated roof repairs

Never walk or kneel on a corrugated roof unless you first place a long scaffold board across. With asbestos/cement and plastic roofs the board should be positioned exactly over the roof joists.

Corrugated iron roofs should be treated regularly with red oxide or bituminous paint. If an asbestos/cement roof has become porous, it can be waterproofed with two coats of liquid bitumen proofing. First remove moss and lichen by brushing with fungicide and repair cracks with mastic, reinforced with metal foil

An iron roof that has rusted in one spot or an asbestos-cement roof that has developed a hole can be temporarily repaired with glass fibre matting which is sold for car repairs. For a permanent repair fit new sheets of corrugated asbestos-

Cutting corrugated plastic sheet with a padsaw

Drill fixing holes into peaks of the corrugations

Screws, screw-nails and washers for fixing sheets

Foam plastic infill is used for eaves gap filling

Roof glazing

Linen tape impregnated with mastic will deal with leaks

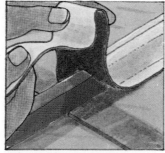

First place the tape on the bead with equal overlap

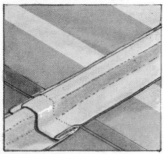

Wrap around the bead and on to the glass either side

At glass joins, double the tape for extra thickness

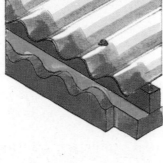

When pressed down, the fold fills the glass step

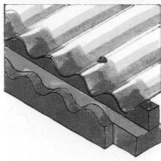

Two types of tape are made; plain and, better, foil back

cement or corrugated plastic. Both can be cut with a pad saw or power jig saw (asbestos: wear breathing mask). Make fixing holes to coincide with roof joists by drilling through raised corrugations. Fix plastic sheets with rust-proof screws with plastic sealing caps and fix asbestos-cement sheets with galvanised screw-nails with soft sealing washers. Neither type should be fitted tight enough to crack the sheeting. Adjacent sheets should be overlapped by two complete corrugations.

Special moulded foam strips are available to draughtproof the corrugations along the eaves. The junction of the roof to the wall is easily sealed with self-adhesive flashing strip.

Glass roofs

Leaking glass roofs on skylights, leans-to and greenhouses, are best repaired by lifting the glass and rebedding it on mastic glazing strip or putty. This provides a chance to chip away the old putty, repaint the bars and renew cracked sheets of glass.

A quicker method is to seal the roof with waterproofing tape run down the glazing bars and along cracks in the glass. Plain tape is messy to handle and it is better to use the more expensive longer lasting foil-covered tape. The tape will stick to any clean and dry surface and is available in a number of widths. It should be wide enough to overlap adjoining surfaces by at least 12mm.

Felt roofs

Sheds are often covered with a single sheet of roofing felt which may tear after a while. Small holes can be repaired by sticking a patch in place with bituminous adhesive. If a larger tear occurs it is best to re-cover the roof. The heavier the grade of roofing felt used, the longer it will wear. If the roof has a minimum slope of 30 degrees you can give it more character with felt slates available in strips of four tiles approximately one metre long by 300mm wide.

Lay sheets of felt along the length of the roof, starting at the eaves and finishing at the ridge. Hold sheets in place with 13mm galvanised clout nails fixed all around the edge. At the eaves and the ends space the nails 50mm apart. Overlaps, which should be at least 75mm, should be secured at 150mm intervals. For an extra strong seal, paint overlaps with bitumen sealer or adhesive before fixing with nails. The ridge should be covered last, with a strip of felt 300mm wide fixed with clout nails 50mm apart.

Sloping or flat roofs of more permanent buildings are often built up from two or three layers of felt and flat roofs are then surfaced with a layer of chippings to give protection from the sun. If this type of roof starts to leak after a time it may be possible to trace the hole and repair it with bituminous mastic reinforced with a patch of roofing felt.

If it is necessary to replace the felt completely, consult the local authority to ensure the felt to be used complies with the current building regulations. The major roofing felt manufacturers have explicit technical booklets which explain how to fix built-up roofing made of two or three layers of felt.

The first layer which usually has an asbestos base is fixed to the roof boards by nailing all over with galvanised clout nails at 150mm centres. The second layer which is also asbestos base is stuck to the first layer with roofing felt adhesive or hot bitumen. The final layer or capsheet may be one, two or three ply felt and is also stuck down. On flat roofs the capsheet is coated with chipping compound which holds a surface of stone chippings in place. On sloping roofs the capsheet is usually mineral-surfaced roofing felt and chippings are unnecessary.

Felt covered roof
Garden workshop and shed roofs are covered with felt. Here is the way the strips should be positioned with at least 75mm overlaps

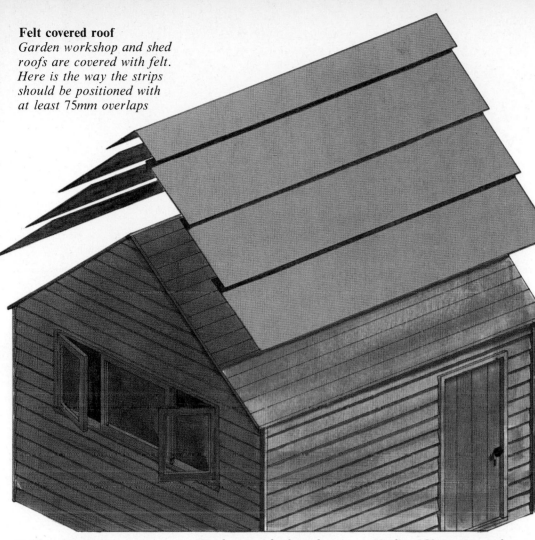

Start re-covering at the eaves, leaving a good overlap

Fold and nail the corners adding mastic for weathering

Work towards the ridge each side, sealing as you go

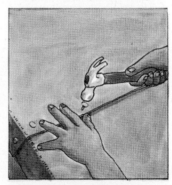

Nail at 150mm intervals using adhesive for sealing

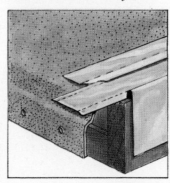

The final strip covers the ridge and meets the sides

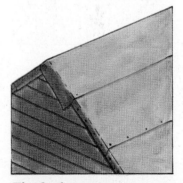

Sloping flat roofs are treated similarly, usually with three layers of felt

The first layer is nailed, the second and third are stuck with roofing adhesive

At verges, flashings are fabricated to protect the timber and meet the felt

The final covering is coated with chipping compound and stone chippings

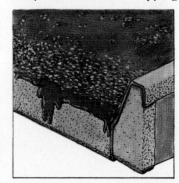

Structure
Floor structure and repairs

Modern floors

Floor construction in a house with cavity walls. First floor is suspended, ground is solid. Joist supports are shown, bottom

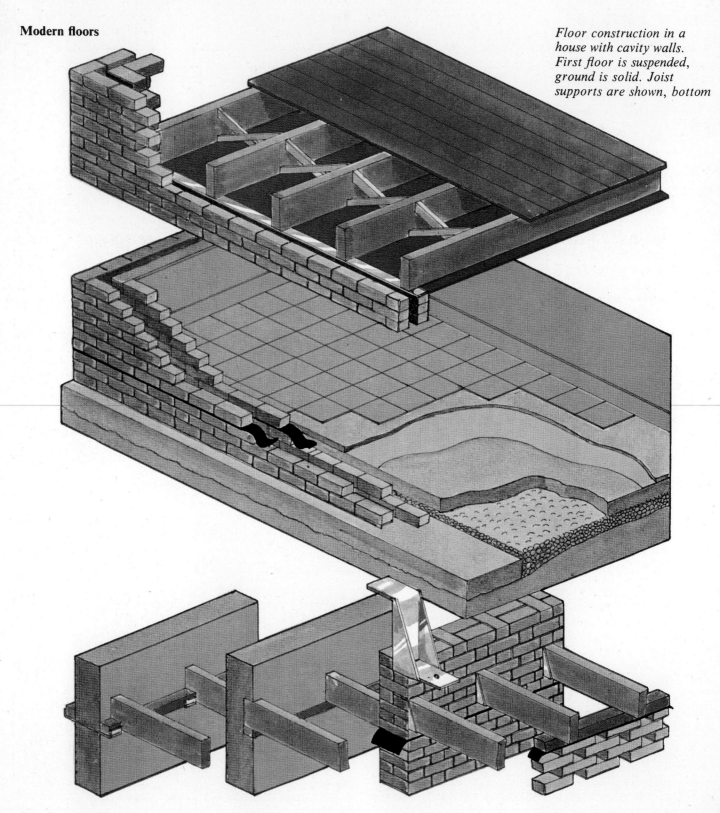

SOLID FLOORS

There are two types of floors found in a house, solid floors and suspended or hollow floors.

Solid floors are laid directly on the ground and consist of a concrete sub-floor laid over rubble. The sub-floor is covered with a damp-proof membrane and surfaced with a thin layer or screed of sand and cement. A floorcovering such as parquet, quarry tiles or plastic tiles is laid over the screed. Solid floors are only at ground level in most houses, but purpose built flats usually have solid concrete floors at all levels.

Smoothing a solid floor

An uneven solid floor such as an old quarry tile floor or a concrete floor with a badly laid screed is dangerous to walk on and will shorten the life of any floorcovering laid over it. The trouble is rectified with modern self-smoothing screeding compounds or underlayments which provide a hard, smooth base for the floorcovering. Most manufacturers supply detailed instructions.

These screeds should be applied in a layer no more than 3mm thick. If this is not sufficient to smooth the floor, then apply two separate layers. Check the evenness of a floor by laying a long straight board in several directions. Irregularities deeper than 6mm should first be filled with mortar. If the floor is in very bad condition, it would be better to resurface it with hardboard or lay a new floor.

Scrape any loose and flaky surfaces first using an old metal scraper. Then sweep the floor and wash if necessary to remove grease and polish. To ensure perfect adhesion especially on nonabsorbent floors such as quarry tiles, prime the floor surface with a floor bonding and priming liquid. Most makers of floor screeds also produce a primer. Apply one coat and allow to dry. With absorbent surfaces such as concrete it is usually sufficient to dampen with water.

Mix the screeding powder in a bucket with water, stirring it thoroughly to a thick, creamy paste. Start at the corner farthest from the door and pour some of the mixture on the floor. Use a steel trowel held at an angle to spread the mixture as evenly as possible over the floor. No finishing off is necessary as trowel marks will disappear as the self-smoothing action of the screed takes place. The screed can be walked on in about an hour and floorcoverings can be laid the next day. Maximum hardness is achieved in a week.

Damp-proofing a solid floor

If a solid floor has been laid without a damp-proof membrane or if the damp-proof membrane has become damaged in some way, floorcoverings and perhaps skirtings will soon show the effects of damp.

In many cases the damp can be cured with two coats of a clear waterproofing treatment. Another method is to apply a pitch/epoxy floor sealer. This forms a tough black film that acts as a physical barrier to the damp and on which any

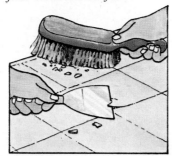

When smoothing a floor first clean the surface

Prepare non-absorbent surfaces with a primer

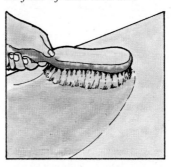

Before screeding, sweep the surface of dust and dirt

Starting at a corner, pour out the screeding compound

Spread the mixture but do not trowel it very smooth

Damp-proofing a solid floor can be carried out with either a clear waterproofer or a pitch/epoxy floor sealer spread with a broom

Flattening floors

The electric floor sanding machine with a dust bag

All nails must be punched well below the surface

conventional floorcovering can be laid. Pitch/epoxy sealer can be applied to a damp or dry floor which is smooth enough to take floorcoverings. The floor should be clean and free from wax, polish and paint. If necessary, skirtings should be removed to allow the treatment to be taken a short distance up walls to link with an existing damp-proof course. Mix the two parts of the sealer and pour some of the mixture on the floor in the corner farthest from the door. Spread with a stiff brush or broom to leave a complete film over the floor area with no gaps or small holes to allow damp to penetrate.

After 24 hours the film can be walked on and floor-coverings can be laid after 48 hours. The film is not fully cured for seven days.

Insulating and smoothing a solid floor

It is possible to insulate and smooth a solid floor using sheets of insulating boards covered with hardboard. The technique is the same as for suspended floors. The only difference on solid floors is that bitumen-impregnated insulating board and tempered hardboard should be used in all cases. The insulating boards must be stuck down using bitumen-base adhesive. If the sub-floor is damp apply a damp-proof membrane first.

SUSPENDED FLOORS

Suspended timber or hollow upper floors are found in nearly all houses and at ground level in many older houses. They consist of timber boards nailed to timber joists. At ground level the joists are often supported on low walls called sleeper walls that run beneath the floors. Alternatively, joists may be built into the wall and supported on a timber wall plate or iron plate which distributes the load along the wall. A more recent method is to support the joists in galvanised steel hangers which are built into the wall. Similar methods are used to support the joists in upper floors.

Sanding a floor

Sanding is the simplest way to level a wooden floor and is particularly useful if the floor is to be sealed and used as a decorative feature. Although floor sanding machines have dust bags, sanding a floor is still a very messy job and it is a good idea to wear a dust mask available from large chemists. If the intention is to level the floor before applying an overall floorcovering it would be better to lay sheets of hardboard over the floor. Prepare the floor for sanding by ensuring that all boards are securely fixed. Punch down all nails and pull out all tacks in case these tear the sanding belts.

Hire a floor sanding machine from a plant hire shop. Floor sanders resemble large and heavy vacuum cleaners. They have a bag to collect the bulk of the dust and a large revolving drum at the front round which are wrapped heavy-duty abrasive sheets. Start with a coarse or medium grade and finish off with a fine grade.

Tilt back the machine before switching on, then gradually lower the machine to the floor when the drum is spinning. The machine tends to pull away from the operator so hold it in check and allow it to move forwards slowly. At the end of a run it will continue to sand if it is pulled backwards. It is best to run the machine backwards and forwards in the direction of the floorboards. If the floor is in bad condition do the first few sandings at 45° to the run of the boards, but avoid using the machine directly across the boards. Each pass should overlap the next by about 75mm. Be very careful when lowering the drum at the start of a run as it is very easy to

Floors in a bad condition, start at 45° to the boards

Continue parallel with the boards, overlapping by 75mm

Intermediate runs can be at 45° but never at right-angles

Close to edges, a small disc or hand sander is used

Squeaks and lifting boards

After removing the nails drill for suitable screws

Drive in, say, 38mm gauge 8 screws to secure the board

Square edge boards are found mostly in older houses. Tongue-and-groove boards are better for insulation

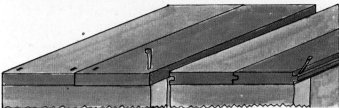

Start lifting boards using a floorboard bolster

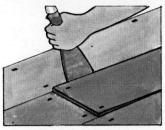

A claw hammer then helps with the levering up

Press down with the foot over a pivot and up pops the other end!

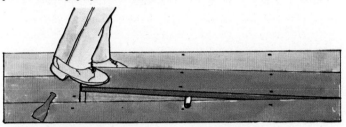

Before cutting tongues switch off the electricity

This is a floorboard saw with teeth on both sides

The floorboard saw will cut through tongues neatly

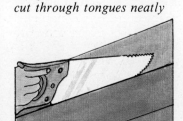

One board up and the claw hammer does the others

make a trough at this point. The machine will leave small areas unsanded near the walls and in awkward areas. Finish sanding with a special edge sander or, if the area is small, by hand with glasspaper and a sanding block.

After sanding, the floor should be swept, vacuum cleaned and mopped over before it is sealed with polyurethane floor sealer or other finish.

Squeaking floorboards

Squeaking is caused by boards rubbing against each other and can often be cured temporarily by dusting the joints with French chalk, talcum powder or graphite powder. For a lasting solution drill the boards and fix down with screws so they cannot move.

Securing springy boards

Springy boards may be cured simply by screwing down, but often boards are springy because the joists below are moving too. Lift the boards to check. Sometimes joists or wall plates are twisted and sometimes mortar has come loose where the joists are set in the wall. It may be possible to secure the joist by wedging it with a scrap of timber or packing pieces of slate under it. If the ends of the joists are rotted deal with them as explained on page 27.

Lifting floorboards

Floorboards are usually square-edged in older houses and tongued and grooved in newer properties.

Square-edged boards are fairly easy to lift by inserting a lever such as a bolster or cold chisel into a gap near the end of the board. Prise the end up until the end of a claw hammer or other lever can be slid under the board. Work along the board with the two levers until it comes free. Alternatively slide a rod under the board to hold up the end, press your foot on this loose end and the nails will give farther along the board past the rod. Subsequent boards are easy to lift, but take care to avoid splitting them.

If the first board will not come up easily, check to see if it is held down with screws. If it is not, then it is probably tongued and grooved and it will be necessary to cut through the tongue before lifting the board. Do this by cutting along the joint with a convex blade flooring saw, a pad saw or a circular power saw set to cut about 20mm deep. Be careful not to cut through any electrical cables. If in doubt turn off the mains before starting. Also avoid cutting into joists which are indicated by rows of floor nails. When the tongue has been cut along its length it should be possible to lever up the board. With one board removed the remaining boards can be lifted with a hammer or lever.

Modern houses are often floored in 2440mm by 600mm chipboard panels. These panels are usually tongued and grooved all round making them very difficult to lift. One way to tackle the job is to saw all round the joints with a circular saw set to cut 18mm deep. If this does not allow the first panel to be lifted by levering, increase the depth of the saw cut to 22mm in case panels of this thickness have been used.

Cutting and replacing boards

When it is necessary to lift only a small section of floorboard, first cut the board close to a joist. The line of the joist can be seen from the row of securing nails and the joist will extend for 25mm to 40mm on either side. Push a blade into the gap between the boards to find the side of the joist and mark across the board at this spot. Drill a number of small holes at

Making an access point

Cut through the floorboard tongues at the access point

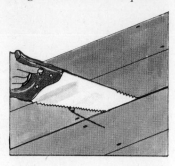

Drill a hole, at an angle, so as just to miss the joist

Use a pad or jig saw to cut the board being lifted

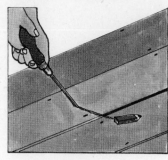

Use bolster and claw hammer to lift the board part way

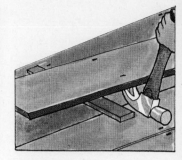

Make the second cut using a batten to steady the board

Refix the remainder of the board using flooring nails

Glue and nail a support batten to the first joist

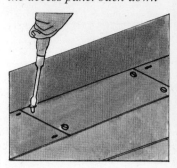

Finally use screws to fix the access panel back down

an oblique angle on one side of this line to make a start for a pad saw.

With the pad saw, cut across the board keeping the saw at an oblique angle so the board is well supported when it is replaced.

Lever the board up past the point where the second cut is to be made and hold it up with a scrap of wood or metal rod. Now cut the board to coincide with the centreline of a joist. That part of the board that was loosened but not removed should be hammered down again and secured with more flooring nails if necessary. A much better method would be to use screws.

Before the short section of board is replaced, additional support must be fixed to the joist where the first cut was made.

Use a scrap of 50mm by 25mm softwood glued and nailed to the side of the joist so it is flush with the top of the joist. After the board has been replaced, screw it down so that it may be removed easily in the future.

Levelling a board

When a board has been replaced it is often not exactly the right thickness. If it is too thin pack pieces of linoleum or hardboard to level the surface. If the board is too thick you may be able to plane it or cut wide, shallow slots to coincide with the joists. Cut the slots slightly wider than the joists and use a chisel to remove sufficient wood from between the saw cuts to allow the board to lie level. A circular power saw, adjusted to make a very shallow cut, makes short work of removing most of the waste wood but take great care when working on site.

Filling gaps

There are several ways of dealing with gaps between floorboards.

The easiest is to fill the gaps with a wood filler or stopper. The cost of these materials limits their use to floors where

there are a few gaps to fill. Papier mâché is cheap and easy to make and is the best material in most cases. It tends to dry greyish-white, but it can be dyed to match the flooring where the boards will be exposed after treatment. Soft white unprinted paper is ideal but newspaper is the most usual material.

Tear paper into scraps and then wet with boiling water while pounding with a piece of timber. Add more paper or water as necessary to make a thick paste. When the paste is cool, add cellulose-base wallpaper adhesive powder to make

New piece of board

When a board is damaged—quite likely in the case of an access panel—a new piece must be fitted. When exactly the right thickness board is not available, to save laborious planing, cut the board to length and width, and cut rebates to fit over the joists

Papier mâché

For most gap-filling between floorboards, papier mâché is suitable. It can be used without colour-matching but water-base stains will make it tone better with the surrounding boards. When dry, it can be sanded smooth, stained, varnished or painted. It makes an excellent draughtproofer

Mix shredded paper with boiling water and pound well

When gaps between boards are really big, the best solution is to relay the whole floor. Occasionally, however, it is convenient to fill such gaps with wood strips. This is not an easy job for each strip has to be planed, preferably to a taper, to fit each gap. So, before adopting this course, see how many gaps there are

Use an adhesive with a nozzle and apply to the gap

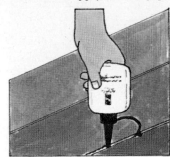

When cool, add cellulose wallpaper adhesive

Work well into gaps with a small trowel and smooth

Tap the prepared strip into the gap with a block

When the adhesive is dry plane the strip flush

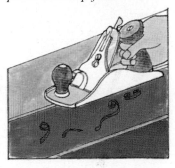

a really thick mixture. After the powder has been added a little more water may be necessary to make the mixture workable. Press it firmly into the gaps with a filling knife and sand it smooth when it has dried out in two or three days.

Gaps larger than about 6mm must be filled with wood strips. Cut these slightly oversize and plane to form a slight wedge.

Apply wood glue along both sides of the strips and tap into place. When the glue has dried the strips can be planed level with the surface of the boards. When strips have to be joined,

make sure that the joints coincide with the joists to give them a neat appearance.

Relaying a floor

Relaying a floor is a hard and lengthy job, but it is worth doing if there are many large gaps between the boards and if some are badly worn and damaged. The worn boards can be replaced and joists can be checked, repaired and treated against woodworm and rot if necessary. While the floor is up underfloor insulation can be installed.

Relaying a floor

Lift the old boards and clean them for reuse

Remove the old nails or, if too tight, hammer home

Now is the opportunity to fit underfloor insulation

If you have no cramps, make a pair of sliding wedges

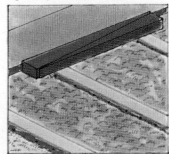

When, say, six boards are down, position wedges thus

Knock the wedges together to produce a cramping action

When secure, nail all six boards before moving on

The last board is cut to size and tapped into place

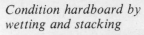

Insulation board topped with hardboard sheets

Condition hardboard by wetting and stacking

Choose board sizes which suit the job in hand

Nail at 100mm centres at edges, 150mm elsewhere

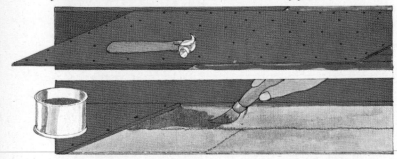

Insulating board can be nailed or stuck down but in the former case ensure the nails enter 13mm of floor

Twisted joists cause many floor problems. One solution is to fit 25 × 50mm struts between them as shown

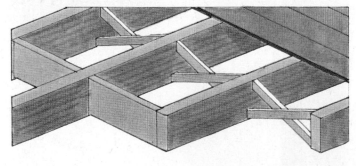

Lift all the boards, remove nails, scrape the edges and stack them on one side of the room. Next examine the joists and remove nails or hammer them home if they are too hard to remove.

At this stage underfloor insulation can be added to a ground floor. A very simple method is to staple paper-face glass fibre flanged building roll between the joists. The roll is available as 50mm, 75mm, or 100mm thick glass fibre mat backed with Kraft paper wider than the insulation to form flanges for fixing.

The boards are replaced from the side lifted last. Normally gaps can be eliminated by pushing the boards together as they are nailed with new floorboards, but if the boards are slightly curved it is possible to tighten them with wedges.

Lay five or six boards in place without nailing. Then place wedges at regular intervals across the joists and nail scrap timber to the joists against the wedges to form a temporary stop. Tension the wedges by hammering the ends together. This forces the boards tight together and they are then nailed down. To finish off, cut a new floorboard to fill the last gap. Make it slightly oversize with its edges planed to slope so it can be tapped home in a tight fit.

Relaying a floor with chipboard

In cases where timber floors are in very bad condition it is best to replace them with new floorboards or with secondhand boards bought from a demolition contractor or with sheets of flooring grade chipboard. Chipboard sheets make up into a very hard, smooth floor. They are difficult to remove so be sure to leave small screwed-down access panels at points where it might be necessary to reach electric cables or water pipes from time to time.

Get tongued and grooved panels if possible. The 18mm thickness is suitable for joist spacings up to 450mm, and the 22mm thick panels for spacings from 450mm to 600mm.

Resurfacing and insulating a floor

Hardboard is an excellent under-surface for all floor-coverings, except ceramic and quarry tiles which need a thicker underlay such as chipboard. If desired, hardboard can be sealed and used as a decorative finish.

Good thermal insulation can be achieved by laying insulating board under the hardboard. Use 12.7mm, 19mm or 25mm thick insulating board according to the degree of thermal insulation required. In kitchens or bathrooms use bitumen-impregnated insulating board.

For the surface use 3.2mm or 4.8mm standard hardboard. Use tempered hardboard in damp conditions or where there will be heavy traffic, for example in kitchens, bathrooms and halls.

First condition the insulation board to avoid the possibility of buckling after the sheets have been laid. Insulation boards should be exposed to the air in the room where they are to be used for 48 hours before fixing. The boards should be separated and stood on edge so the air can circulate freely. In a well-heated older building it will be sufficient to treat hardboard in the same manner, but increase conditioning time to 72 hours. In new buildings and damp situations such as kitchens and bathrooms in older buildings, hardboard must be water conditioned. Do this by sprinkling the rough sides of the boards with water and leave them stacked back to back on a flat surface for 48 hours or for 72 hours for tempered boards.

Fix the boards immediately after conditioning. If insulating boards are to be used, lay these first. Start in the middle of the room and work outwards so only the sheets round the edge of the room need to be trimmed. Lay the sheets in brickwork fashion so the joints are staggered. Sheets up to 2440mm by 1220mm can be used, but sheets 1220mm by 610mm are much easier to handle.

Insulating boards can be stuck down with bitumen or contact adhesives, but on a timber floor it is more usual to fix them with rust-resistant ring shank or screw nails. These should be long enough to penetrate the timber base by not less than 13mm. Set the nails 13mm from board edges and then across joints. Spacing should be every 100mm on edges and at 150mm elsewhere.

Hardboard sheets are laid over the insulating boards, but are staggered so the joints do not coincide. Stick them down with bitumen or contact adhesive. The sheets should be laid rough side up unless they are to be used as a decorative finish or sub-floor for thin vinyl tiles.

REPAIRS TO JOISTS

Straightening joists

If joists are twisted, or bounce when walked on, the reason could be that struts which stabilise the joists are required between them. Straight struts of 150mm by 25mm timber wedged between the joists and nailed in place are the simplest to fit. Alternatively use 50mm by 25mm struts fixed diagonally between the joists in an X formation.

Replacing joists

Joist trouble is frequently indicated by a bouncing floor near to the walls of a room. Joists are most prone to decay from wet and dry rot, also woodworm near to their ends. Lift the floorboards to ascertain the extent of the trouble and take steps to remedy the damp, if this is the cause. Replace the entire joist if possible or bolt a new end piece on to a sound section of the joist.

On the ground floor support the joist with a car jack while the end is sawn off and a new section bolted in place. Remove all the rotted part and at least one metre of sound timber and then treat the joist and all cut surfaces with wood preservative. The new section should overlap the existing joist by at least one metre and should be bolted in place with three 9.5mm bolts and with square toothed-plate timber connectors sandwiched between the joists.

At the wall end the joist should be supported in a galvanised steel joist hanger, which can be fitted after any recess in the wall has been bricked up. Alternatively a low sleeper wall with damp-proof course and wall plate can be built to support the end of the joist. In this case there should be a clearance of about 20mm between the joist end and the wall.

When a joist in an upstairs floor is to be replaced some ceiling damage will result, but holes are easily repaired by nailing plasterboard into place after the new joist has been fitted. In the case of upstairs floors, joist ends must be supported in joist hangers or built into recesses in the wall.

If a new end is to be bolted to a joist, use adjustable steel props in the room below to support the joists while work takes place. Spread the load by wedging the props between thick pieces of timber at floor and ceiling. Props are available from plant and tool hire shops.

You may come across electrical wires under the floors. Turn off the mains and work around them carefully. Where the cable runs across a replaced joist drill a hole in the joist and cut a wedge above it which can be glued back in place after the wire has been placed in the hole.

When joists of a suspended floor fail, the usual reason is rot at the ends. No need to replace the whole joist, just the end. Here is one method, where a new section is added and supporting side pieces are bolted to the old and new timbers. On the right is a joist hanger. Below is a method of joining joists. Bottom shows cable fitting

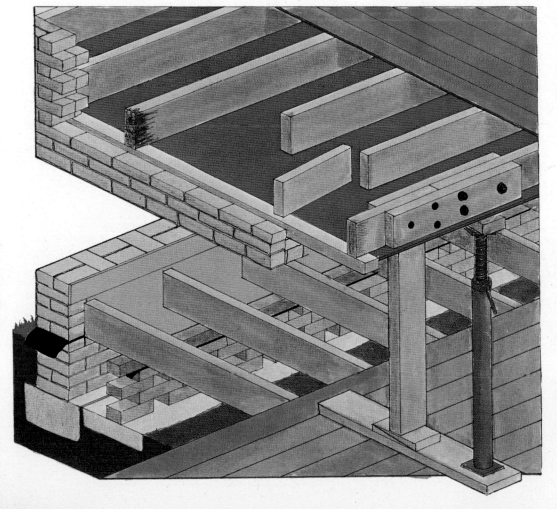

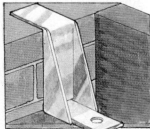

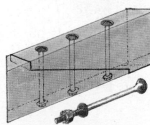

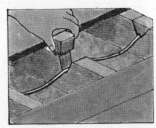

Structure
Working with concrete

Concrete is a useful and relatively inexpensive building material that is suited to many types of household projects such as laying foundations and floor slabs and for making drives and paths. It is made up of three basic ingredients: cement, water and aggregate. These are combined in various proportions depending on the strength of concrete required.

Cement

Ordinary cement, called Portland cement, will be appropriate for most jobs. It is sold in 50kg bags, although smaller quantities are available from do-it-yourself shops.

Coloured cement

The traditional grey colour of concrete is not to everyone's liking for a path or patio. Other colours can be made by introducing coloured Portland cement into the mix.

When using coloured cements make sure to keep the various cements well separated. Uniformity of mixing is more important with coloured cement since adding too much or too little to different mixes will result in a blotchy finished effect. If an exact colour is required, remember that coloured concrete dries to a paler shade than it was when wet.

Admixtures

Admixtures are available which accelerate or retard the setting rate of concrete. When incorporating these into a mix, precise measurement is important to achieve the desired effect. Colourants are also available.

Aggregates

Aggregate adds bulk and strength to the concrete. There are three types – coarse, fine and combined. Ordinary concrete contains a mixture of coarse and fine aggregate, but mortar used in brickwork contains no coarse aggregate. Coarse aggregate is made up of gravel and crushed gravel or stones. Fine aggregate is very coarse sand. Combined aggregate which is easier to mix is sometimes called all-in ballast.

Specify that you want washed ballast. Avoid as-dug ballast which is not suitable for concrete work as it is sold in the state that it is dug from the ground.

If you intend to mix your own concrete, you can order the cement and aggregate and mix it yourself with a shovel or with the aid of a concrete mixer.

Ready mix concrete

Ready mix concrete is a more expensive method of obtaining the material and is not economical for small jobs. It is loaded in a special lorry in precise proportions and delivered already mixed to the right consistency ready to pour. If expense is not important, ready mix is very convenient, but remember that concrete is very heavy. A three cubic metre load, for example, weighs 7 tonnes. It takes only a couple of hours for the ready mix to set, so it has to be transported and poured into the formwork quickly. It's not a job that can be done single-handed. A couple of helpers are needed, especially if the delivery lorry cannot reach the site and the concrete has to be transported in wheelbarrows.

Equipment you may need for concreting, say, a garden path. Extra items are boards and pegs for making shuttering

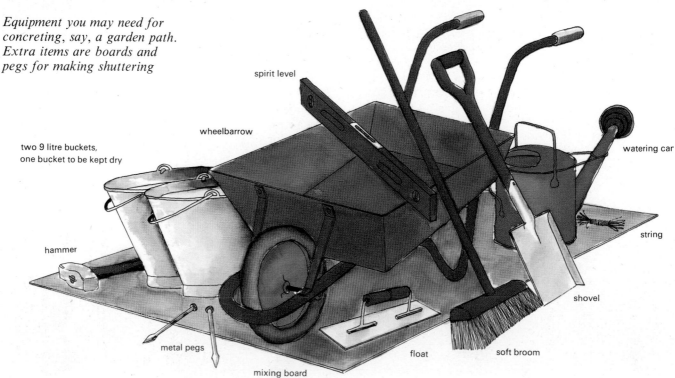

spirit level

wheelbarrow

two 9 litre buckets, one bucket to be kept dry

watering car

string

hammer

shovel

metal pegs

float

soft broom

mixing board

For really big jobs, needing at least 3 cu m, a ready-mix concrete lorry can save a lot of work – but several helpers may be needed

Many firms operate on a minimum charge of 3 cu m. Larger jobs might not work out more expensive when compared with mixing your own concrete with a hired mixer. It is therefore important to estimate the amount of concrete needed for the job.

The ready mix supplier will need to know when to deliver the concrete and if it is merely to be dumped in a pile or poured into the formwork. Since this will govern the time that the delivery takes, the cost will probably be affected. Most suppliers allow for last-minute cancellations in the event of rain.

There are other points to take into account. Your garden gates, for example, should be wide enough for the lorry to get through and any existing driveway strong enough to withstand its weight. Concrete can be damaged by frost

which causes it to crack up. If your job is being done at a time of year when these conditions are likely, try to order warm ready mix. This sets more quickly and reduces the risk of frost damage.

Dry mix concrete

There are various brands of dry mix available which contain cement, sand and aggregate mixed together in the correct proportions. Water is added and the concrete is mixed with a shovel. This eliminates the need for calculating proportions of cement and aggregate and is sometimes the best solution for small jobs.

Calculating amounts required

When using ready mix, estimating amounts of cement, sand and aggregate needed is not a problem. The supplier will just want to know the total amount of concrete required in cubic metres.

When mixing by hand, you will have to calculate the exact requirements in terms of bags of cement and cubic metres of both sand and coarse aggregate. This is made easy by using the table on the following page.

Using the table

First establish the dimensions of your project and calculate the area. Then read across from the area scale on the left of the table to the particular thickness you are using. From this point move straight down to the bottom scale and read off the total volume of concrete required. After choosing the appropriate mix, continue reading straight down to arrive at the number of bags of cement and the volume of sand and coarse aggregate required.

If you intend using ready mix concrete, simply order the total quantity of the appropriate mix. If you are mixing the concrete by hand buy the quantities of cement, sand and aggregate.

As an example consider making a driveway, say, 2.5m wide, 8m long and 100mm thick using Mix A. The total area is $2.5 \times 8m = 20m^2$. Find $20m^2$ on the left, read across to the 100mm line and directly down to give the total volume

Mixing concrete; dry mix, add water, mix thoroughly

Push-along and electric drill-operated concrete mixers

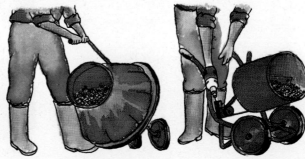

of concrete, 2m². Next read downwards to Mix A which shows that you will need 12, 50kg bags of cement, 1 cu m of damp sand and about 1.6 cu m of coarse aggregate. It is wise to order slightly more to allow for wastage.

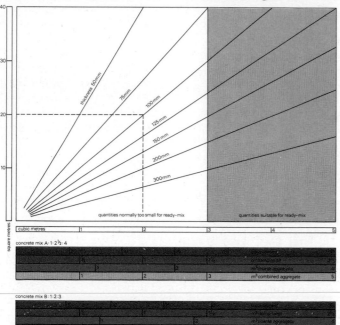

Square-end shovels are needed for the mixing and shovelling the mix into a wheelbarrow. Again, keep one shovel for using with cement. A sturdy wheelbarrow may be required to transport the concrete. An ordinary garden rake is useful to roughly level out the concrete once deposited in the formwork. A steel trowel or wood float is required depending on the type of finish desired. Some finishes are achieved by brushing with a soft or stiff broom. A watering can is necessary for adding water to the mix.

Mixing concrete by hand

It is best to mix concrete in small batches to avoid problems of interruptions or bad weather.

Path laying; compacting, formwork, levelling, concreting

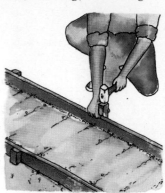

Mixes

Mix A, 1:2½:4, consists of 1 part cement mixed with 2½ parts damp sand and 4 parts coarse aggregate, all measured by volume. It is suitable for circumstances where a thickness of 75mm or more is needed. Foundations, floor slabs and driveways come into this category. Mix B, 1:2:3, is stronger and is suitable for paths and small sections or slabs thinner than 75mm.

If all-in ballast is used, then for Mix A use: 1 part cement to 5 parts combined aggregate; for Mix B use: 1 part cement to 3¾ parts combined aggregate.

Damp sand which is normally supplied is quoted in the tables. If dry sand is used, reduce the quantity of sand in each mix as follows: For Mix A use 2 parts, for Mix B use 1½ parts of dry sand.

Tools and equipment

Mixing and laying concrete requires only ordinary tools. All equipment should be washed thoroughly at the end of a work session to remove all traces of concrete. If it sets on tools it will have to be chipped off.

Two 9 litre buckets will be needed to measure out the ingredients accurately. Keep one bucket only for cement.

Concrete must be mixed on a firm, level and clean base such as a forecourt. Make sure that all drains are covered to prevent any concrete from running away and setting in them, causing blockages later. If there is no convenient mixing area near the site, make a wooden mixing platform out of a piece of 19 or 25mm plywood.

Measure out the aggregates and cement by filling a bucket and levelling off with a shovel. For example should a 1:2:3 mix be needed, then each batch will be made by adding the ingredients in these proportions. That is, one bucket of cement, two buckets of sand, three buckets of coarse aggregate. All the buckets will be filled to the same level. Thus, assuming same-size buckets are used, you will be guaranteed an accurate mix.

Remember to keep one shovel solely for handling cement. Keep the second shovel for the sand, aggregate and the mixing. Pour out the buckets of coarse aggregate in a small circle on the ground and add the sand. Dump the cement on top of the aggregate and mix well until it is the same colour overall.

Form a crater in the centre of the pile and add water. It is important to use only clean water or the concrete will not set properly. The amount of water added to the mix determines the consistency. If the mix is too wet the concrete will be weak. The ideal consistency is evenly moist. If in doubt, aim for a drier rather than a wetter mix. The important thing is that the concrete is workable and can be placed and compacted in the formwork easily.

Add a little water at a time and turn over the mix so that the water is gradually absorbed. Before adding more water, form a crater in the centre of the mix. Keep turning over the mix with a chopping action until the consistency is correct.

Concrete mixers

POWERED CONCRETE MIXERS ARE POTENTIALLY DANGEROUS MACHINES. KEEP CHILDREN AWAY AND USE WITH CARE.

By renting a power mixer the strenuous job of mixing concrete can be made quicker and easier. Where a large expanse of concrete is required a mixer is probably essential.

The simplest mixer available consists of a mixing drum set on a trolley. The cement, aggregate and water are tipped into the drum and mixed by pushing the drum back and forth on a level surface. Another mixer is operated by an electric hand drill. The drill connects to a gearbox from which a drive belt runs and operates the mixing drum. There are larger, electrically operated mixers and types with a four-stroke petrol engine as well as diesel mixers suitable for very large jobs.

Tamping a path and a drive. Right: making a joint

Preparing the site

First outline the area to be worked by driving pegs at each corner and tying strings taut between them. For curved paths, mark the ground with chalk or sand roughly to outline the path. Concrete can be laid directly on to firm ground after any vegetation has been removed and soft spots replaced with compacted rubble. On soft or loose soil, lay a thin layer of hardcore such as broken bricks or other clean rubble and compact well with a roller. Be careful not to leave air gaps.

If you plan to make the top surface of the slab flush with the surrounding ground, remove 50 to 100mm of top soil as

required. In soft soil remove an extra 25 to 75mm of soil and backfill with hardcore as before. Generally the thicker the concrete the more hardcore is required.

Building the formwork

A wooden frame called formwork is constructed to contain the concrete while it sets. The 25mm thick timber must be of a depth equal to the intended thickness of the concrete. Thus 25 × 75mm timber will be used for a 75mm thick slab.

The formwork will have to withstand a fair amount of pressure from the concrete, so stout support pegs should be knocked into the ground at one metre intervals and nailed to the formwork if necessary. Use two pegs behind formwork joints to make sure there are no gaps between the boards.

Check the level with a spirit level. For level slabs, check both along and across the formwork. Paths and drives should allow a crossfall for drainage by making the formwork 25mm lower on one side.

To check for crossfall accuracy, place a 25mm shim on the lower formwork. Lay a straight-edge across the formwork with one end resting on the shim. Check for level by placing a spirit level on the straight-edge. Repeat this procedure at several points along the path. For sloping paths keep the same crossfall and make sure that the two sides slope evenly.

To bend the formwork for curved paths, simply use thin boards bent to the required curve. If the boards are too stiff, either soak them in water to make them more pliable or use hardboard well supported with pegs.

Long concrete slabs need expansion joints every 3m to prevent cracking. Place formwork stop-boards across the slab with the support pegs on the other side of the area to be poured first. Make sure these stop-boards are level with the main formwork.

Laying the concrete

Pour the concrete into the formwork and spread it out evenly to a thickness 25mm higher than the edges of the timbers to allow for compaction. Make sure that the concrete works its way down to fill all corners and edges of the formwork. The concrete is compacted and levelled with a tamping beam made of a stout length of timber 150 to 300mm longer than the width of the formwork.

On long slabs place, but do not nail, a 9mm thick board in front of the stop-board to form an expansion joint.

When the formwork is widely spaced, it is necessary to fit handles on either side of the tamper to make it easier to lift and operate. Use the tamper with a straightforward chopping action. Lift and drop it back on to the edges of the formwork so that it compresses the concrete. Move across the formwork in stages of about half the thickness of the tamper.

Making concrete non-slip. Protect against heat and frost

31

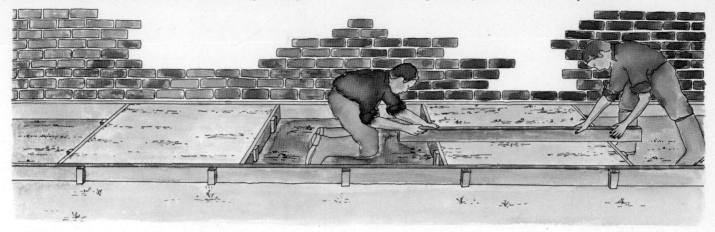

Where access is restricted or inconvenient, paths and drives can be dealt with in bays. When the first bays have set, the in-between ones can be completed. If needed, expansion joints can be incorporated

Tamping leaves a corrugated surface on the wet concrete. In some circumstances this is left to set but usually a smoother surface is required. Work over the area again using the tamper in a sawing action. Let it rest on the formwork and gradually push it back and forth. This will level off any high spots or ridges. Any depressions should be filled with concrete and brought level using the tamper. The concrete should then be fairly smooth and level with the top edges of the formwork.

Now remove the stop-board, if any, leaving behind the 9mm board and pour the next bay. Repeat the same procedure of placing the 9mm board at each stop-board. Leave the 9mm board in the slab to create a flexible gap which prevents large slabs from cracking as the concrete expands and contracts with the heat.

Concrete finishes

The concrete finish will depend on how the area is used. Paths and steps should have a textured surface for safety during icy periods. Concrete floors should be as smooth as possible to facilitate cleaning. The surface can be left with the rippled texture after tamping, but for a less slippery surface, brush the concrete with a stiff broom.

To expose the aggregate, brush finish the surface when the concrete has just been compacted. Leave it to set partially so that the particles cannot be dislodged easily and then spray with a watering can fitted with a fine rose and at the same time sweep with a soft broom. The water sprayed in this way creates a fine slurry. Soft brushing will remove the slurry and leave the aggregate slightly exposed.

A smooth surface is achieved by using a wood float in wide, circular sweeps over the fresh concrete. The technique of leaving an all-over, semi-smooth surface without exposing too much aggregate takes some practice.

For a really superb surface, the concrete can be finished with a steel float, but for outdoor work this shouldn't be necessary.

Protecting fresh concrete

In warm weather the danger is that the concrete will dry too quickly. Always cover the concrete with damp hessian or sacking or polythene sheets anchored down with bricks.

If work is being carried out when there is a possibility of frost, cover the fresh concrete with a layer of straw, hessian or sacking. Cover the straw with polythene anchored with bricks.

In warm weather the curing process takes about four days.

Allow twice as long in cold conditions. When the curing period has elapsed, remove the formwork. If it is taken off too early the edges and corners of the concrete will be weak.

CONCRETE PROJECTS

Laying a path

First establish the direction of the path and mark the outline using taut strings if the path is straight. For curved paths, mark the outline with powdered chalk or sand. Garden paths should be 50mm thick and made using Mix B. They can be laid directly on top of firm ground but remember that any vegetation or soft spots must be removed and backfilled with rubble. For soft ground, lay a hardcore layer compacted to 25mm thickness, then prepare the formwork for the 50mm thick slab.

Keep the path as level as possible but it must, of course, follow the contours of the ground. Remember to allow for a 25mm crossfall across the width of the path for drainage.

Add expansion joints every 3m along the length, but if the path slopes steeply, put them at 2m intervals and pour the concrete as stiff as possible.

If the path is to be laid along an existing wall, the tamping procedure must be changed since you can't lay the tamping beam across the path.

By pouring the concrete in alternative bays, the tamping beam can first be used across the stop-board. After two days of curing these boards are removed and tamping of the final bays is achieved by standing on the cured concrete.

Before placing stop-boards place a 50mm wide strip of thick bitumen felt to form a continuous joint between the wall and the concrete slab. Also ensure that the path is well below the wall d.p.c. level.

Base for a small shed

Lay out the area, and prepare the site and formwork for a 75mm slab. On soft clay increase the thickness to 100mm. In either case use Mix A. It is advisable to lay a damp-proof course (see following page).

The base can be made in one slab provided that the maximum dimension does not exceed 3m and the length is not more than twice the width. The area must be subdivided into two or more slabs with joints if the area is larger. These individual slabs should be roughly square and equal in size.

To make sure that the main formwork is square, lay it out with a builder's square. You can make your own square by

A builder's square is most useful for all d-i-y work. Make it as big as possible, based on sides of 3, 4, 5

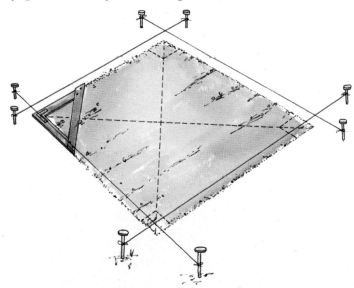

Setting-out a shed or garden workshop base. Keep the pegs well clear of the working area

using three lengths of timber in the precise proportions of 3:4:5. After laying out the formwork, check that the diagonals are equal using a long board or steel tape.

Making a builder's square

Cut 2m of good straight 25 × 75mm softwood into three pieces each 450, 650 and 850mm long. Butt join the two short pieces with an L-bracket, then accurately measure out 450 and 600mm along the outer edges.

Mark the long piece with two marks 750mm apart.

Lap join the triangle, as shown, left, ensuring that the marks coincide to form a 450, 600, 750mm triangle. Use two screws at each end of the cross piece.

Larger structural bases

A structural base is set out the same way as the garden shed base using Mix A. But a large base needs a sounder sub-base. If the subsoil is soft clay or is inconsistent across the site, dig 75mm farther down and fill with well-compacted hardcore. A 100mm thickness of concrete is normally sufficient.

It's always advisable to check the positions of underground drains at the planning stage in case any need to be relaid.

Lay a 1000 gauge plastic sheet as a damp-proof barrier under the slab. Spread a layer of sand over the subfloor to protect the sheet from any sharp stones. The sheet should be laid over the base and the formwork, extending about 100mm on all sides. When sheets have to be joined, overlap edges in a double fold at least 150mm wide. If the slab is laid against a wall always include the damp-proof membrane and at exterior walls the plastic damp-proof membrane must join the damp-proof course of the wall.

Driveways

A 100mm thick concrete slab using Mix A will withstand the weight of normal cars. If heavier vehicles are using the drive, add an extra 50mm of concrete.

If possible, allow the drive to slope away from the garage. Follow instructions for a sloping path and use as stiff a mix as possible. If the drive must be level, plan a crossfall of about 50mm from side to side for drainage.

Allow at least 14 days to elapse before driving on the concrete. In cold weather, or if heavy vehicles are to be driven on the concrete, the full 28 days curing time should be allowed.

Slope a drive away from the garage. Incorporate a drainage gulley where two slopes meet

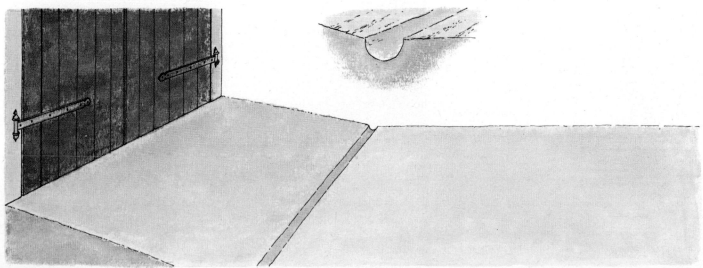

Structure
Brickwork

Techniques for building with bricks and blocks are similar. Learning these techniques will enable the householder to tackle many useful and money saving construction and repair jobs.

Types of bricks

There is a large variety of colours and textures of bricks available. Most good builders' merchants stock a standard selection of brick types and secondhand bricks, but other types can usually be ordered. For practical purposes two types of bricks are most often used, facing bricks and common bricks.

Common bricks are made of fletton clay and are used for all building work which is not visible, such as walls that will be plastered over.

To finish off the tops of walls, there is a variety of coping bricks to suit almost any style desired

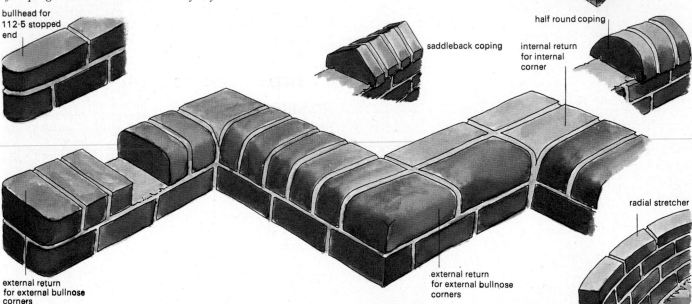

bullhead for 112·5 stopped end

saddleback coping

half round coping

internal return for internal corner

radial stretcher

external return for external bullnose corners

external return for external bullnose corners

A two-brick thick wall in English Garden Wall bond

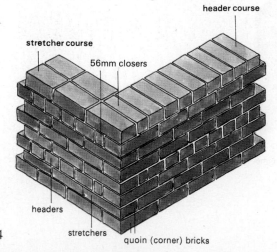

header course

stretcher course

56mm closers

headers

stretchers

quoin (corner) bricks

A similar wall but in Flemish Garden Wall bond

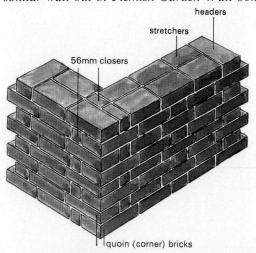

headers

stretchers

56mm closers

quoin (corner) bricks

Facing bricks are used in situations when the appearance of the brickwork is important. The most widely used are made of fletton clays which have been faced with mineral granules or coarse sand burnt into the clay. Bricks are available which have been faced on all six or only three sides.

Secondhand bricks available from demolition sites and some builders' yards are cheaper and better suited for jobs in which the brickwork is to match an existing area. Any mortar on used bricks can be removed with a trowel or by rubbing two mortar surfaces together. Patches of thin mortar will not affect the use of the bricks.

Brick sizes

Bricks now conform with the British Standard size of 215mm long, 65mm high and 102.5mm wide, which corresponds with the old Imperial nominal size 9 × 4½ × 3in.

These dimensions are 10mm smaller than the working or nominal size of 225 × 112.5 × 75mm which includes the thickness of the mortar. The working size is used in estimating jobs.

A brick has a vee-shape indentation in one face called the frog. It holds a good amount of mortar and forms a better grip than would be possible by joining two flat surfaces. Laying the bricks with the frog up is traditional.

In addition to the standard rectangular shape bricks you can also buy special-purpose bricks. These include coping bricks of various shapes used for the top courses of garden walls and curved bricks for arches and curved walls.

Mortar

For most jobs use a mix of one part Portland cement, one part hydrated powder lime and six parts clean sand. Exposed garden walls require a stronger mix of one part cement to three parts sand. Make sure that no stones are included in the mixture.

The night before work starts, soak the lime in a bucket of water and pour off the surplus water the following morning. Mix one part of lime with six parts of sand adding enough water to achieve a stiff consistency. This mixture is called coarse stuff and can be mixed in advance and kept for weeks if covered.

When ready to start work, add the cement to the coarse stuff, adding more water if necessary.

The mortar must be used within two hours of mixing. In very hot weather, mix up small batches of mortar at a time as it will set quickly.

For smaller jobs use one of the ready mixed mortars which guarantee consistent strength, colour and workability. A 20 kilogram bag contains sufficient mortar for about 80 bricks.

Types of bonding

All brickwork must be bonded with the bricks laid in a pattern so that the vertical joints of each course or layer of bricks do not lie above each other. This would structurally weaken the wall.

Stretcher bond is the simplest and most common bond. The bricks are laid lengthwise so that vertical joints in one course fall on the centreline of the bricks in the courses above and below. This bond is used for walls using one thickness of bricks and for cavity walls which are two thin walls with an airspace between them.

In English bond one course of stretchers alternates with a course of headers (bricks placed end facing outward). This is a strong type of bond.

Flemish bond which is more decorative, consists of a sequence of headers and stretchers in each brick course. English Garden Wall bond uses a course of headers to three courses of stretchers and Flemish Garden Wall bond uses one header to three stretchers in each course.

These bonds can add considerably to the cost of the wall since facing bricks are used as headers.

Walls such as garden walls that are 215mm thick have special corner bonding arrangements. With both bond styles, a narrow piece of brick called a closer must be placed next to the quoin (the corner header) so that a quarter bond is produced between the bricks in the courses above and below. A closer is nominally 56mm wide.

FOUNDATIONS FOR BRICKWORK

Planning the trench

Foundations are needed for any brick wall. For garden sheds the walls can be built directly on the concrete slab, but elsewhere a trench is required. The depth of the trench varies with the nature of the subsoil and the weight of the wall.

In firm subsoils a light garden wall requires a 300mm deep trench. On weaker subsoils such as soft clay, dig down to 450mm. If the subsoil is still too soft, dig down to a firmer level and replace the soil with a layer of well-compacted hardcore.

Tool kit for brickwork and blockwork

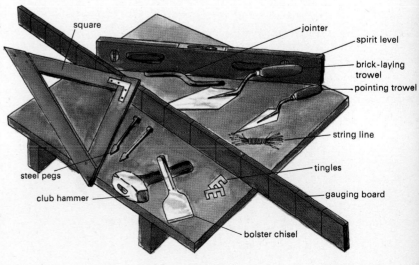

square — jointer — spirit level — brick-laying trowel — pointing trowel — string line — tingles — gauging board — steel pegs — club hammer — bolster chisel

On firm subsoil a light wall does not require a concrete strip foundation. Instead lay a course of bricks side by side in the trench. But in most cases fill the trench with concrete using Mix A: 1 part cement, 2½ parts sand and 4 parts coarse aggregate.

If in doubt about the nature of the subsoil, seek expert advice before proceeding.

Setting out the trench

To mark out the area to be dug out, place two pegs at either end. Tie a taut string indicating the outline of the trench which should extend about 120mm either side of the wall. Thus for a 225mm wall the strip will be 120 + 225 + 120mm = 465mm wide. For larger projects use easily constructed profile boards instead of pegs to hold the taut strings.

Excavate the trench using the strings as a guide, and level the bottom to the correct depth.

Concrete foundation strip

To establish levels, drive a datum peg into the ground in a safe place about 450mm from the trench. For a garden wall the top of the peg should extend about 150mm, but for a shed or building the top of the peg should be set at the planned level of the floor slab. Then using a straight-edge and spirit level, a constant level can be established by measuring up or down from datum level.

Before pouring the concrete, drive two or three pegs in the trench indicating the exact depth of the concrete. Check that the pegs are all level with a board and spirit level.

For garden sheds or buildings, the top of the concrete should be a multiple of 75mm below the datum so that the brick courses line up with the slab level. Set the tops of the pegs between 150 and 300mm below ground level.

The concrete can now be poured into the trench. For quantities over 3 cu m you may want to use ready-mixed concrete, provided there is proper access. Work the concrete so that it is level with the top of the pegs. On a sloping site stepped foundations are necessary. Make sure each step overlaps the next (see p. 39).

Laying bricks

The first course is most important since if this course is level and straight it will be much easier to lay the following courses accurately. (Follow the diagrams, opposite.)

First determine the wall line by using taut strings between pegs or between the profile boards used before. Transfer the line to the top of the concrete by using a spirit level vertically. You can draw a straight line on the concrete between two points by using a chalk line.

A chalk line is a simple device which contains replaceable chalk which is deposited on the string as you pull it out. Have

Setting-out details for foundations

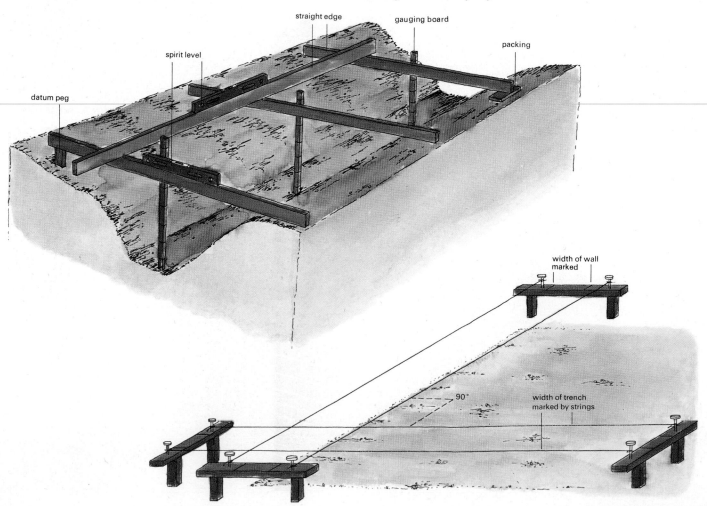

a helper hold the end of the string firmly on one point on the concrete as you walk to the other point unrolling the string.

To mark the line, pull the string very taut and hold the end with your thumb over the point on the concrete. When you lift the string with your other hand and let it go with a snap on to the concrete, the chalk mark is left. Alternatively, lay a little mortar and mark the line in it with a trowel.

Laying a straight garden wall is easy, but for a garden shed the exterior outline of the brickwork must be laid out so that the sides of the rectangle are square. Plan the lengths of the walls to be multiples of 225mm if possible. Then use a builder's square to make sure the sides are square. Check that the diagonals are equal.

Remember to refer to the local authority in case planning permission is required.

Start at an end or a corner and spread a layer of mortar with the trowel to bed the first brick. Lay a second brick a few feet along the line and bridge the two bricks with a straight-edge. Place the spirit level on the straight-edge and make any adjustments to the higher brick to bring the two level.

It's not easy to lay a uniform thickness of mortar. A gauge rod made of a wooden batten marked with course depths will be helpful.

Spread a layer of mortar a little more than 10mm thick, then draw the trowel through to make a valley. When the next brick is placed, the mortar will be compressed and the valley filled up. Any excess that squelches outside the building line is trimmed off with the side of the trowel.

Lay a band of mortar about 300mm long for each brick and the excess can be turned up on to the edge of the brick to form the vertical joint. Tap down the brick with the handle of the trowel.

Continue in this way until the first course of bricks is laid along the line. Build up the corners in steps four or five courses high, checking level and plumb and diagonal with the spirit level. Knock in any bricks that are out of place.

To lay the second course stretch the bricklayer's line between the corners. Use tingles to prevent sagging.

If the mortar is uneven, skim off the excess and use it to fill the cavities. If the mortar is too thick and will not compress, remove the brick and scrape some off. If the mortar has dried and the brick is not fixed firmly, do not be too concerned as it will be gripped on three other sides. If the mortar has no grip, scrape it off and start again. On a hot day it's worth wetting the bricks before laying them. This will ensure that moisture from the mortar is not absorbed too quickly by the bricks causing the mortar to lose its grip.

If the layer of mortar is too thin, remove the brick and add more. The brick may not be gripped as well as before, but for the occasional brick this will not be critical. Check each complete course for height with the gauge rod and use the spirit level vertically, horizontally and diagonally to check that all the bricks are in line.

Using a hammer and bolster

To cut a brick, mark the brick on the face side with a pencil. Put the brick on a firm surface and hold the bolster along the line to be cut while striking it one hard blow with the hammer. Clean up the edge by hacking with the edge of the trowel.

On garden walls the top layer of bricks, called the coping course, protects the wall from the elements. These bricks should, therefore, be facing bricks. A neat finish is to stand bricks or halved bricks on end in a row or to use one of the special-purpose coping bricks available in various shapes.

Flush pointing

This is the type of pointing used where appearance is not too important. It is relatively quick and easy to do even for the inexperienced worker

Weathered pointing

This method of pointing is the most difficult but is probably the neatest when well done. The trowel, bottom right, is often used instead of the Frenchman

Hollow pointing

A popular method of finishing which is easy to do even on facing brickwork. The dressing tool is simply made from a piece of iron rod about 10mm diameter

Pointing brickwork

There are three common joint finishes, flush, weathered and round or hollow. The process of making the joints neat and weather-resistant is called pointing and is done as the bricks are laid or when the wall is completed.

Flush joints are made simply by scraping away any excess mortar using the edge of a trowel to leave the joints flush with the face of the brick. If you are not sufficiently skilful with the trowel, rub the mortar with a narrow strip of wood wrapped in sacking. Take care not to smear mortar on to the face of the brickwork.

Weathered joints are the most difficult to make. Fill the cavity with mortar so that it protrudes slightly beyond the surface. Place the hawk against the wall below the joint to collect any droppings. Complete each vertical joint first, working in an area of about a square metre. The object is to wipe the trowel at an angle along the joint. Draw the trowel downwards, resting the left-hand edge of the trowel against the inside face of the left-hand brick, with the right-hand side of the trowel pressing flat against the right-hand brick. When doing the horizontal joints, slope the mortar out towards the bottom edge by pressing inwards with the top edge of the trowel.

A small tool called a Frenchman can be used to skim off excess mortar and leave a neat finish. It is made from a metal strip bent and filled to a point at one end. Move the tool along a straight-edge held in line with the joint.

A rounded length of metal is used for round or hollow joints. This bar is pressed along the joint to leave a smooth, concave band of mortar.

Repointing brickwork

Chip out the old mortar with a chisel and club hammer or raking tool and brush all dust from the cavity. Soak the cavities with water to prevent the bricks from absorbing too much moisture from the mortar. Then proceed with pointing as required.

Working with blocks

Building blocks and screen wall blocks are used widely by the home handyman for constructing buildings and decorative walls. Their obvious advantage over bricks is that, being larger, there are less of them to lay for a given size wall.

Standard concrete building blocks are 450mm long × 225mm wide in a range of thicknesses up to 225mm. 400 × 200mm blocks are used for small walls. Remember that these are nominal sizes which include the 10mm thickness of mortar. The actual size of a 450 × 225 × 100mm block would, therefore, be 440 × 215 × 100mm.

There are several different grades. Lightweight plain wall blocks are not weather-resistant and need a protective rendering. Aerated and textured lightweight blocks also need to be protected with rendering but they are easier to cut and groove for electric cables. Dense concrete plain wall blocks are weather-resistant and do not need further protection.

Plain wall blocks are usually built to a stretcher bond system. Half blocks are available to eliminate cutting.

Foundations

The same foundation techniques used for a brick wall apply to block walls. But when a wall is over 2m high, piers are built in for stability. To allow for piers, the foundations should be twice as wide as the thickness of the blocks. The base of the trench must be a minimum of 350mm below the ground and a concrete layer of at least 150mm is needed. To reduce the risk of the foundations being weakened by digging at a later stage, ensure that one course of blockwork is set below ground level. On a sloping site, stepped foundations are required. Each step should equal the height of one block, and each step must overlap the next.

Setting out a strip foundation for blockwork is exactly the same as for brickwork but keep in mind that wall lengths should be in multiples of 450mm wherever possible.

Concrete and mortar

The concrete for the foundations should be Mix A: $1:2\frac{1}{2}:4$, but for light walls on firm ground leave out the sand and use one part cement to five parts coarse aggregate.

For the mortar mix follow the recommendations of the block manufacturer but if in doubt use a mortar of one part cement, one part lime and six parts sand. Other mortars such as 1:2:9 or a cement, sand and special plasticiser mixture can also be used.

Notice that masonry cement is specified for the mortar. This provides a mix which is weaker than the blocks. If minor settlement problems arise later, any cracks will follow the line of least resistance through the joints. These can then be repointed.

Table A
Maximum dimensions for free-standing block walls

Actual block thickness	*Max. height*	*Max. spacing between piers*
75mm	1.5m	3.0m
90mm	1.75m	3.5m
100mm	2.0m	4.0m
140mm	2.5m	5.0m
190mm	3.0m	6.0m

Wall heights and pier spacing

All external walls must be strong enough to resist lateral forces such as wind. Table A gives recommended maximum

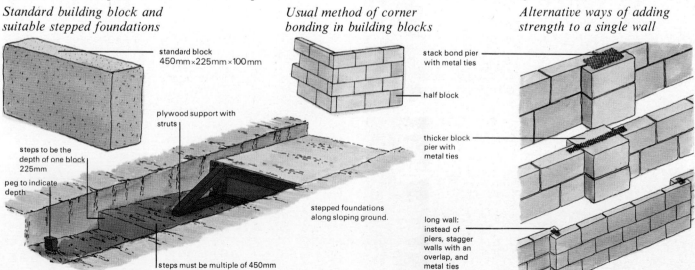

Standard building block and suitable stepped foundations

standard block
450mm × 225mm × 100mm

plywood support with struts

steps to be the depth of one block 225mm

peg to indicate depth

steps must be multiple of 450mm

stepped foundations along sloping ground.

Usual method of corner bonding in building blocks

half block

Alternative ways of adding strength to a single wall

stack bond pier with metal ties

thicker block pier with metal ties

long wall: instead of piers, stagger walls with an overlap, and metal ties

heights for free-standing garden walls. Depending on the thickness of the block wall, lateral bracing is needed at distances given in the table. Internal walls are braced by other intersecting walls but external, free-standing walls need piers.

Generally, piers should be spaced at a maximum distance of twice the height of the wall. Thus a 100mm free-standing block wall can be up to 2m in height but it must have piers at least every 4m. In windy, exposed areas, use these guidelines conservatively, reducing them by two-thirds.

Building piers

A pier can be built in several ways. It can be stack bonded and tied to the wall with metal bonding ties at every other course. Press the metal well into the mortar so that each tie is well covered The long dimensions of the diamond shapes in the mesh should lie at right angles to the joint.

Or a pier can be formed from a stack of thicker blocks with reinforcement at every other course.

For long walls, instead of building piers, build the wall in panels to the allowable length and stagger and overlap these panels tying them together with metal ties at alternate courses.

Building with plain blocks

The basic brickwork techniques are used for building with blocks. Start at the ends of the wall building up about four courses at a time. Check each block for vertical plumb against surrounding blocks. Complete the courses between the corners, checking for level and plumb and following the string guide line pinned to the ends of the wall.

Spread the mortar on the blocks below and on one side of the block being laid so that horizontal and vertical joints will be made as work proceeds. Tap the block into place making sure it is well bedded down. The mortar joint should be 10mm thick. Check it with a piece of 10mm thick wood if necessary.

When a wall is to be higher than four courses, a couple of days should be allowed for the mortar to harden before building further courses.

Screen wall blocks

The advantage of screen wall blocks, apart from their decorative appeal, is that they define an area without completely enclosing it. Used as fencing they allow plenty of light and air through to plants and vegetables.

Screen wall blocks are manufactured in various patterns. Most builders' merchants will carry a stock. The most common block size is 300 × 300 × 100mm. Matching pilaster (pier) blocks and coping slabs are also available. Pilaster blocks are grooved so that the wall units will slot in securely.

Screen wall blocks are usually stack bonded with each block exactly on top of another so that vertical joints are created. Horizontal reinforcement is therefore required.

The foundations for screen walls are laid out the same way as for other brick and block walls. Make the trench about 300mm wide but, since the wall is very light, a shallower strip foundation may be used.

Building with screen blocks

Small screen walls can be built without pilasters at either end For a low garden wall or a screen around dustbins, for example, follow the instructions but omit the pilasters.

A wall with pilasters takes a little more planning since the pilaster at the starting end may need to be reinforced with a length of reinforcing bar or angle iron stuck vertically into the strip foundation at the time of pouring concrete. Check the manufacturer's details for advice. The maximum distance between pilasters without reinforcement is about 3m.

Start at one end, threading pilaster blocks over the reinforcement and laying it on a bed of mortar. Check that the block is level in both directions. Lay two or three more pilaster blocks and fill the cavity with fairly fluid mortar made from one part cement to three parts coarse aggregate. Check the level of the blocks and after three blocks check plumb on both faces.

Now lay the first screen block on a mortar bed and fit it into the pilaster groove with a mortar joint. Continue by laying the rest of the first course without mortar, leaving a 10mm gap between each block. Check the gap with a 10mm thick piece of wood. Find the location of the pilaster at the other end and lay the first pilaster block, checking level with the first pilaster block at the other end. Stretch a string between the bottom blocks after adding two more blocks and checking level and plumb. Now lay the first course of screen blocks on a mortar bed with 10mm mortar joints, following the line. Make sure to check level and line frequently, tapping blocks into place where necessary. Continue laying each course moving the string up and adding pilaster blocks as you build up.

When the desired number of courses have been laid, add coping slabs and pilaster caps to protect the wall.

Rendering

The external faces of block walls used in buildings must be rendered with a mixture of cement, lime and sand to keep out moisture.

To make the job of getting a smooth finish easier, fix vertical battens to the wall to form a series of bays. When the mix has been applied in a bay, a straight-edge can be rested

Starting building a block wall to a string line

Using a spirit level to ensure a wall is vertical

Some of the screen block patterns that are available

A neat way of concealing the household dustbin

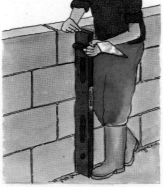

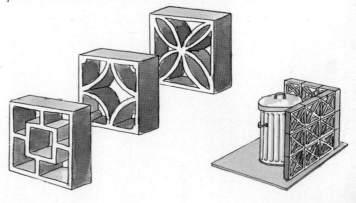

on the side battens and drawn upwards to level off the rendering. When the bays are completed, the battens are removed and the remaining spaces filled up. Corner battens are critical. Fix these at an accurate vertical using a spirit level.

Three coats of rendering material are applied. The first

Bedding the first pilaster block with reinforcing rod

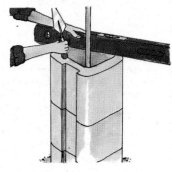
Adding more blocks and ensuring they are level

The screen blocks fit into the pilaster block groove

The first course of screen blocks laid to a line

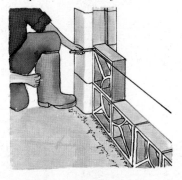
Fix the string line to match the pilaster block joint

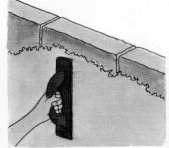
Finish off the wall with purpose made coping blocks

which is a mixture of 1 part cement, 6 parts sand and 1 part lime is applied with a steel trowel to a thickness of 6mm. After smoothing each bay with the straight-edge, comb the surface with a tool called a scratcher to form criss-cross diagonal lines. Allow 12 hours to dry.

The second or floating coat is 12mm thick and is sometimes applied as two 6mm coats. After smoothing, the surface can be keyed using the scratcher to form horizontal lines. Flatten out any ridges using a wood float.

The final coat depends on the finish to be used. Cement fining is the most common finish and achieved by using a wood float followed by a sponge used in a light, circular movement. A mixture of two parts sand to one part cement is used for this.

Tyrolean finish

This finish which is available in several colours is fairly simple to achieve. The final effect is very attractive and offers good weather resistance. With blockwork a suitable base can be provided by brushing down the surface and applying a slurry of sand and cement with a soft brush. This fills in the texture of the blockwork surface and leaves a smooth finish. Use a mix of one part Portland cement to two parts fine sand mixed to a fluid consistency. Dampen the blockwork so that water from the mix will not be absorbed too quickly. Use a soft brush to work the mix well into the texture of the blocks and then rub the surface with sacking. Brush an area about two courses by 3m before rubbing.

When the wall is finished and the slurry has set, cover it with polythene sheets for a few days to allow it to cure.

Alternatively, apply an undercoat with the Tyrolean mixture. Brush this well in with a soft brush. This has the advantage of providing an undercoat of the same colour as the final finish.

If you omit the preparation stage, the Tyrolean finish can still be applied to blocks which are not too dense. The Tyrolean finish is bought in bags of ready mixed ingredients to which water is added. It is applied with a hand-held machine which can be hired.

The finish is applied to a dry, reasonably absorbent surface. Keep moving the machine without varying its distance from the wall.

The final finish is built up in three layers, each applied by using the machine at a different angle to the wall to ensure good coverage. At the end of the first application the surface will look speckled.

Each application must be allowed to set before the next is applied. Intervals between coats depend on the absorbency of the surface and the weather. A final light spraying with water will allow the finish to harden more quickly.

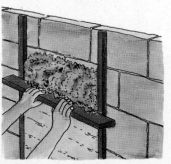
Ruling off a bay with a timber straight-edge

Smoothing with a wood float. Blocks are shown for clarity

Wall preparation for applying a Tyrolean finish

A hand-operated Tyrolean machine can be hired

Structure
Treating Decay

DAMP

The walls, floors and roof of a house must be constructed to keep out moisture and keep in heat. Moisture is always present in the ground and in the air and a house must be built with moisture barriers to prevent it from entering the house. The damp-proof membrane, below the ground floor is usually a thin plastic sheet which prevents the moisture from rising through the concrete slab. The damp-proof course, D.P.C., is a thin, impervious layer built into the lower part of a brick wall to prevent the porous brickwork from soaking up moisture from the ground. These layers must be overlapped to provide a continuous barrier.

Rain falling on to roofs or being driven by the wind into walls quickly finds its way into the house if there are structural defects such as loose roof tiles or defective flashing. Metal or asbestos/bitumen flashing strips are placed where low roofs meet walls to prevent water from getting in. The flashing, which is held in the brickwork joints, channels the water on to the roof. Other main causes of damp are leakages from internal pipes, storage tanks or radiators, condensation on cold interior surfaces and waterlogged brickwork.

Damp creates a musty smell, spoils decorations and leaves a cold, unhealthy atmosphere in a house. And damp results in attack by fungus diseases which can cause structural decay to the house.

Older houses, built without a damp-proof course and the protection of the double skin of a cavity wall are most likely to become damp. Modern houses are also subject to damp mainly through neglect. The whole house should be inspected for damp at least once a year so that any problem will be discovered before extensive damage is caused.

Damp caused by roof defects/chimney stacks and pots

The first place to inspect for damp is the roof. Before climbing on to the roof, stand back and view the chimney stack and pots through a pair of binoculars. Look for missing pointing, damaged flaunching, damaged brickwork, cracked, damaged or missing pots and defective flashing. If the stack is seriously damaged, the brickwork will have to be dismantled and the stack rebuilt. Should the chimney become saturated, damp will soak down and appear on the chimney breast below. Since the flue is chilly, a downdraught may be created.

Before attempting roof repairs, obtain a roof ladder designed to hook over the roof ridge. If the flaunching mortar around the chimney is cracked and loose, remove it with a hammer and cold chisel. Clean away loose mortar and lay new flaunching. The thickness at the pot must be at least 50mm, sloping down to about 12mm at the edge of the stack.

If the stack and flaunching are sound, remove loose bricks, clean and reset them replacing any which are broken or badly chipped. Rake and brush out decayed joints to a depth of at least 12mm before repointing.

A cracked or broken pot must be replaced. Chimney pots are heavy and it is a good idea to use a rope to lower it to the ground. If the pot is loose, reset it with the base at least one brick course down.

Flashing is used to make a watertight junction between the chimney stack and the roof. Defective flashing allows rainwater to seep in, which spoils the ceiling and chimney breast below. If decayed jointing mortar has caused flashing to pull away, push it back in and replace the mortar. New flashing can be cut in lead, zinc or aluminium. Alternatively, the complete flashing can be replaced with a proprietary

There are so many places where damp can make its presence felt – here are some likely places and causes

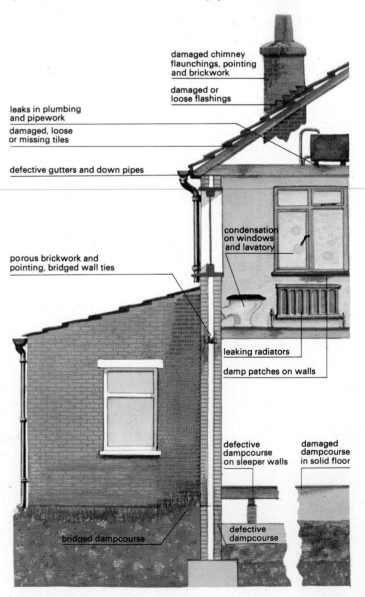

damaged chimney flaunchings, pointing and brickwork

damaged or loose flashings

leaks in plumbing and pipework

damaged, loose or missing tiles

defective gutters and down pipes

condensation on windows and lavatory

porous brickwork and pointing, bridged wall ties

leaking radiators

damp patches on walls

defective dampcourse on sleeper walls

damaged dampcourse in solid floor

defective dampcourse

bridged dampcourse

asbestos/bitumen material using the old flashing as a pattern. Seal slight gaps or cracks in the flashing with a bituminous mastic compound applied with a trowel.

In some older houses, chimneys have a cement mortar fillet instead of proper flashing. Point gaps which open up under the fillet with a stiff mastic or fit flashing in these places.

If damp patches have appeared on a chimney breast, repair the cause of the damp and then apply two coats of good quality sealer over the surface of the inside wall or line the wall with aluminium foil held in place with a rubber/bitumen adhesive. Apply a lining paper before repapering or painting.

Tiles and slates
Inspect and repair roof tiles and slates from within the loft if possible, to avoid the hazard of working on the roof. In a modern house the roof will be felted and this will not be possible. A pair of binoculars are useful for inspecting the roof. Look for cracked, dislodged or missing tiles or slates. It may be necessary to go into the loft during a heavy rainfall to find the cause of the leak as often water coming through the roof is deflected by the rafters and the leak appears elsewhere on the ceiling. Repair or replace slates and tiles following the procedure in the section on roofs.

Gutters and downpipes
Damp patches which appear just below ceiling level on the inside of walls during heavy rain indicate damaged or blocked gutters and downpipes. Eaves gutters and downpipes can overflow and soak walls if they are not kept clean and free of obstructions. It is possible for the gutters to become full of sediment particularly with tiled roofs. Use a ladder which extends three rungs or more above the guttering to inspect the area. Lash the ladder to a ring bolt screwed into the fascia board which holds the gutter brackets.

Clear the gutter of any leaves, moss growths and other rubbish which has gathered in it and check for birds' nests in downpipes. If any are found, clear them out and fit wire cages over the pipes to restrict further entry. To check that there is an adequate fall towards the downpipe, pour water into the gutter at the farthest end from the downpipe and check whether it runs freely along the gutter and down the pipe. If it gathers in pools, adjust the gutter brackets until it flows smoothly. If water overflows from the top of a downpipe which is not blocked, the problem may be caused by a blocked gully, drain pipe or soakaway. (See page 78.)

If water drips from the joints between lengths of cast iron or asbestos cement guttering, the joints will have to be remade. Bed them on mastic jointing compound or on a layer of mastic-impregnated linen tape. Repair cracks or broken gutters with a proprietary resin filler following manufacturer's instructions.

In cases where cast iron or asbestos cement guttering must be replaced, fit one of the modern plastic gutter and downpipe systems. (See page 72.)

Damp caused by wall defects
Walls absorb a great deal of water and rely on the wind and sun to dry them out. External walls can become damp on the inside and, if this damp is not detected and cured, it can extend over the complete surface of the walls. It is therefore essential to find the cause of the damp and take immediate remedial action.

There are two types of brick and block walls: solid and cavity. Older houses were built with solid walls, whereas most modern houses have cavity walls in which the outer and inner walls are separated by an air cavity which provides better

Even a simple chimney stack offers several opportunities for damp to penetrate. Check these points

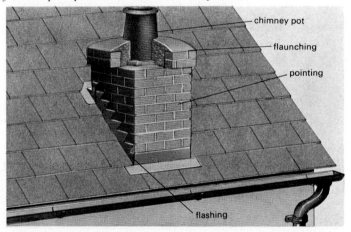

chimney pot
flaunching
pointing
flashing

insulation. Cavity walls are held together by galvanised steel ties, designed to prevent water from creeping across to the inner wall and causing damp on the inside surface. When these walls are built, mortar must not be allowed to drop down between the walls and catch on the galvanised ties. As mortar is porous it will act as a bridge allowing water to pass through it along the ties and into the inner wall.

Solid walls of brick, concrete or stone absorb water at different rates, depending on the porosity of the material and the quality of the pointing. Most ordinary materials used in house construction are of medium to high porosity. Heavy driving rain will gradually penetrate and damp will appear on the inside of walls. Walls facing the prevailing rainbearing winds from the south-west are the most vulnerable. If damp appears on walls, check for defective pointing on external walls. Make good any defects by raking out the old mortar to a depth of about 12mm before repointing.

Damp around windows and doors
The woodwork around window and door frames can shrink and pull away from the surrounding brickwork, leaving cracks where damp will penetrate. These gaps should not be sealed with cement or putty as this hardens and will only crack again. A mastic compound gives a permanently flexible

Seal gaps between window frames and walls with mastic

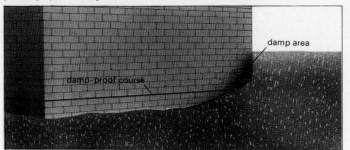

Earth piled up over the dpc of a house wall gives a passage for damp to enter and ruin decorations

damp area

damp-proof course

Gravity injection of dpc fluid into a brick wall

seal regardless of slight movements. Mastic can be bought in cartridges for use in an applicator gun, similar in action to a grease gun, or it is available in cans and is applied with a trowel.

Inspect drip grooves under window sills. If they become clogged with paint, water will run over the grooves and on to the brickwork of the walls. Clean out accumulations of paint to restore the groove. Pin a painted batten along the underside of window sills if there is no drip groove. Water will then flow off the top of the sill and along the batten to the ground rather than running on to the wall.

Preventing damp in walls

There are several precautionary measures which can be taken to prevent damp in walls. Cement rendering gives good protection and is an ideal all-over covering for walls which are unattractive. Roughcast and pebbledash are mixtures of stone chippings or small pebbles which are thrown on to a cement and sand rendering to give a more decorative covering. These decorative finishes are not waterproof but if they are free of cracks they greatly reduce damp absorption. (See page 40.)

If a wall has become damp because of a cracked decorative finish, fill the cracks with mortar. Cut out damaged or loose material and repair with fresh rendering and finish. If the surface is sound but damp problems persist, paint over the decorative finish with a cement or stone base paint. These paints which are bought as powder and are mixed with water, are used to protect and decorate. An alternative paint for this purpose is exterior-grade emulsion. Gloss or bitumen paint is expensive and unattractive and traps any existing damp in the wall thereby driving it into the house.

For exposed brickwork, coat the walls with a silicone water-repellent. This colourless liquid seals the brickwork against further damp penetration while allowing it to breathe so that trapped moisture can escape.

Rising damp

Damp patches which appear at skirting level on the ground floor, usually indicate that moisture is rising up through the walls from the ground below. To prevent rising damp, a damp-proof course usually of slate, engineering bricks or felt is fitted between the brick courses as an unbroken barrier right around the house.

If soil or sand is piled against the wall above damp-proof course level, water can penetrate the walls. Removing the soil or sand will remedy this problem.

If there is no damp-proof course then either a conventional one can be inserted or one of the various liquids available for treating walls against rising damp can be used.

Treating rising damp

If the problem is not too serious, treat with a damp repelling liquid on the bare bricks of external walls and the plaster on inside walls. The liquid will seep through up to 225mm of brickwork to form a barrier which is impervious to damp.

The silicone injection method involves drilling holes into the walls around the outside of the house, about 150mm above ground level and injecting a water repellent solution which spreads throughout the brickwork to form an effective barrier against rising damp. A system of wall ventilation or atmospheric damp proofing using porous earthenware tubes inserted in the wall at the level of the original damp-proof course is often used in conjunction with silicone injections. The tubes are sloped downwards towards the ground outside and a grille is fitted to the outside wall to keep out rainwater.

With this siphonage method the air in the tubes absorbs moisture from the wall and, as it is cooled, the air becomes heavier and more dense. Consequently it flows out of the tubes and is replaced by fresh air. In this way a constant circulation is set up in the tubes and each becomes a drying centre. With the Electro-Osmosis system, which is a trade, not a D.I.Y. process a copper strip linked to an earth rod driven deep into the soil is introduced into the wall at damp-course level. The minute electrical charges in the wall are discharged, preventing moisture from rising.

Damp caused by defective solid floors

In solid floors a badly installed or damaged damp-proof membrane will allow damp to rise to the surface of the floor. Before deciding on any course of treatment, make absolutely certain that the problem is as a result of rising damp and not condensation. These can easily be confused. One positive test for this is to bed a small piece of glass on a ring of putty and lay it on the floor so that the putty excludes all air. After about 24 hours, check. Rising damp will be trapped under the glass and condensation will be on the outside.

If the trouble is slight, cover the dry, smooth floor with two or three coats of liquid bitumen. Epoxy resins are also successful as surface treatment.

When rising damp becomes more serious, a sandwich treatment is used. At least two coats of liquid bitumen are first applied to the floor. While it is still wet, sprinkle the top coat with sharp, washed sand which prevents damage and forms a key for a 50mm layer of screed on top. Brush off surplus sand when the top coat of the bitumen is dry. Take bitumen up the wall to tie in with the wall damp-proof course.

If rising damp is extreme, it will be necessary to take up the concrete floor and lay a new one which incorporates a suitable damp-proof membrane. If an old timber floor has rotted and needs replacing, it is as well to consider laying a concrete floor with a damp-proof membrane instead.

Siphonage method; porous earthenware tubes set in a wall will remove damp

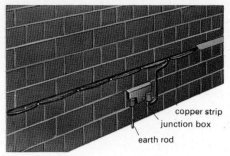

Electro-Osmosis—earthing the electric potential stops damp being drawn up

copper strip
junction box
earth rod

Up to 225mm of wall penetration is claimed for brush-applied treatments

Treating damp in internal walls and basements

In addition to liquid treatments for use as damp-proof courses, there are liquid treatments which can be used on internal walls and in basements to prevent damp from spoiling decorations. Some simple treatments can be painted over wet or dry plaster and can then be painted or papered over. This type of treatment only seals the surface. It does not cure damp or prevent condensation.

Another method of resisting but not curing damp to plastered walls is to line the walls with a waterproof laminated paper or aluminium foil. Some of these materials contain a specially formulated primer and adhesive, which combine to bond a roll of waterproof laminated covering to a damp surface. A strong fungicide is incorporated in the adhesive to prevent fungal attack. This type of treatment not only seals the surface to prevent damp from showing through, but also resists alkalis and efflorescence.

The only permanent way to cure damp on internal walls is to trace the cause of penetration, remedy the fault and renew all damaged plaster. Damp walls cause plaster to crumble or perish. If plaster is cracked, the cracks can easily be filled. Large areas of defective plaster will have to be hacked away and joints in the brickwork raked out to form a key for new plaster. With smooth bricks, either score them to make a key for the plaster or use a PVA bonding agent which gives good adhesion.

Plastering is a skill which requires a great deal of practice. There are pitch impregnated fibre based materials which are corrugated to form dovetail keys to hold plaster on one side making the job easier. Used as vertical damp-proof courses, these are fixed direct to brickwork or masonry with galvanised nails. If condensation rather than damp is the problem, use a special plaster which resists condensation.

CONDENSATION

Condensation is often mistaken for penetrating damp, but its causes and cures are quite different. It occurs when warm, moist air comes in contact with cool surfaces. The beads of moisture on wall tiles and windows in kitchens and bathrooms are examples. An indication that the problem is caused by condensation is when external walls are damp inside on cold, dry days. Condensation also appears as sweating under floorcoverings laid over concrete or tiled floors or on cold floor tiles. To cure condensation, rooms must be kept warm and well-insulated with adequate ventilation to allow steam and water vapour to escape.

Condensation presents the greatest problems in kitchens and bathrooms. Generally, bathrooms are quite small and, when the bath is run, a great deal of steam is released into the air. A solution is first to run cold water, and then run hot water in under the cold water through a rubber hose to minimise the amount of steam. Ventilation can be provided in kitchens and bathrooms by air bricks or louvre windows. On dry, sunny days an open window will help steam to escape.

If steam problems are not acute, a fixed louvre ventilator installed in a wall, window or above a door may suffice. A strategically placed electric fan will help to disperse concentrations of steam towards an air brick or open window.

A cooker hood is a useful attachment for removing steam, grease and other smells from the kitchen. If the cooker is not placed against an outside wall, fit trunking to convey the fumes to the nearest point of extraction. Cooker hoods either disperse fumes through an outlet in the wall or recirculate the air after it has been filtered through a charcoal filter.

Extractor fans

An extractor fan will keep the air moving and remove heavy concentrations of moist air. For maximum benefit, the fan should be near the cooker or other source of steam and must be very high up in the room. It is important to fit a large enough extractor fan. It must be able to produce enough force to drive against an oncoming wind. For a guide to buying the correct size fan, multiply the volume of the room by the number of air changes required. Air in a kitchen

A floor damp-proof membrane should join with the wall dpc.

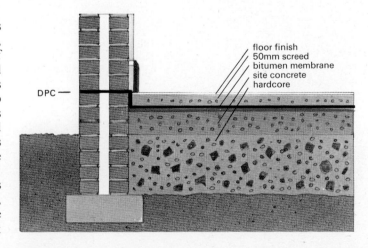

DPC

floor finish
50mm screed
bitumen membrane
site concrete
hardcore

should generally be changed about 15 times an hour. A 150mm model with an extraction capacity of 280 cubic metres/hour is the smallest size which should be considered.

There are extractor fans designed for wall or window fitting and others for mounting in roof lights, pitched roofs and ceilings directly below attics. Back-draught shutters are built into many extractor fans, which prevent cold blasts from entering a room when the fan is switched off.

When buying an extractor fan for fitting in a window, seek the advice of a glass merchant. It is important that the glass is strong enough to carry it. Seek expert advice, too, if a kitchen has a boiler in it: an extractor fan can starve a boiler of vital combustion air and cause dangerous fumes.

Condensation on walls and ceilings

The best way of dealing with condensation which has formed on internal walls is to provide thermal insulation and to increase the room temperature. Paint kitchen and bathroom ceilings with an anti-condensation paint. As well as providing thermal insulation, the paint absorbs moisture when the humidity is high and releases it when the air is drier.

If condensation is more severe as it may be when a non-porous material such as gloss paint has been put on the ceiling, the best solution is to cover the surface with expanded polystyrene tiles or sheet. This provides good insulation and condensation will not form easily on it. (See page 108.) Choose a non-flammable grade, to cut down fire risk. Sheet material can be covered with a ceiling paper and tiles can either be left plain or painted with a fire-retardent or emulsion paint.

In living rooms and bedrooms the amount of water vapour present is far less. One of the main contributory factors may be a blocked off fireplace which reduces or cuts off ventilation completely. In this case install an air brick or drill holes in the covering material. The ideal dry heat for a room is produced by radiators, infra-red heaters or electric fires and convectors.

If these initial measures do not completely overcome the problem, affected walls must be insulated. Cavity infill in which foamed plastic or mineral wool are blown into the cavity wall is a popular method, but requires specialist equipment. (See page 106.) Another method is to line walls internally, but the lining must not be so thick that it obstructs the operation of doors and windows. An easier way to produce thermal insulation and thereby reduce condensation, is to line the walls with sheet expanded polystyrene. It is sold in rolls and is easy to fix. (See page 108.)

If a wall has mould, mildew or fungus, it must be treated before redecorating. Strip off wallpaper and apply a fungicidal wash. Ordinary washing will have no effect on combating fungus spores. If the wall is being painted, use a mould-resistant paint.

To cure condensation problems on external walls, fit a tubular strip heater at the base of the wall. These are also effective in keeping the chill off cold walls in bathrooms.

Condensation on floors

Condensation on solid concrete floors often is mistaken for rising damp. A sure test to distinguish the difference, is the glass and putty test described on page 44.

Laying some form of insulation over the floor is the simplest way to cure condensation. Use wood blocks or a carpet with a good quality underlay. When a floor must be easy to clean, sheet vinyl or vinyl tiles with built-in foam or other type of underlay is the best covering.

Condensation on windows

Even windows which have been double glazed attract a great deal of moisture. Only an hermetically sealed unit, where the space between the two panes of glass has been evacuated and then filled with dry air or inert gas, will be reasonably condensation free.

With most of the other types of double glazing, if moisture is evident between the panes of glass, drill a few small holes through the frame and into the cavity from the outside. (See page 111.) These act as drains for any condensed moisture which may collect and allow for circulation of exterior air to minimise condensation. Alternatively, place silica gel crystals between the panes to absorb the moisture. Once the crystals are saturated they must be removed and dried before re-use.

WOOD ROT

For any type of pest decay, whether it be mould, insect or fungus to take hold, the wood must be fairly moist. Precautions such as the insertion of air bricks to prevent moisture from entering the house or penetrating exterior woodwork are therefore very important. If moisture does penetrate, the cause must be found and remedied and the wet timbers must receive immediate attention. Roof timbers, joists, skirting boards, window frames and sills, cellar timbers, fences and garage doors are all vulnerable.

Dry rot

The first visible sign of rot is a spreading mass of mycelium which are white, grey or brown sheets of soft threads with a cotton wool texture. Mycelium occurs as a result of dry rot spores being allowed to grow on moist timber. These spores germinate on wood with more than about 20% moisture content. Fruiting bodies form like giant toadstool caps, which then release more spores. They are spread on to new sites by air currents, by tools and even by feet.

The mycelium can spread considerable distances and does not stop where the damp ends. It can travel over dry wood and through plaster, brick, concrete and stone. The threads carry their own supply of water to create ideal conditions for spreading the fungus to new sites. If the fungus is not detected and eradicated, it can soon climb from a cellar into the attic. It can even come through a party wall from the next house.

There are various indications of dry rot. Rooms take on a musty, mushroom-like smell. Timber appears warped and paint begins to flake. Bare timber splits both longitudinally and across the grain to form large cubes. Damp patches or fungi appear on plaster. The growth can easily take place out of sight, so if dry rot is suspected, lift floorboards to check for rot and look behind cracked and distorted skirtings. The decayed timber will usually be dusty brown and crumble into a dry powder when touched.

Remove and burn all affected timber and cut timber back at least 1 metre beyond the farthest sign of attack. Remove panelling or plaster for at least 1 metre around the affected area to expose brickwork and check that the dry rot strands have not spread further.

Kill surface spores, which look like rusty-red dust and strands on brickwork and sub-floor, by sterilising with a blowlamp. Thoroughly clean away and burn all debris. Paint the sub-floor, brickwork and timber within about 2 metres of the attack with a good quality dry rot fluid. To ensure that the brickwork and mortar joints are sufficiently soaked, drill 12mm diameter holes down into the wall at a slight angle.

Dry rot fruiting body producing spores

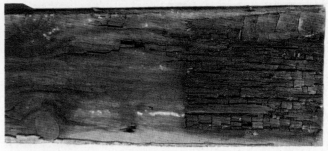

Timber affected by wet rot (photographs, Wykamol)

Woodworm

Woodworm are the grubs of various beetles which lay their eggs on timber. The grubs hatch and burrow into the timber to emerge as new beetles. Woodworm attack is recognisable by the holes and fine dust nearby. If the attack is active, there will be fresh holes showing clean, white wood inside and heaps of dust outside.

The most common wood boring insect which accounts for most woodworm damage, is the furniture beetle. It attacks not only furniture, but structural timbers, joinery, plywood, wickerwork and wattle fencing. Other insects which damage wood are the powder post beetle, longhorn beetle, death watch beetle and weevil. All these are treated in the same way.

Apply a reputable brand of insecticide to cracks, holes and joints. This is available in cans and is brushed or sprayed on. Special plastic nozzles are sometimes provided and there are aerosols designed for injecting the fluid into holes.

To treat roof timbers, remove loft insulation materials so that ceiling joists and laths can be reached. If there is severe damage to structural timbers, they may have to be strengthened or even replaced. Before starting work, read the instructions for the insecticide carefully and be sure to wear adequate protective clothing. The fluid can affect the insulation of some electric wires and these must be protected. The vapour is explosive so switch off power to electrical circuits in the area and work by an extension light connected to a socket outlet outside the area. Do not smoke near the treatment area.

Apply a proprietary woodworm fluid through a garden pressure sprayer which produces a moderately coarse spray. Spray all timber surfaces and apply the liquid liberally into open joints, crevices and end grain surfaces. The spray which filters through should take care of attacks in ceiling laths. Mayonnaise woodworm killers are easier to use. A paste is spread on top of the timbers with a knife or brush and it slowly penetrates.

Vapour fumigant smoke generators and slow-acting woodworm killers which are left in the loft, will prevent a beetle invasion and kill off minor infestation but these are only superficial treatments.

Lift floorboards at frequent intervals to check for woodworm attack and treat with either spray or paste as for roof timbers. Leave floors which have been treated with a woodworm fluid uncovered for at least four weeks before laying vinyl floorcoverings. Remove affected panelling and joinery to expose uncoated surfaces such as studding timber unless infestation appears only very slight. Treat by brushing or spraying with fluid and inject fluid into holes in painted or varnished surfaces. In all cases inspect regularly after treatment. If there are no signs of fresh attack after about a year, then the trouble has been eradicated.

Wet rot

Wet rot is less serious than dry rot, because the fungus will not spread beyond the damp timber. It flourishes only on timber which is wet. Once eradicated, the wood must be treated with a preservative because the drying wood may still be wet enough for stray spores to germinate.

Stained black wood with dark brown threads is a sign of wet rot. These can often be mistaken for the mycelium threads of dry rot. Check nearby wood, plaster and brickwork. If these are dry, wet rot fungi will not cross them. Sometimes cracks appear along the grain of decayed timber and there may also be cross-grain cracking although the cubes are not as large as with dry rot. Yellow or brown streaks or patches are often found in decayed timber.

Wet rot fungus stops growing once the moisture is removed. Cut infected timber back to sound material, eliminate the cause of damp and treat the surrounding timber with preservative. Where the surface of timber is so decayed that it can be scraped away, remove as much decayed material as possible then apply preservative. If fence posts have rotted through at their base, cut off the rotten length and reset the posts on concrete spurs so that the wood is above ground and out of moisture. (See page 51.)

Blue-grey to black streaks and patches on new softwood indicate moulds. These are harmless in themselves, but they indicate slight dampness which could become severe. Brush them off and prime, undercoat and top coat the wood for future protection. If desired, preservative can be applied before painting. The preservative makes the timber poisonous to whatever feeds off it. There are also water-soluble and organic preservatives and tar oils available for this purpose.

The common furniture beetle; it lays eggs on most timbers

Injection of woodworm fluid

Spray application of fluid

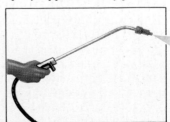

Structure
Fencing

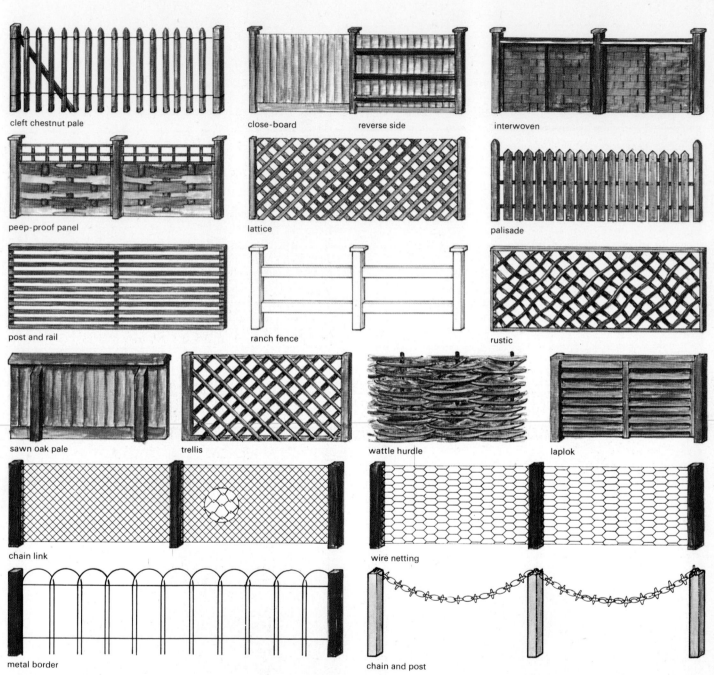

cleft chestnut pale

close-board   reverse side

interwoven

peep-proof panel

lattice

palisade

post and rail

ranch fence

rustic

sawn oak pale

trellis

wattle hurdle

laplok

chain link

wire netting

metal border

chain and post

Cleft chestnut pale: *Suitable where light and air are needed for plants.* Close-board: *For privacy and security.* Interwoven: *Inexpensive but needs regular maintenance.* Peep-proof: *Often called rustic lap.* Lattice: *Similar to trellis but more rigid.* Palisade: *For fresh air and sunlight.* Post and rail: *In several styles. Rail width and spacing*

variable. Ranch fence: *Available in timber or PVC.* Rustic: *Peeled and treated poles arranged in a criss-cross pattern.* Sawn oak pale: *Attractive although expensive.* Trellis: *Plastic or timber – inexpensive and easy to erect.* Wattle hurdle: *Interwoven twigs of alder, hazel or chestnut with vertical supports. Extremely*

durable. Laplok: *Panel fence for use with timber or concrete posts.* Chain link: *Inexpensive – made in galvanised steel, aluminium or plastic coated chain.* Wire netting: *Cheaper and in various patterns.* Metal border: *Rolls of various lengths and heights offered.* Chain and post: *Steel or nylon – more decorative than functional*

The fences forming the boundary to a property play an important part in the appearance of both the house and garden.

There are many types of fences available ranging from a simple chain-link type which is popular on housing estates, to high screen timber fences that provide complete privacy. Among the more popular types are close-board, split chestnut paling, woven larch panels, wire net, trellis and rigid PVC posts and rails. The type you choose depends on various factors; privacy desired, ease of maintenance, protection against the elements and cost.

Where privacy is a prerequisite, a solid close-board or woven fence is ideal. This acts as a windbreak and keeps children and pets in or out of the garden. Light reaching plants growing near to the fence will, however, be reduced by this type of fence. To resist buffeting from a strong wind, a solid fence must be anchored more securely than an open fence.

Timber fences made from thick boards will last longer than those made from thin wood slats. Every piece of fence made from softwood, whether posts, rails, panels or boards, must be treated with a wood preserving solution every year to prevent deterioration.

Even hardwoods, although much more resistant to attack, should be protected. Take particular care where timber is buried in, or comes into contact with, the ground.

Erecting a fence

Before erecting a fence check the Building Regulations regarding the height and type of fence allowed in your district.

Digging post holes

The most difficult part of building a fence is digging the holes for the posts. This work can be simplified with a hand-operated post hole borer which works on the same principle as a corkscrew. Large tree roots and stones will have to be broken up or dug out by other means. Dig new post holes at least 300mm from existing holes to avoid concrete or other material which may have been used to support the old fence.

A string line is essential as a guide to the line that the fence will take. Dig the hole for the first post and install the post. Then drive a peg into the location of the last post and secure a taut string line between them. On a sloping site, install the first post at the lower end of the slope.

If digging all the post holes at once, use a batten to mark out post centres along the string line. Manufacturers' catalogues often give guidance on exact centres or they can be calculated by measuring the exact width of panels and allowing for connections.

Remove the string while digging the holes, then re-tie it before proceeding. Check the string against a spirit level so that it can be used later as a guide to erecting the panels horizontally.

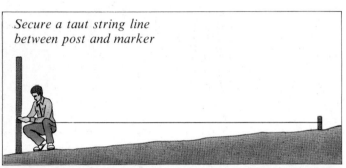

Secure a taut string line between post and marker

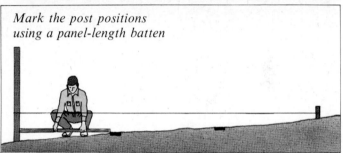

Mark the post positions using a panel-length batten

Ensure the string line is level, to guide the panels

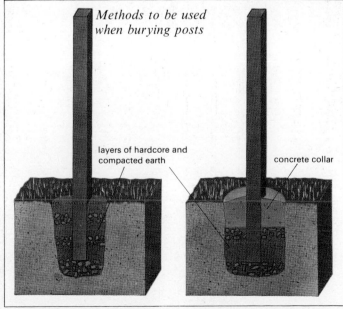

Methods to be used when burying posts

layers of hardcore and compacted earth

concrete collar

Each panel and its adjoining post is then installed in turn. Make sure that the posts touch the string line and that the tops of the panels are level.

Fixing timber posts

The usual method for fixing a timber post is to stand the post in the hole on top of a layer of rubble and pieces of brick to allow good drainage. The hole can then be filled to the top with alternate layers of well-compacted earth and rubble and finished with a layer of earth. If the ground is weak, add a 250mm thick layer of concrete forming a 250mm diameter collar around the post. Use a mix of one part cement to four parts all-in ballast for the concrete keeping it on the dry side. Alternatively, to prevent the post from rotting, use concrete spurs embedded in concrete.

Generally a 450mm deep hole is sufficient but, in very weak soils, holes as deep as 900mm may be necessary. Dig the holes first, then determine the length of the post allowing for the depth of the hole and the panel plus 75mm if the post is to protrude above the panel.

Fixing fence panels

When the first post is positioned and backfilled in its hole and the vertical is checked, fix the first panel. Use 65mm long gauge 12 galvanised or aluminium alloy nails spaced about 600mm apart. Place pieces of brick beneath each end of the panel for extra support and to ensure that the base of the panel is at least 50mm above the ground.

Position the end of the panel in the centre of the post and knock in nails on both sides of the panel. Space the nails at about 600mm centres on both sides. Position the next post and nail the panel to it. Continue until all the posts and panels are erected. Be sure that the top of each panel is level

with the string guideline. When the fence is completed, fix post caps.

Erecting a close-board fence

Follow the same procedure for setting out a string line and digging post holes. As each post is fixed in the ground, set the arris rails in the post. The other ends of the rails are set in the next post before the hole is backfilled. Gravel boards should also be fitted if there are recesses in the posts to house them.

When all posts and arris rails are up, the vertical boards can be fixed, overlapping by about 19mm. This overlap must be consistent along the entire run of the fence. The first board in each section must be fixed vertically or else the following boards will be out of line. Use a spirit level to check the position while nailing boards into the arris rail. Position the thick edge of each board over the thin edge of the previous board and nail through both edges.

Preservatives

Most fence panels and posts are sold already treated with preservative. Western red cedar and oak have greater resistance to rot than softwoods and should therefore be used for the posts. However, any timber will rot after a few years without protection. Although some manufacturers state that further preservative treatment is not necessary for a few years, it is a sensible idea to treat the fence at least once every year.

And it is a good idea to apply preservative yourself before erecting the fence. Stand the dry posts overnight in a large container filled with preservative so that the part of the posts that will be below ground is immersed. If you paint the posts, apply the paint a few inches above ground so that the bare stumps can later be treated with preservative.

There is a definite sequence of operations for erecting a fence. With kits, exact details are usually provided by the supplier. Here is an outline of the methods for a panel fence and a board fence

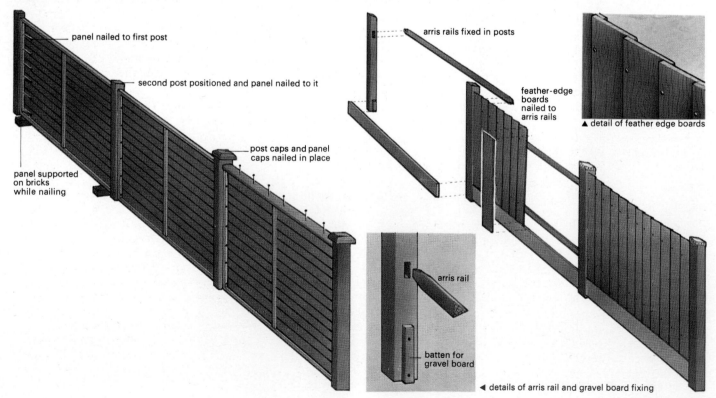

panel nailed to first post

second post positioned and panel nailed to it

post caps and panel caps nailed in place

panel supported on bricks while nailing

arris rails fixed in posts

feather-edge boards nailed to arris rails

▲ detail of feather edge boards

arris rail

batten for gravel board

◄ details of arris rail and gravel board fixing

Repairs are frequently needed to keep the fence in good condition. When the bottom of the post rots, it can be cut off and a concrete spur fitted (left). Replace a timber post with a concrete one set in concrete (right) to avoid recurrence of the trouble. When a timber post is fitted, use one of the methods shown on page 49

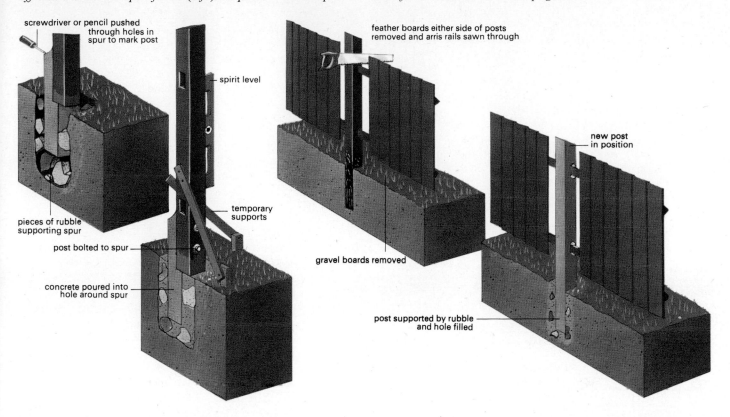

screwdriver or pencil pushed through holes in spur to mark post

spirit level

pieces of rubble supporting spur

post bolted to spur

concrete poured into hole around spur

temporary supports

feather boards either side of posts removed and arris rails sawn through

gravel boards removed

new post in position

post supported by rubble and hole filled

Repairs to fence posts

The posts support the whole structure and must be well maintained. They are susceptible to rot as they are in contact with the ground. Inspect the posts regularly especially near ground level.

If slight decay is noticed in a timber post, it might be possible to arrest the rot before it spreads. Dig around the post to a depth of at least 250mm and apply preservative to the stump. A couple of applications in dry weather followed by pouring preservative into the hole so that the liquid soaks down into the remainder of the stump is the best method. Remember that creosote will damage nearby plant life so select a preservative which is harmless to vegetation for use in a garden.

If there are signs of rot, take action quickly. If the rot has not spread too far up the post, the damaged wood can be removed and the sound section set on a concrete spur fixed in the ground.

Concrete spurs

Concrete spurs are available at builders' merchants complete with bolts already positioned. Measure the dimensions of the post to order the correct size bolts and washers. Do not dismantle the fence until you have obtained the spur.

Before cutting off the damaged section of the post, arrange temporary support for the panels on either side. Make sure that you cut right back to sound timber and apply a generous coat of preservative to the end grain of the post.

Dig out a hole around the post and hack the stump out as best you can. With an obstinate stump, some sort of lever will be needed to exert sufficient force.

A hole at least 450mm deep is needed for the concrete spur.

To bring the spur up to the required height for the base of the posts, fill the bottom of the hole with rubble. It is important carefully to mark the positions of the bolt holes on the post. Place the spur temporarily in its proper location under the post and push a screwdriver or pencil through its holes to mark the holes on the post. Remove the spur and drill the holes.

Fill the hole with concrete and seat the post on the spur. Secure the post with the bolts and washers and check for vertical with a spirit level. Attach temporary supports nailed to pegs to hold the post in position until the concrete has set.

Replacing fence posts

Concrete spurs are not very attractive. If this is a consideration, posts can be replaced with new timber or concrete ones. A new post must be the same size as the old one.

If the post is being removed, the arris rails and gravel boards will also have to be removed. To remove the arris rails of a close-board fence, first remove one board on either side of the post by extracting the fixing nails. It will probably be necessary to saw through the arris rails as close as possible to the post to free it unless the post can be pushed sideways to free the tenon intact. The alternative is to take down the complete panels on either side of the post. This way the tenons on the ends of the arris rails can be freed from the mortises in the posts. Install the new post in the old hole, securing the arris rails with dowels if necessary.

Concrete posts are available to suit different fence styles. These come with ready drilled holes, slots or recesses for wire fences, panels or arris rails. About one third of the post should be underground.

Arris rail failure at mortises can be repaired with purpose-made brackets. If timber battens are used, the first board will have to be shaped as shown. Rail breakage can be made good with a bracket. Post caps protect post end grain, but gravel boards have to be replaced from time to time

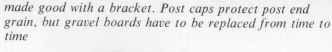

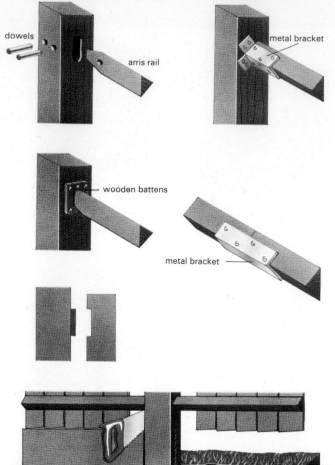

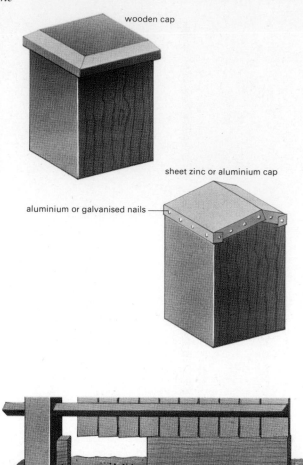

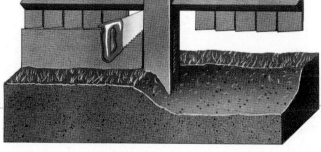

gravel board sawn off   trench dug and board removed

50×50mm batten   board replaced and   trench filled in
screwed to post   fixed to batten

Insert the post in its hole and use timber wedges or stones to keep it vertical while pouring in a mix of one part cement to five parts all-in ballast. Fill to just below ground level, tamp the concrete well down and keep the post supported until the concrete has set.

Arris rails

Loose arris rail joints or split rails should be repaired. If the tenon at the end of the rail does not fit snugly in the post mortise, drill holes through the post and arris rail and insert dowels to hold the rails securely in position.

The alternatives are to fit a proprietary bracket to anchor arris rail to post or to make a framework from 25mm thick battens around the hole. Screw this framework to the post and screw the rail to the framework. Apply preservative to the battens especially the end grain before fixing. Splits in the middle of the rail can be fixed with another type of proprietary bracket. If a new rail is needed, measure the distance between the posts and add 75mm to allow for the tenons which enter the posts. Fitting a new rail is easy if one of the fence posts is sufficiently loose for it to be pushed sideways allowing the tenons to slot into the mortises.

If the posts are solidly fixed you can install the arris rail by cutting off one tenon and fixing that end with a bracket.

Post tops

Square sawn post tops look attractive but if left unprotected they can cause the post to rot from the top downwards. The simplest form of protection is to saw the top off at an angle creating a slope so that water cannot collect. This is not a complete protection and a capping material such as timber or metal should be screwed or nailed in place.

A metal cap cut from a sheet of zinc or aluminium must have its edges folded over the sides of the post and should be secured with aluminium or galvanised nails.

If the post has been in position for a while, it has probably deteriorated somewhat already. Check the timber and cut back to sound wood. Rot can also occur in the tops of feather-edge boards. These can be capped like posts.

Gravel boards

Gravel boards prevent the fence from contacting the ground but they are subject to rot. It is easier and less expensive to replace the gravel boards than the fence.

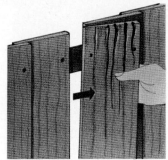
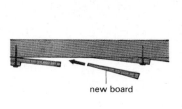

new board

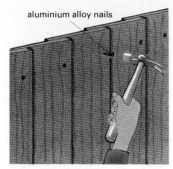

aluminium alloy nails

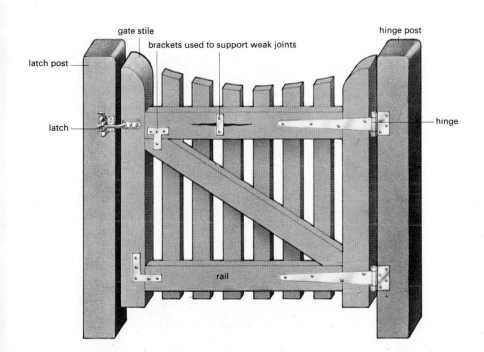

gate stile
brackets used to support weak joints
hinge post
latch post
latch
hinge
rail

The usual method of fixing gravel boards is to slot them into holes made in the fence posts while the fence is being erected. Replacement gravel boards are secured to timber battens screwed to the posts. First remove the old board, digging a hole around it to get it all out. Saw off the ends where they enter the posts. Once the board is clear, dig out a small trench to fit the new board. Screw on a 50 × 50mm batten at the base of each post to create an anchorage point for the new board. Keep the tops of the battens in line with the bottom of the fence panels or boards.

The new gravel board then can be positioned and screwed to the battens flush with the fronts of the posts. Then fill the trench and clear away any build-up of earth or vegetation around the board to prevent further deterioration.

Replacing feather-edge boards

Feather-edge boards are nailed to the arris rails. When preservative has not been applied, these boards will become brittle and eventually pull through the nails. Often they can simply be nailed back into place using aluminium alloy nails. Replacement will eventually be necessary. One board can be removed and replaced without dismantling the whole section.

If the nails holding a board to the arris rail are difficult to budge, hammer them into the rail using a nail punch to set the heads below surface. When the board is free, slide the thin edge of the replacement board under the thick edge of the next board. Drive aluminium alloy fixing nails through both edges into the arris rail. Remember to treat any new timber with preservative.

Gates

Most manufacturers sell gates to match their fences. Gates are simple to install. When laying out the fence posts allow for the gate instead of a panel between two of the posts. The space should be wide enough for the gate plus about 10 to 20mm clearance.

Make sure the posts are exactly vertical before fitting the gate with strong galvanised hinges.

To fix a sagging gate, first determine the cause. Loose screws or worn hinges can be replaced using longer screws or screws with wall plugs if necessary.

A sagging gate is often caused by a loose or tilting post. The remedy is to remove the gate and secure the post in concrete or on a concrete spur.

Domestic plumbing layout; two-pipe system

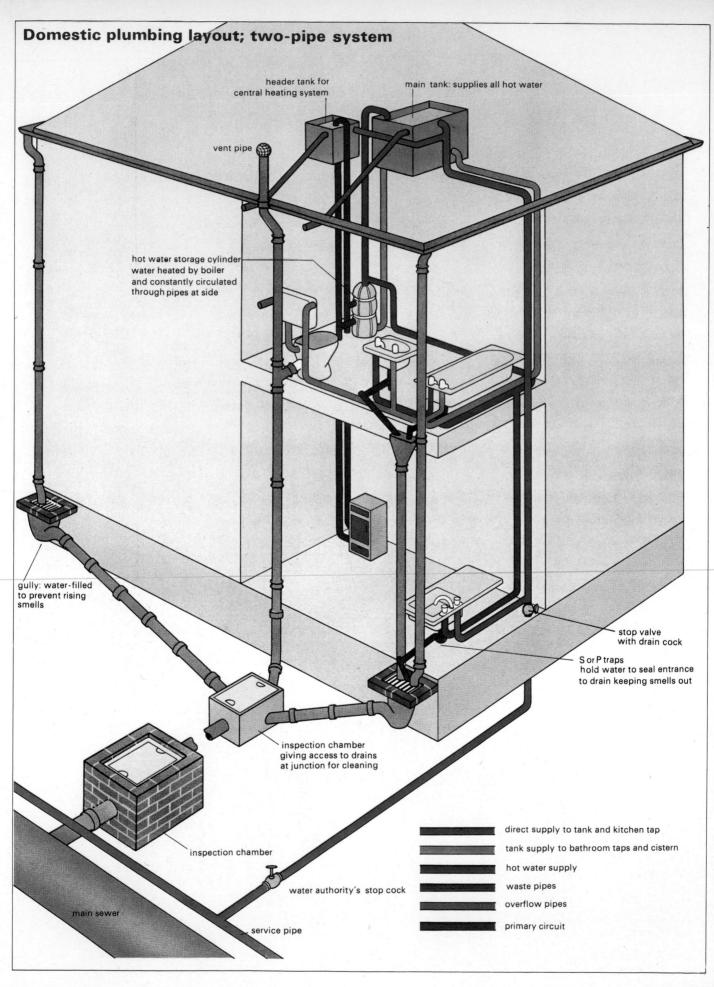

header tank for central heating system

main tank: supplies all hot water

vent pipe

hot water storage cylinder water heated by boiler and constantly circulated through pipes at side

gully: water-filled to prevent rising smells

stop valve with drain cock

S or P traps hold water to seal entrance to drain keeping smells out

inspection chamber giving access to drains at junction for cleaning

inspection chamber

water authority's stop cock

main sewer

service pipe

direct supply to tank and kitchen tap

tank supply to bathroom taps and cistern

hot water supply

waste pipes

overflow pipes

primary circuit

Plumbing systems, repairs and projects

Plumbing seems quite mysterious to the beginner but once the techniques and basic principles are familiar, the handyman can undertake many money saving repairs and improvements to the plumbing system of his home.

COLD WATER SYSTEM

The main artery of the plumbing system is the service pipe or rising main which connects the domestic plumbing system to the water authority's main which runs under the pavement.

The householder's responsibility for this pipe begins at the water authority's stop-cock, usually provided in a purpose-built pit in the footpath outside the house. This will probably have a specially shaped shank that can be turned on and off only by one of the authority's turn-keys. This pipe is usually lead or copper tubing and enters the home through the kitchen floor – generally under the sink.

Just above the floor at the foot of this pipe is the householder's main stop-cock, often combined with a drain-cock that will permit the rising main to be drained when required.

Stop-cocks have arrows engraved on their bodies. When fitting a stop-cock it is important to make sure that this arrow points in the direction of the flow.

At least one branch pipe will be 'teed off' from the rising main a few feet above the floor. This is the branch pipe which supplies the cold water tap to the kitchen sink and provides pure water for drinking and cooking. It is important that this water be supplied direct from the main and not from a storage cistern.

Another branch may be taken from the rising main within the kitchen to supply a garage or garden tap. This should be provided with its own stop-cock to enable the external water supply to be cut off and drained during frosty weather.

In some homes the cold water supply pipe to the bathroom, serving the bath, wash basin and wc flushing cistern, is also teed off from the rising main. This is referred to as a 'direct' system. However, most homes use an 'indirect' system in which bathroom cold water services are supplied from a main storage cistern, usually located in the loft. The indirect system is designed to ensure that there is no possibility of contamination of the drinking water from the bathroom or toilet. The rising main is taken up an internal wall of the house to supply the cistern and the flow of water is controlled by a ball or float valve which closes automatically when the water reaches a set level.

Storage cisterns

Domestic cold water storage cisterns are now standardised to a nominal capacity of 227 litres. Older cisterns were made of galvanised steel but are being replaced by asbestos, reinforced plastic or polythene cisterns which are lighter and not subject to corrosion.

The top and sides of the cistern but not the base should be protected from frost by means of a lagging jacket made of glass fibre or slabs of expanded polystyrene. The cistern should be fitted with a removable cover to keep the water clean. If insulation has been placed between the joists, it should be omitted from the space beneath the cistern.

In addition to the ball-valve inlet, there will probably be at least three pipes connected to the cold water storage cistern. The overflow pipe is taken from a point not less than twice the diameter of the pipe from the top of the cistern to discharge in a conspicuous position outside the house. This pipe will be a minimum of 22mm in diameter and should be extended inside the cistern with a bend taking its inlet about 50mm

Below: modern plastic cold water storage cistern. When installed, it must be mounted on a flat base. Bottom: square galvanised steel cistern. Both types should be well insulated

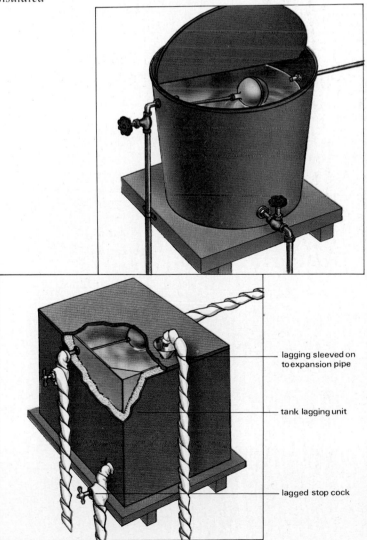

lagging sleeved on to expansion pipe

tank lagging unit

lagged stop cock

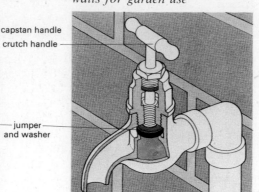

Conventional pillar tap fitted with capstan handle and easy-clean cover

capstan handle
crutch handle
jumper and washer

Crutch head bib tap as usually fitted to outside walls for garden use

Modern pillar tap with acrylic handwheel. Conversion kits are available

handwheel
washer

Sink mixer with separate hot/cold channels for cold mains, hot tank supplies

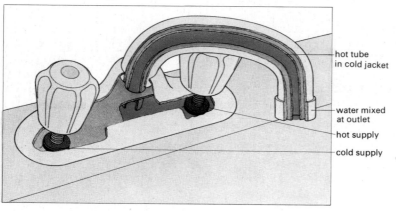

hot tube in cold jacket
water mixed at outlet
hot supply
cold supply

Distinctive looking Supatap – washer-changing without turning off the main supply

check valve
jumper and washer
anti-splash device

below water level. This provides a water seal that will prevent icy draughts blowing up the overflow pipe into the roof space. If an overflow pipe is not dipped in this way, extension pieces can be purchased that will screw on to the internal end of the pipe to provide this water seal.

The other two pipes connected to the storage cistern supply the cold water and the hot water systems. Both should be taken from a point 50mm above the bottom of the cistern to reduce the risk of grit from the mains being drawn into the pipes.

The cold water supply to the bathroom will be in 22mm tubing which will have two 15mm branches taken from it by means of reducing tees to supply the wash basin tap and the flushing cistern of the wc.

Taps and mixers

Most taps operate in the same way as the screw-down stop-cock. Turning the handle raises or lowers a valve to open or close the waterway. Bib taps have horizontal inlets for fixing to a wall above an appliance and pillar taps vertical ones which is fixed directly to the appliance.

On some modern tap designs the handle and cover are made as one unit. The mechanism is, however, similar to the traditional tap.

Bath and basin mixers may be regarded as two taps with a common spout from which a mixture of hot and cold water can pass. Bath mixers often incorporate a means of diverting the mixed water from the spout to a shower connection.

Sink mixers are different as it is illegal to combine in one

plumbing fitting water from the main with water from a storage cistern. Sink mixers therefore have two separate water channels, one for hot and one for cold water. The two streams of water mix in the air as they leave the spout of the mixer.

One type of patented tap called Supatap operates in a different way. The actual nozzle of the tap is turned to turn water on or off. Supataps incorporate check valves which enables washer changing to take place without cutting off the water supply.

Flushing cisterns

There are two kinds of flushing cistern used for lavatories. The older bell type of cistern is today used mainly for an outside toilet. It is made of cast iron with a well in its base which contains a heavy iron bell. A lever operated by a chain raises the bell and then releases it suddenly.

The more modern, direct action, flushing cistern usually has a flat base. It can be made of metal, plastic or ceramic and can be used for either high level or low level lavatories.

HOT WATER SYSTEMS

The most common hot water system uses a storage cylinder with a supply pipe carrying water from the cold water cistern to the cylinder. The water in the cylinder may be heated by means of an electric immersion heater or by a boiler using either solid fuel, gas or oil. A common arrangement combining these methods uses a boiler to heat water and provide central heating during the winter months and an immersion heater for use during the summer.

If the hot water system is to be combined with a central heating system, an indirect hot water system should be provided. This system has two separate circuits, a primary system supplied from a feed and expansion tank and the domestic hot water system supplied from the main storage cistern. In the first, the primary system, the water is heated by a boiler and passes continuously through the central heating system. It also flows through the main storage cylinder where it heats the domestic hot water indirectly. The water in the primary system is used over and over again which prevents corrosion and the build-up of scale.

Since the supplies to the hot water taps are taken from above the storage cylinder, the cylinder cannot be drained from these taps. A direct cylinder which is heated by a boiler is drained from the drain-cock beside the boiler. An indirect cylinder, or a direct cylinder heated by an electric immersion heater only, must be provided with a separate drain-cock usually fitted into the cold water supply pipe to the cylinder at its lowest point.

There are a number of patented self-priming indirect cylinders on the market which offer a simple means of conversion from direct to indirect hot water supply. These need no separate feed and expansion tank and the cylinder incorporates a special inner cylinder. As the system is filled with water this overflows from the outer part of the cylinder into the inner cylinder and then to the primary circuit.

A number of packaged or two in one hot water systems have been produced in which the cold water storage cistern and the hot water storage cylinder are brought into close proximity to form one unit. Some of these have a small 68 litre capacity capable of supplying only the hot water system. Others described as packaged plumbing systems have a standard 227 litre cistern capable of supplying bathroom cold taps and lavatory flushing cisterns as well as the hot water system.

The cylinder, whether direct or indirect, should be fitted with an efficient lagging jacket to conserve heat. This is particularly important when the water is heated by means of an electric immersion heater. For optimum fuel economy the lagging jacket should be 75mm thick regardless of the type of insulating material used.

Other hot water systems

Instantaneous multipoint gas water heaters can be connected direct to the water main to provide whole-house hot water supply. The development of the balanced flue makes it possible to install one of these heaters unobtrusively in any room with an external wall. With a system of this kind it is possible to dispense altogether with the cold water storage cistern. If permitted by the local water authority, hot and cold water taps can both be supplied direct from the main.

Small instantaneous gas or electric water heaters can also be used to supply individual fittings although electric water heaters have a lower rate of delivery. These are useful to supply spray wash-hand taps or showers in places not easily reached by gas heaters.

Another type of water heater that can be connected direct to the mains is the small open-outlet storage gas or electric water heater. The control valve is fitted on the inlet side of these heaters to control water flowing into them. As cold water flows in at the base it displaces the hot water in the upper part of the appliance which overflows down a standpipe to the open-ended spout. These can be particularly valuable in supplying hot water to a point remote from the main hot water supply system, for example to provide hot water over the wash basin in an outside or cloakroom toilet.

DRAINAGE

Drainage is at least as important to a household plumbing system as the water supply. All the water that flows into a house must eventually be disposed of in some way.

Single stack drainage

The old-fashioned two-pipe system which distinguished between soil fittings for lavatory waste and waste fittings for sinks, basins, baths and bidets has been replaced by single stack drainage. The two-pipe system is found in most older houses but is no longer installed largely as a result of the Building Regulations of the 1960s which required the soil and waste pipes of new buildings to be contained within the perimeter of the walls.

Packaged plumbing units are useful for installations where headroom is restricted. Cold water cistern and hot water tank, complete with immersion heater, are combined

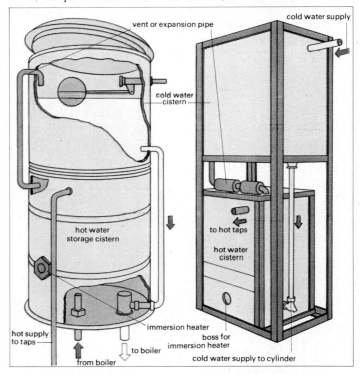

On the left is the old-fashioned well-bottom toilet cistern – often called the pull-and-clank! Right is the modern direct-action version

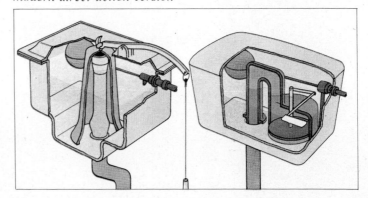

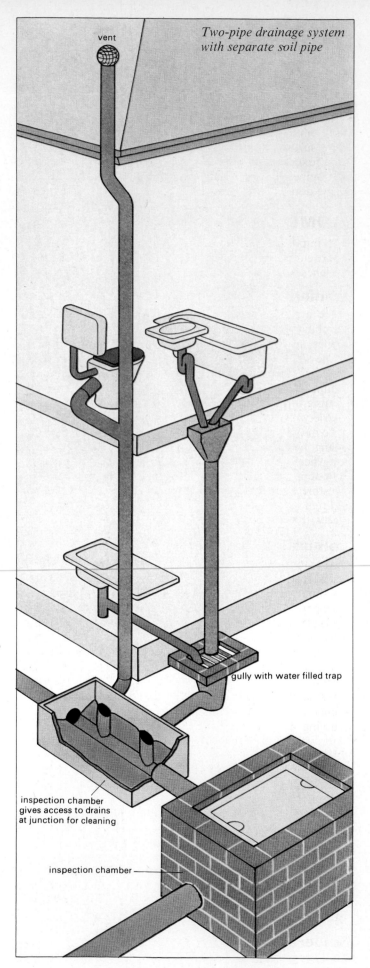

vent

*Two-pipe drainage system
with separate soil pipe*

gully with water filled trap

inspection chamber
gives access to drains
at junction for cleaning

inspection chamber

Single stack drainage makes no distinction between soil and waste appliances. All wastes are discharged directly into a single 100mm main waste stack. This stack is contained within the house and is visible from outside only as a few inches of pipe extending from the slope of the roof. Safe and efficient single stack drainage demands very careful attention to design to avoid problems of siphonage from one trap to another.

Waste pipes, particularly from the wash basin must be kept as short as possible and must have a minimal fall. The connection of the bath and basin wastes must be made to the main stack in such a way as to prevent the possibility of their outlets being fouled or blocked by discharges when the wc is flushed.

Traps to plumbing fittings

The outlets from all plumbing fittings must be provided with traps to prevent smells from the drains from entering the rooms in which the fittings are installed.

The simplest form of trap is a U bend in the pipe designed to retain water after the appliance has been used. A wc trap is built into the appliance. Bath, basin, bidet and sink traps are fitted between the appliances and the waste outlets. Traps with horizontal outlets are called P traps and those with vertical outlets are called S traps.

The seal of the trap is the vertical distance between the normal water level in the trap and the upper part of the U bend.

With the two-pipe drainage system, traps normally have 50mm seals. The single stack drainage system requires a deeper seal of 75mm. All traps require some means of access in case of stoppage.

Gullies

With a two-pipe drainage system gullies are provided for the collection of rain and surface water and for the collection of the wastes from sinks, baths, bidets, wash basins and similar non-foul wastes.

Even with the single stack system it is not unusual for waste pipes from ground floor appliances to be taken to a gully rather than to the main stack. Where this is done the waste pipe should discharge above the level of the water standing in the gully but below the grid. This ensures that the flush of the discharging water is available for cleansing the gully and prevents the risk of flooding as a result of the grid becoming blocked.

Underground drains

The underground drains are laid in straight lines to a self-cleansing gradient. There should be means of access usually in the form of inspection chambers or manholes at all junctions and major changes of direction. These are constructed of brickwork, precast concrete sections or plastic reinforced with glass fibre.

Modern homes probably have drains of polyvinyl chloride or of pitch fibre instead of the old-fashioned salt-glazed pipes. PVC pipes are connected by means of simple push-on O-ring joints and do not require a concrete base for support.

In older properties there may be an intercepting or disconnecting inspection chamber near the front boundary of the property.

This chamber will have an intercepting trap at its outlet. The purpose of the intercepting trap was to prevent sewer gases from entering the house drains.

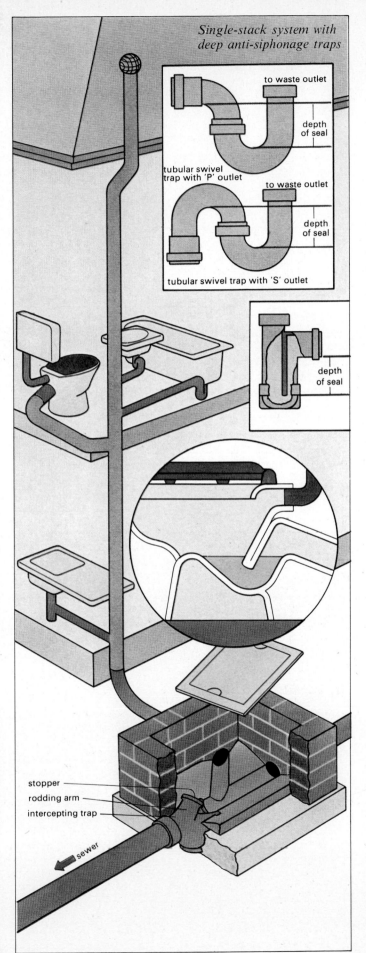

Single-stack system with deep anti-siphonage traps

to waste outlet

depth of seal

tubular swivel trap with 'P' outlet

to waste outlet

depth of seal

tubular swivel trap with 'S' outlet

depth of seal

stopper
rodding arm
intercepting trap

sewer

Roof drainage

Rainwater is collected in the gutters along the roof lines and is discharged into vertical drain-pipes. The disposal of rainwater will vary according to area. In some districts householders are required to provide a soakaway for roof and yard drainage.

A soakaway usually consists of a pit 1.5m or more deep and 1.5m square in plan. This is filled to within about 300mm of the surface with broken bricks and other builder's rubble, and the surface soil is then replaced. In other areas rainwater drain-pipes lead into gullies which can be connected directly to the domestic drainage system.

PLUMBING TECHNIQUES

It is important to check with your local water authority before embarking on plumbing work to be sure that the work complies with regulations.

Joining pipes

There are a number of simple techniques necessary for plumbing work. These are primarily the means by which the copper, stainless steel or PVC tubing is cut and joined.

The sizes of copper tubing suitable for most household projects are 15mm, 22mm and 28mm. Steel tubes are sized as 15mm, 20mm and 25mm. These pipes may be joined by means either of compression or soldered fittings available in a variety of sizes and shapes.

To make either type of joints with copper or stainless steel tubing, first cut the tube to length with either a fine hacksaw or a wheel tube cutter. A wheel tube cutter makes it easier to cut copper tubing absolutely square and is a worth while investment for a major plumbing job. Keep the ends square and remove the rough edges with a file. Clean the end of the pipe with wire wool or sandpaper.

Compression joints

Non-manipulative compression joints and fittings are the easiest for the home plumber with a minimal tool kit as they are simply tightened together. The compression joint has three parts: a body, a soft copper ring or olive and a coupling nut that is tightened to make the joint secure and watertight. First loosen the coupling nut of the compression joint. With most types of joint there is no need to remove it altogether. Insert the tube end through the coupling nut and compression ring as far as the tube stop within the body. After hand tightening, hold the body of the fitting with a wrench and tighten the coupling nut with a spanner. The coupling nut compresses the soft copper ring against the outer wall of the tube to make a watertight joint.

When you use a spanner to tighten the coupling nut it is nearly impossible to over-tighten. Since stainless steel is a harder material than copper, a little more force will be needed.

Many plumbers smear the tube end with Boss White or some other jointing paste before inserting it into the fitting. This isn't necessary but it will ensure a watertight joint.

It may be necessary to connect metric copper or stainless steel tubing to Imperial size tubing. With compression fittings this presents no problem. 15mm and 28mm fittings can be used directly with $\frac{1}{2}$in and 1in size tubing and 22mm fittings can be adapted for use with $\frac{3}{4}$in tubing.

Soldered capillary joints

Soldered capillary joints are not more difficult to make and

ASSEMBLY OF COMPRESSION FITTINGS AND SOME COMPONENTS

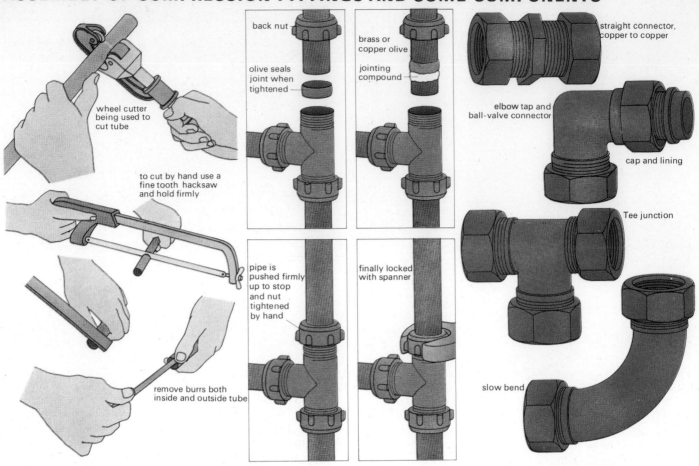

wheel cutter
being used to
cut tube

to cut by hand use a
fine tooth hacksaw
and hold firmly

remove burrs both
inside and outside tube

back nut

olive seals
joint when
tightened

brass or
copper olive

jointing
compound

straight connector,
copper to copper

elbow tap and
ball-valve connector

cap and lining

Tee junction

pipe is
pushed firmly
up to stop
and nut
tightened
by hand

finally locked
with spanner

slow bend

Making an integral–ring capillary joint

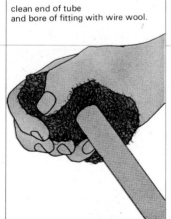

clean end of tube
and bore of fitting with wire wool.

apply flux sparingly to the inside
of the fitting, and outside of tube ends.

Making an end–feed capillary joint

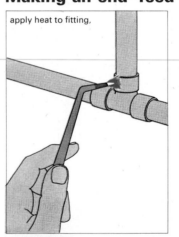

apply heat to fitting,

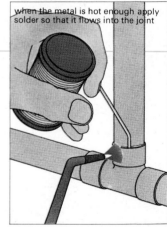

when the metal is hot enough apply
solder so that it flows into the joint

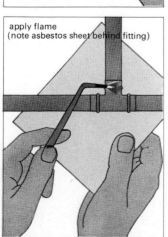

apply flame
(note asbestos sheet behind fitting)

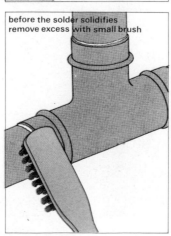

before the solder solidifies
remove excess with small brush

Components of a compression joint

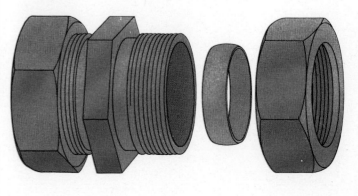

Making an O-ring joint

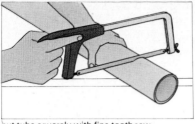
cut tube squarely with fine tooth saw

chamfer tube end

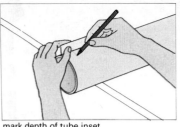
mark depth of tube inset

insert rubber ring seal

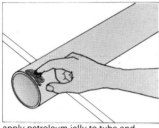
apply petroleum jelly to tube end

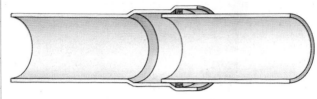
align tube end to socket and push home

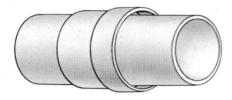
completed joint

are less obtrusive and less expensive than compression joints. There are two types of this joint available, integral ring fittings and end-feed fittings. Integral ring fittings incorporate sufficient solder to make the joint. With end-feed fittings the user must apply solder as he makes the joint.

To make a soldered capillary joint with copper tubing, cut, finish and clean the tubing. Smear a little flux on to the bore of the fitting and the ends of the tube and insert the tube end into the fitting as far as the tube stop. Apply the flame of a blow-lamp first to one end of the fitting until solder appears all round the fitting. Repeat for the other end of the joint.

With an integral ring fitting the solder contained within the fitting will melt and spread by capillary action between the tube end and the internal surface of the fitting. The joint is complete when a bright ring of solder appears round the mouth of the fitting. Clean off excess solder with a small brush while it is still hot leaving a fillet around the end of the fitting.

End-feed joints are made in the same way except that after heating the tube and the fitting, an appropriate length of solder wire is applied to the end of the fitting and heated to flow into the space between tube end and fitting. It is a good idea to bend over the end of the solder wire to the length that you will need before beginning work. The solder wire should be about as long as the size of the fitting.

When more than one joint has to be made with one fitting, it is best to make all joints at the same time. If this cannot be done, wrap any joint already made with damp cloth so that reheating the fitting does not melt the finished joint.

Always exercise extreme care when using a blow-lamp near timber or skirting boards. Place a sheet of asbestos or a pad of glass fibre between the fitting and any wooden surface immediately behind it.

There are slight differences of technique that must be observed when making soldered capillary joints with stainless steel tubing. Phosphoric acid flux must be used and the blow-lamp flame should be applied only to the fitting, not to the tubing.

Metric capillary joints and fittings cannot be used with Imperial size tubing. Conversion fittings are available but a simpler method, especially when connecting to 1in or $\frac{1}{2}$in tubing, is to use a compression joint for the actual connection between the old Imperial and the new metric tubing and then to continue the plumbing project with metric capillary fittings.

Bending metal pipe

A variety of bends are available in the catalogues of manufacturers of compression and capillary fittings. It is, however, possible to make easy bends in 15 or 22mm copper and 15mm stainless steel tubing by hand. It is necessary to insert a steel bending spring to support the walls of the tube and prevent them from collapsing. Grease the spring to facilitate removal and insert into the tube beyond the point at which the bend is to be made. Bend over the knee, overbending at first and then bringing back to the curve required. To remove the spring insert a screwdriver through the metal loop at its end. Twist anticlockwise to reduce the spring's diameter and pull.

Pipe-bending can save money. The bending spring is removed by twisting as shown

The correct spring for the pipe in use is inserted up to the point of the bend

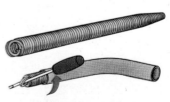

The pipe is bent over the knee, but sharp bends are to be avoided if possible

Over-bend and return to correct position for easy spring removal from pipe

61

Plastic tubing

Polyvinyl chloride (PVC) tubing may be used for cold water services, for waste and stack pipes and for underground drainage. PVC tubing used for cold water services is joined by solvent welding. Waste and drain pipes of this type may be joined either by the same means or with push-on ring seal joints. In practice it is usual for smaller diameter pipes such as branch wastes to be joined by solvent welding and stack pipes and underground drains by ring seal joints.

Solvent welding

To cut plastic pipe for solvent welding the tube end is cut square with a hacksaw and the burr and rough edges are removed from the inside and outside with abrasive paper.

Chamfer the outer edge of the pipe end to an angle of about 15° with a file. Insert the tube into the solvent weld socket and mark the depth of the tube in the socket with a pencil. Roughen the pipe end and the interior of the socket with fine abrasive paper and degrease both of these surfaces with a suitable cleaning fluid as recommended by the manufacturer.

Apply an even coat of solvent cement to the interior surface of the fitting, using a lengthwise brush stroke. In the same way apply a thicker coat to the tube end as far as the pencil mark. Push the pipe end into the socket immediately without turning it. Hold in position for about fifteen seconds and then wipe off surplus cement from the mouth of the fitting. Do not disturb the joint for five minutes and do not use the pipe for twenty-four hours.

Ring seal joints

Prepare the pipe as for solvent welding. Draw a line round the pipe 10mm from its end and chamfer back the pipe to this line with a rasp or shaping tool. Insert the pipe end into the socket and mark the depth of the insertion. Make another mark 10mm nearer to the pipe end than this point. This allows 10mm for expansion.

Insert the joint ring after cleaning the recess provided for it in the pipe socket. Lubricate the pipe end with petroleum jelly and push firmly into the socket through the joint ring. Adjust the pipe position so that the insertion depth mark is level with the socket edge.

SOME PLUMBING PROJECTS

Replacing a wc

The first step is to choose the type of wc you want to install. The most familiar is the ordinary wash-down kind which is available in both high and low level types. It depends for its flushing action upon the volume of the flush. It is available with either an S or a P trap and with a straight outlet or an outlet bent in various directions to suit the position.

The other two kinds of wc work by siphonic action. The contents of the pan are pushed out by atmospheric pressure when the flush is operated. Both types of siphonic wc give a total clearance of the pan, eliminating the possibility of the flush failing to cleanse the pan properly. They also permit the use of close coupled lavatories in which flushing cistern and wc pan form one unit and in which the conventional short flush pipe of the low level wc is completely eliminated.

In addition, the double trap siphonic suite has the advantages of a large water area and a very silent action. It is, of course, more expensive than a straightforward wash-down suite and it projects farther from the wall. There are some small wc compartments in which it can't be fitted.

Removing the existing wc

Removing the flushing cistern should present no special difficulty. Cut off the water supply to the cistern and flush to empty. The threaded tail of the ball-valve inlet will be connected to the water supply pipe by means of a ball-valve connector or cap and lining joint. Unscrew the securing nut and pull the water supply pipe away from the ball-valve.

A similar joint will connect the threaded outlet from the cistern to the upper end of the flush pipe. Unscrew the nut and disconnect the flush pipe in the same way. The overflow pipe is disconnected by unscrewing the retaining back-nut inside the cistern. The cistern can now be lifted off its bracket supports or unscrewed from plugs in the wall and removed altogether.

Disconnect the lower end of the flush pipe from the flushing horn at the back of the wc pan and remove it. Unscrew the brass screws holding the pan down to the floor. Upstairs lavatories are usually connected to the branch soil pipe with a mastic joint. By moving the pan to and fro it should be possible to pull it out of the soil pipe socket.

A ground floor wc may be cemented on to the solid floor and have a cement joint connecting its S trap outlet to a stoneware branch drain. This will be more difficult to remove.

Unscrew and remove any brass floor fixing screws. Deliberately break the pan outlet immediately behind the trap. Drive a cold chisel under the base of the pan and break the cement joint with the floor. Pull away and remove the front part of the pan, leaving a few inches of jagged pan outlet protruding from the drain socket.

Stuff a wad of cloth or newspaper into the drain socket to prevent pieces of broken stoneware and cement from falling into the drain. Then work on the pan outlet with a cold chisel and a hammer. Work carefully and patiently, keeping the point of the chisel pointing towards the centre of the pipe.

Try to break the pan outlet right down to its base at one point. The remainder and the jointing material can then usually be dug out fairly easily. Then carefully remove the wad of cloth or newspaper.

Installing the new wc

The installation of a new wc is carried out in reverse order from the removal of the old one. The new pan is fitted first.

Do not set the pan of a ground floor wc in a bed of cement and sand. It has been established that the setting of this mixture can set up stresses that could damage the pan. Remove every trace of sand and cement left on the floor and ensure that it is level.

Hold the new pan up to the drain socket so as to establish its position on the floor. Mark through the screw-holes in the base of the pan. Remove the pan. Drill and plug the floor at the points marked.

To make it easier to position the screw-holes exactly over the plugs, insert short lengths of wire such as straightened out paper clips into the plugs so that they project vertically from the floor.

You may wish to remake the pan connection with a cement joint. If you do this, place the pan in position with the pieces of wire projecting through the screw-holes. Remove the wire and screw down with brass screws, using a lead washer to protect the ceramic surface of the pan.

Check with a spirit level that the pan is perfectly level. It may be necessary to pack slivers of wood or pieces of linoleum under one side to level it.

Dampen some newspaper and push it down hard into the drain socket so that this newspaper caulking extends for a

Replacing a wc

Break the pipe just before it enters the drain socket

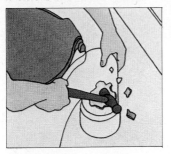

Stuff a wad of newspaper into the drain socket

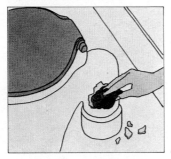

Complete the break, remove the screws and the pan

Carefully chip away the remaining pieces of pipe

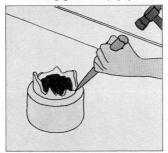

Clean away the old mortar on the floor

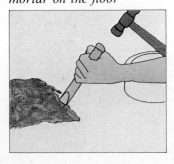

Take care not to over-tighten the nut

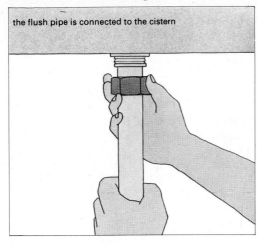

the flush pipe is connected to the cistern

Use packing pieces – not mortar

make sure that the new pan is set level

This is an easy cap-and-lining joint

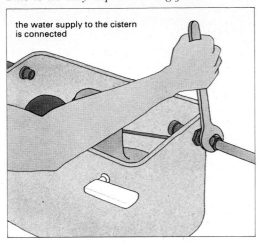

the water supply to the cistern is connected

A snug fit makes the joint watertight

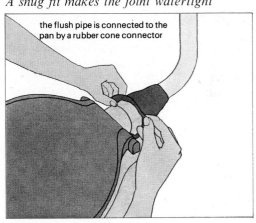

the flush pipe is connected to the pan by a rubber cone connector

The Fordham Flush Panel is button-operated

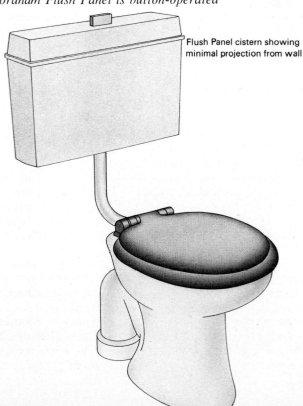

Flush Panel cistern showing minimal projection from wall

Speed is essential, so if the old cistern is a high level one it can be disconnected, but left in place until the new one is in working order. If you do accidentally break the drain socket, don't worry; patented push-on plastic connectors will make good the damage

depth of about 12mm all round the pan socket. This will prevent cement from being squeezed through into the drain which can cause drain blockage.

Neat cement may be used for the joint but a mixture of three parts cement to one part sand will give best results. Make sure that you fill every part of the space between pan outlet and socket and haunch up to a neat finish. Do not disturb or use for twenty-four hours.

Alternatively a mastic joint or a patented push-on plastic drain connector may be used. If you use a push-on joint, this should be made before the pan is screwed to the floor.

Connectors of this kind are particularly useful to the amateur plumber. Unlike any other form of jointing they can be used even if in removing the old wc pan you have damaged the drain socket.

An in situ mastic joint may be made by fixing the wc pan in position and screwing down to the floor. Then bind two or three turns of a waterproofing building tape around the pan outlet and caulk down hard into the drain or soil pipe socket. Fill in the space between outlet and socket with a non-setting mastic jointing material and complete the joint with another couple of turns of waterproofing tape.

A mastic or push-on joint should always be used for upstairs lavatories or for ground floor lavatories on wooden boarded floors. Vibration of the wooden floor will inevitably result in a cement joint cracking and leaking. Many manufacturers of PVC single stack drainage systems supply their own patented wc connectors. The methods described can, however, be used as an alternative.

Make sure that the flush pipe inlet connects squarely to the flushing horn at the back of the wc pan. Some pan manufacturers provide a connector in which the end of the flush pipe is held firmly in position by a rubber O-ring gripped by a device bolted to the pan. The alternative is to use a rubber cone connector. The smaller inlet of the cone is pushed over the end of the flush pipe and the other end over the flushing horn of the pan.

The old-fashioned plumber's rag and putty joint should never be used. It is leaky, unhygienic and a frequent cause of faulty flushing since putty is often carried through into the flushing rim of the pan.

Fitting the new flushing cistern should present no special difficulty. Modern cisterns are usually supported by concealed screws. Hold the cistern up to the wall at the correct level. Mark the position of the screws and drill and plug the wall. Make sure that the base of the cistern is at the level recommended by the maker above the pan inlet.

The flush pipe connection will probably be made with a screw-up cap and lining joint similar to that used for the old cistern. However, some modern cisterns have a simple ring sealed push-in connection.

Next, simply connect the cap and lining ball-valve connector to the ball-valve inlet and screw up the cap nut. The cap and lining joint incorporates a fibre washer that ensures a watertight connection. If the level of the water supply inlet needs to be changed, the water supply pipe should, of course, be shortened or lengthened as required.

It is not unusual for wc flushing cisterns to be supplied with a standard high pressure ball-valve. Check on this as a high pressure ball-valve fitted to a wc cistern supplied from a main cold water storage cistern can result in extremely slow filling. Similarly, a low pressure valve used with a cistern connected direct to the rising main can result in constant overflows.

Check the water level as the new cistern fills. The ball-valve should close when water level reaches the water level mark within the cistern. If there is no mark then it should close when water level is about 12mm below the overflow outlet.

Modern ball-valves have a means of adjusting the water level in the cistern. The older type of valves can be adjusted by unscrewing and removing the ball float and by taking the float arm firmly in both hands. Bend the float end of the arm upwards to raise the water level or downwards to lower it.

Converting a wc from high to low level

This apparently simple task can be made very awkward since the low level cistern may prevent the seat from opening completely.

There are several solutions to this problem. Moving the pan farther away from the wall is very cumbersome and replacing the wc completely with a new double trap siphonic suite is very expensive. The simplest and cheapest solution is to use the slimline flushing cistern or Flush Panel.

The slim brief case dimensions of the Flush Panel mean that it is usually possible to replace an old high level cistern without the need to move the position of the wc pan. With the cistern in position the wc seat can still be raised.

Installing a wash basin

Wash basins are available in ceramic materials, plastics or enamelled pressed steel. Ceramic basins are either wall hung or mounted on a pedestal support. Pedestal basins are most suitable for bathroom use and wall-hung basins for cloakrooms and wc compartments. Before choosing a wall-hung basin, be sure that the wall will support its weight. Plastic and pressed steel basins are usually fitted into the upper surfaces of vanity units. These are most commonly found in bedrooms. Small, built-in wash hand basins are now available which make it possible to provide hand washing facilities in even the smallest wc compartment.

Water supply and drainage

Water supplies for an upstairs basin can usually most conveniently be taken from the plumbing in the roof space. The cold supply may be taken direct from the cold water storage cistern by means of a separate 15mm branch or it may be teed into the bathroom cold water supply pipe. It must not on any account be taken from the cold supply from the cold water storage cistern to the hot water cylinder.

The hot supply may be taken by means of a tee junction from the hot water supply pipe to the bathroom or from the vent pipe from the cylinder below the base of the cold water storage cistern.

If water supplies are taken from the roof space, the pipes will descend the wall in a corner of the room, perhaps concealed by an airing cupboard or built-in wardrobe, and then lie horizontal at or below floor level to the fitting. Neatest results will be obtained by taking the supply pipes under the floor boards to rise vertically just beneath the basin. This is essential with a pedestal basin as a main purpose of the pedestal is to conceal the plumbing.

If your home has a two-pipe drainage system, the waste pipe from the basin will be taken through the wall to discharge over an existing gully or hopper. Connection to a single stack system may be more difficult and should not be undertaken without first consulting the building control officer of your local district or borough council. Unless certain design considerations are met there is a serious risk of the trap siphoning out on discharge and allowing drain air into the bedroom or bathroom.

Installing a wash basin

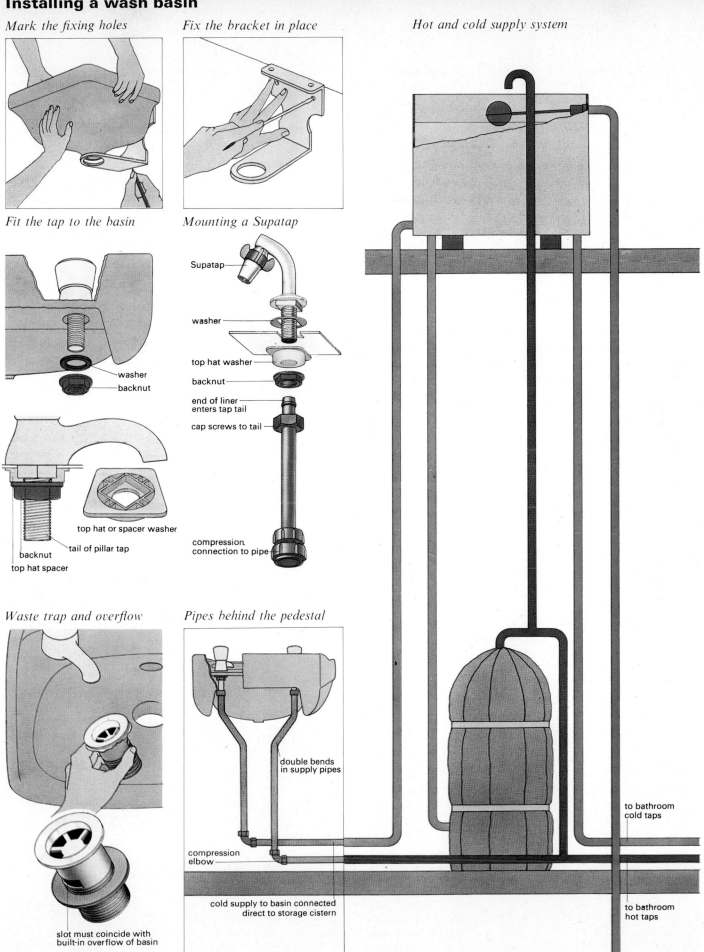

Mark the fixing holes

Fix the bracket in place

Hot and cold supply system

Fit the tap to the basin

Mounting a Supatap

— washer
— backnut

top hat or spacer washer

tail of pillar tap

backnut

top hat spacer

Supatap

washer

top hat washer

backnut

end of liner enters tap tail

cap screws to tail

compression connection to pipe

Waste trap and overflow

Pipes behind the pedestal

double bends in supply pipes

compression elbow

cold supply to basin connected direct to storage cistern

slot must coincide with built-in overflow of basin

to bathroom cold taps

to bathroom hot taps

The branch waste pipe must be laid at a very slight fall and should be as short as possible. If it is longer than 1.6m it may be necessary to provide a small vent pipe rising from immediately behind the trap to a point in the main drainage stack at least a metre above the level of the junction of any waste inlet.

Having decided on the route of the water supply and waste pipes, leave the actual connection of these pipes until the end so that the remainder of the household plumbing services is disrupted for the shortest possible time.

Fitting the basin

Both pedestal and wall-hung basins are normally provided with concealed brackets or hangers for wall fixing. Hold the basin up to the wall and mark the positions at which the wall has to be drilled and plugged. The level of a pedestal basin will be decided by the height of the pedestal. Wall hung basins are usually fixed with their rim at about 800mm from the floor but there is no reason why this height should not be varied.

Drill and plug the wall at the points marked and screw the brackets or hangers firmly to it. Before hanging the basin in position, fit the taps.

You may want to use either individual 12mm pillar taps or a basin mixer. In either case a flat plastic washer is slipped over the tap tails before thrusting them through the holes provided in the top of the basin. With a ceramic basin another flat plastic washer is then slipped on to the tail under the basin and the back nut screwed up firmly behind it. Tighten sufficiently to hold the tap firmly in place but do not overstrain.

If the basin is made of thin material such as plastic or enamelled pressed steel, a plastic top hat or spacer washer must be used instead of a flat one to accommodate the projecting shank of the tap. Once the taps have been fitted the basin can be placed in position on its brackets.

Fixing a waste outlet

Wash basins usually have a built-in overflow and a slotted waste outlet must therefore be provided. Apply a layer of non-setting mastic filler around the outlet hole of the basin. Bed the flange of the waste outlet down on to this mastic base, making sure that the slot in the waste outlet coincides with the built-in overflow of the basin.

A trap must be screwed to the tail of the waste. A plastic bottle trap with a P outlet is ideal. These are neat in appearance, take up little space and are easily dismantled in case of blockage.

Plastic traps are readily connected to a PVC waste pipe. Any joins or bends necessary in this pipe can be made with solvent weld sockets.

Connecting the water supply

Work backwards from the taps towards the main supply pipes. A tap connector or cap and lining must be screwed to the tail of each tap. This useful fitting incorporates a fibre washer so that no other means of waterproofing the joint is necessary.

A double or swan neck bend will be necessary in the lengths of pipe connected to the taps to bring them back to the wall for the wall-hung basin or to the centre of the pedestal. Compression or capillary bends can be used to do this but the spring-bending technique can be used for easy jobs of this kind for a neater and cheaper job.

At skirting or below floor board level fit a compression or

Bidet installation

The hot and cold supplies to a rim supply bidet have to comply with certain rules. Main points are shown here

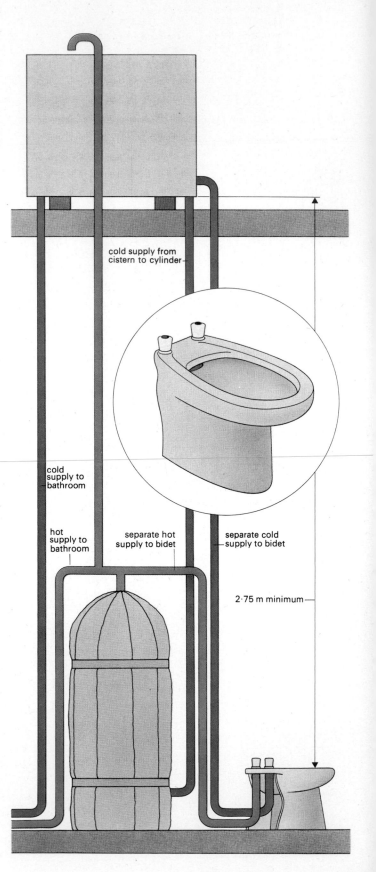

cold supply from cistern to cylinder

cold supply to bathroom

hot supply to bathroom

separate hot supply to bidet

separate cold supply to bidet

2·75 m minimum

capillary elbow and then take the supply pipes horizontally to the corner of the room from which the pipe is to rise into the roof space. Secure the pipes to floor joists or skirting board with pipe clips at regular intervals. Finally fit another elbow to direct the supply pipes up into the roof space to connect with the source of supply. Drain the main hot and cold water supply pipes before making the connections, by turning off the stop-cocks and letting the bathroom taps run until the pipes are empty.

If there are no stop-cocks other than the one on the rising main, tie up the arm of the ball-valve serving the cold water storage cistern so that no water can flow in. Then open the bathroom cold taps and drain the pipes and the cistern. There is no need to drain off the hot water from the hot water storage cylinder. Once the taps cease to run, open the hot taps to get rid of the water in the pipes above cylinder level.

Make the tee joints, using adaptors to metric sizes if necessary, by cutting off the required length of the supply pipe, and following instructions for either capillary or non-manipulative compression joints.

Before turning on the water supply again make sure that all lagging is replaced on existing pipes and that the new branches in the roof space are also thoroughly lagged.

Open up the new taps as you reinstate the water supply and allow the new branch supply pipes to flush through for fifteen minutes or so before turning the taps off. If flow is stopped by an air lock, connect one end of a length of hose to the cold tap over the kitchen sink which is direct from the main and the other end to the tap giving trouble. Turn both taps on full and the mains pressure will blow any air bubbles causing a blockage out of the system.

Where the provision of hot water supply to a new basin would involve a pipe run of more than 6m it is best to supply the cold tap direct from the main and to use a small gas or electric heater connected direct to the main for hot water supply. But the water authority will have to approve this.

Installing a bidet

There are two types of bidet, the over-rim supply and the rim supply model. The first of these is more basic. As far as plumbing is concerned it resembles a wash basin in every respect and can easily be installed in any bathroom that has the space to accommodate it.

The over-rim bidet

Like a wash basin, an over-rim supply bidet has either hot and cold taps or a mixer that are fitted in exactly the same way as the taps of a ceramic wash basin.

The waste may have an independent plug secured by a chain or like some wash basins it may have a pop-up waste operated by a control knob between the taps. Because of the limited space in which to work beneath and behind a bidet, it is wise to fit the waste and trap before screwing the appliance to the floor.

Water supplies to the bidet taps are connected in the same way as for a wash basin. The branch hot and cold supply pipes can be teed off by means of reducing tees from the water supply pipes already in the bathroom.

If the house has a two-pipe drainage system, regard the bidet as a waste and not as a soil fitting. Its waste should discharge over a gully, not directly into the drain or soil pipe.

The rim supply bidet

The rim supply bidet is more sophisticated and its water supply presents special problems. Rim supply bidets have a flushing rim, not unlike that of a wc and a spray head in their base from which a jet of water can be directed upwards. The flushing rim serves the dual purpose of filling the bidet and warming the seat for the user.

Special regulations apply to this kind of submerged inlet appliance designed to prevent any possible risk of the contamination of other water supplies. Hot and cold water supplies to a rim supply bidet must not be teed off existing bathroom or any other supply pipes. The cold supply must be taken by means of a separate branch supplied direct from the cold water storage cistern. The hot water supply must be taken from a separate branch connected directly to the hot water storage cylinder. As a further precaution, the base of the cold water storage cistern must be at least 2.75m above the level of the inlet to the bidet.

If the cold water storage cistern is immediately above the bathroom and the cylinder is in the bathroom or immediately adjacent to it, the fitting of a rim supply bidet is not a difficult project. It is, however, a more complicated and expensive job than installing an over-rim appliance.

Installing a bath

It is often necessary to remove an existing bath before fitting a new appliance.

Removing an existing bath

Remove the bath panels if any. You will then see that the water supply and waste connections are all made in an extremely confined space between the end of the bath and the wall. There probably won't be room to turn an ordinary wrench or spanner. A purpose-made bath or basin wrench which can be used in a vertical position will make the disconnection of the supply pipes easier.

Turn off the water supplies to the hot and cold taps and drain the taps to empty the pipes. Unscrew the cap nuts connecting the water supply pipes to the tails of the taps. Do not attempt to unscrew the back nuts of the taps until you have moved the bath from its present position.

The bath may have an overflow pipe leading straight through the wall to discharge outside. If so saw off this pipe as close to the wall as possible. Unscrew the nut connecting the trap to the bath outlet waste.

The bath can now be moved but, before doing so, turn the adjustable screws on the feet to lower it. This will permit you to move it without damaging the wall tiling. Don't attempt to move heavy cast iron baths without help.

Fitting the bath

Because of the limited space at the back of the bath it is wise to assemble the plumbing as completely as possible before moving the bath into position. Fit the bath taps or mixer using a top hat or spacer washer underneath to accommodate the shank of the tap, before screwing up the back nuts.

Ensure that the water supply pipes are cut to the right length and fitted with cap and lining connectors ready for fitting on to the tails of the taps.

With an acrylic bath it is wise to use a plastic trap and waste pipe. The bath could be damaged by a metal waste as a result of the stresses set up by expansion and contraction.

Bath traps are normally provided with a flexible overflow pipe to connect to the overflow outlet. Before fitting the waste fitting into its hole, spread non-setting mastic sealer around the hole. Connect up the trap but do not connect the flexible overflow pipe to the bath until the bath is in position.

Before putting the bath in position bring the waste pipe to the point at which it will connect to the trap. When the bath is placed in position connect the trap to the waste pipe and the overflow to the bath outlet. Finally connect the two taps to the water supply pipes.

Installing a shower

Shower installation is one of the most worth while plumbing projects that a householder can undertake. An independent shower saves space and money but it must comply with certain quite specific design requirements.

For a conventional shower installed in conjunction with a cylinder storage system of hot water supply there are two essential requirements. The first is that the hot and cold supplies of water to the shower must be under equal pressure. Since the hot water in the storage cylinder is under pressure from the main cold water storage cistern, the cold supply to the shower must also come from this cistern. It is both illegal and impracticable to connect the hot side of the shower to water from a storage cylinder and the cold side direct to the rising main.

The second essential is that this pressure should be adequate. This will depend upon the height of the cold water storage cistern above the shower sprinkler. The level of the

Bath installation

Easiest type of bath to fit is a plastic one – it is a lot lighter than other types. Here are the basic details

This is how a basin spanner is used in a tight space

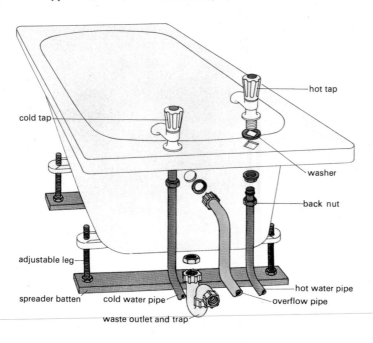

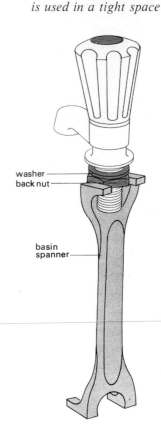

Plastic baths need accurate support, so the legs are adjustable. The overflow on modern baths is built-in

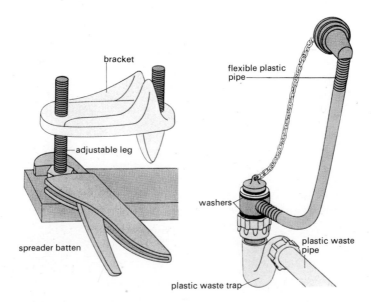

cylinder doesn't matter. It may be above, below, or at the same level as the shower.

For best results, the vertical distance between the shower sprinkler and the base of the cold water storage cistern, the head of water, should be about 1.5m. Where pipe runs are short with few bends it may be possible to obtain a satisfactory shower with a head as low as 1m, but this is an absolute minimum.

A further safety requirement is that the cold supply to the shower should be taken by means of a separate branch supply pipe direct from the cold water storage cistern. If it is taken as a branch from a pipe supplying other fittings then the water supplied from the same pipe will result in loss of pressure on the cold side of the shower. This could result in sudden and dangerous scalding.

In circumstances where there is not enough head a shower can still be installed. Electric shower pumps operated by a flow switch requiring only a few inches head of water are available. These switch on as the shower mixing valve is opened and boost the water pressure. But they do, of course, add considerably to the cost of the installation.

If it is not possible to install a conventional shower in your home you can consider fitting one of the versatile instantaneous electric water heaters with shower attachment.

Water supply is taken to these appliances by means of a 15mm branch supply pipe teed off the rising main. In connecting the electric power the same precautions must be observed as with any other bathroom electrical appliance.

Shower mixing valves

The simplest kind of mixing valve is provided by the two bath taps. These may supply a rubber demountable shower by means of push-on tap connectors. A better arrangement is to provide a special bath/shower mixer. This has a spout for filling the bath and a 15mm shower connector above the spout. The flick of a knob diverts the mixed water from the spout upwards to the shower sprinkler. With either of these arrangements the flow and temperature of the water is controlled by adjusting the bath taps.

A better arrangement is the provision of a manual shower mixing valve. This is a single valve to which hot and cold supplies are connected. Water temperature and in some cases flow are determined by the user turning a control knob. Mixers of this kind are standard equipment for independent showers and models are available for over-bath use.

Finally there is the thermostatic mixing valve which eliminates all risk of either danger or discomfort from the shower suddenly turning hot or cold in use. A thermostatic valve delivers water at a predetermined temperature. If there is a drop in pressure on one side of the valve the pressure on the other side will be automatically reduced to match it. A thermostatic valve eliminates the necessity of taking a separate cold supply pipe from the cold water storage cistern to the shower sprinkler.

Shower in bath *vs* independent shower

If your shower is fitted over an existing bath no special arrangements will need to be made for drainage. You will, however, have to provide plastic shower curtains or a glass panel to prevent water from splashing on to the bathroom floor. Plastic curtains are the cheaper solution but a glass panel has a much neater appearance.

An independent shower unit consists of a shower tray of either ceramic, plastic or enamelled steel enclosed by a shower curtain or a purpose-made shower cubicle. Waste

fittings are provided to the shower tray as for a wash basin except that as shower sprays have no overflow an unslotted waste will be used.

As with other sanitary fittings a shallow 50mm seal trap can be used for connection to a two-pipe drainage system. For connection to a single stack system a deep seal 75mm trap must be used.

Water supplies to an independent shower are taken in 15mm tubing to connect to the 15mm inlets of the shower mixing valve. It is usual to take the supply pipes to the valve in chases cut into the wall plaster. The plaster is made good afterwards and tiled to conceal the pipes.

Shower installation

Water pressure – or head of water – is important for showers, even the one, right. Here are the details

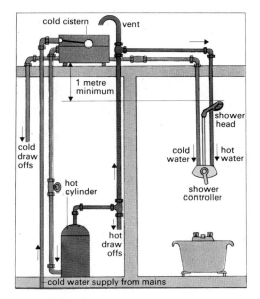

Ways of getting a shower; the first can be fitted only on a bath. The others can be in a bath or shower cubicle

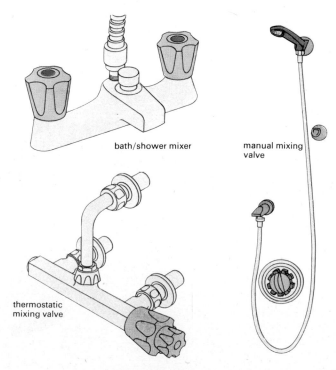

Installing a sink unit

Changing from an old ceramic sink to a modern stainless steel unit transforms a kitchen

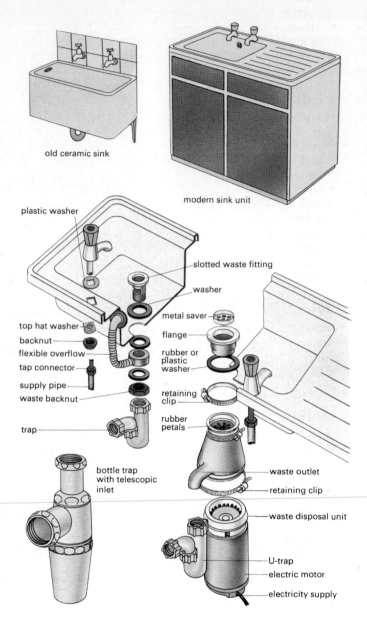

old ceramic sink

modern sink unit

plastic washer

slotted waste fitting

washer

metal saver

top hat washer

flange

backnut

rubber or plastic washer

flexible overflow

tap connector

supply pipe

retaining clip

waste backnut

rubber petals

trap

bottle trap with telescopic inlet

waste outlet

retaining clip

waste disposal unit

U-trap

electric motor

electricity supply

Many older homes had deep, glazed enamel sinks with a weir overflow and a detachable wooden drainer. The sink was supported by iron cantilever brackets built into the kitchen wall. Bib taps supplying hot and cold water projected from the glazed tiles of the wall above it.

The standard modern sink is made of enamelled pressed steel or stainless steel. It incorporates a drainer or drainers of the same material and is supported by a sink unit incorporating drawer and cupboard space.

Removing an existing sink

Remove the draining board of the old sink and unscrew the cap nut securing the trap to the waste outlet. The old sink can now be levered away from the wall and removed. Don't attempt to lift it single handed as it will be very heavy. It is

probably easier to cut the cantilever brackets off flush with the wall than to attempt to remove them.

Cut off the water supply to the taps and drain them to empty the supply pipes. The existing supply pipes may be buried under the wall plaster. Excavate them from the wall with a cold chisel and pull them forward.

Unscrew and remove the old taps and cut the supply pipes sufficiently to permit the new sink to be placed in position above them. Don't cut off too much from the pipe ends. It will prove easier and cheaper to make another cut later than to extend pipes that have been cut too short.

Installing the new sink

Before placing the sink unit in position fit the new pillar taps into the holes provided at the top of the sink. If you fit a mixer make sure that it is a sink mixer with separate channels for the hot and cold water supplies and not a basin mixer.

A flat plastic washer should be slipped over the tails of the taps or mixer before inserting them into the holes. A top hat or spacer washer is then slipped on underneath to accommodate the projecting shank of the tap before screwing up the back nut.

The waste outlet should also be fitted into the hole provided for it before moving the unit into position. This is bedded down on to non-setting mastic. Most stainless steel and enamelled pressed steel sinks have an overflow outlet which connects to the waste outlet and must be fitted to a flexible overflow pipe.

Place the sink unit in position and hold up a cap and lining tap connector to the two tap tails. This will tell you where you must cut the two supply pipes to make the compression or capillary connection between the pipes and the tap connectors.

Cut the pipes at the points marked, fit the tap connectors to the pipe ends and screw the connectors to the tails of the taps. A basin spanner will make this task easier.

It may be possible to fit the trap of the old sink to the new waste outlet. If not, use a bottle trap with an adjustable inlet which gives the extra tolerance that is needed to permit connection to the old waste pipe.

Even with a single stack drainage system it is advisable to take the sink waste to an outside gully rather than to make a connection to the main soil and waste stack.

Sink waste disposal unit

In a really up-to-date kitchen an electric sink waste disposal unit may be provided instead of the normal waste outlet. These units dispose of all the soft kitchen wastes. Grinders operated by an electric motor reduce these wastes to a slurry that can then be flushed down the drain by running the cold tap.

Installation of a waste disposal unit requires a sink outlet of 87.5mm instead of the usual 38mm outlet. Outlets of stainless steel, but not enamelled pressed steel sinks can be enlarged to this size by means of a hole cutter that can be borrowed or hired from the supplier of the disposal unit.

Waste disposal units are fitted by placing a rubber or plastic washer round the outlet hole before inserting the flange of the unit. Depending upon the make of the unit, the connection is made beneath the sink either with bolts or with a snap fastening.

The outlet of the disposal unit is then connected to a P or S trap in the usual way. A conventional trap should be used. Manufacturers of waste disposal units do not recommend the use of bottle traps at the outlet of their appliances.

Installing a washing machine

As the washing machine will almost certainly be located adjacent to the kitchen or bathroom sink, water supplies to the machine can most conveniently be taken from the pipes supplying the taps. These pipes can usually be tapped beneath the sink at a point where the actual connections will be screened by the sink unit.

You will need two 15mm compression tees with all outlets equal, two lengths of 15mm copper tubing sufficiently long to extend beyond the side of the sink unit to a point adjacent to the washing machine and two purpose-made washing machine stop-cocks.

Plumbing-in a washing machine adds greatly to convenient working in the kitchen. Here are the details

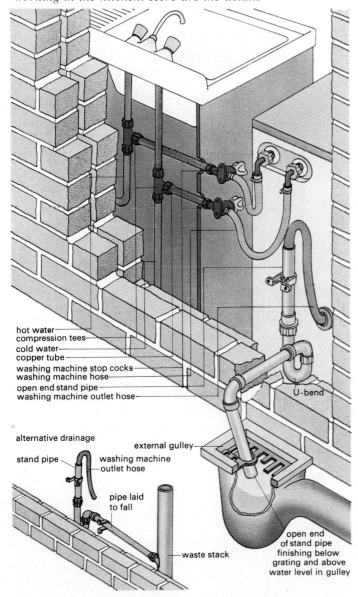

hot water
compression tees
cold water
copper tube
washing machine stop cocks
washing machine hose
open end stand pipe
washing machine outlet hose

U-bend

alternative drainage

external gulley

stand pipe

washing machine
outlet hose

pipe laid
to fall

open end
of stand pipe
finishing below
grating and above
water level in gulley

waste stack

Compression tees are suggested rather than capillary soldered ones because these will be suitable for making the branch connections whether your existing supply pipes are in Imperial or in metric tubing.

Turn off the water supply to the sink taps and run them to empty the supply pipes.

Hold up the tee joints to the water supply pipes and mark the points at which they will need to be cut before attaching the compression tees.

Insert the lengths of copper tubing into the branch outlets of the two tees. Tighten the branch cap nuts securely.

The washing machine stop-cocks can then be connected by means of their compression joint inlets to the farther ends of the copper tubing. Once these are fitted and the two stop-cocks turned off the water supply can be turned on again. The washing machine hoses clip on to the stop-cock outlets and the stop-cocks are then used as taps to fill the washing machine when required.

Providing for drainage

The simplest way to deal with the drainage from the washing machine is to hook the outlet tube over the edge of the sink and drain the machine into the sink. This is possible in most cases and requires no plumbing.

If this cannot be arranged a 35mm diameter open-ended standpipe may be provided and the washing machine outlet hose hooked over that. The standpipe must have its open end at least 600mm above floor level.

Manufacturers of PVC waste systems make suitable standpipes with traps at their base suitable for discharge over an external gully or for connection to the waste stack of a single stack drainage system.

Providing an outside tap

An outside tap with a hose connector can be extremely useful for watering the garden or cleaning the car. Most water authorities permit the connection of such a tap to the rising main though they will probably make an annual charge for its use.

Installing the tap

Turn off the main stop-cock and drain the rising main from the drain-cock provided immediately above it. If there is no drain-cock at this point you can still proceed but be prepared for some water to leak out from the rising main when you cut it.

Connect a compression tee with all ends equal to the rising main about 600mm above floor level.

Fit a short length of 15mm copper tubing into the branch outlet of the tee. Then fit an ordinary brass screw-down stop-cock with compression joint inlet and outlet on to the other end of this tube. When fitting this stop-cock make sure that the arrow engraved on its body points in the direction of the flow of water, that is away from the rising main.

Once this stop-cock has been securely fitted and turned off, the main stop-cock can be turned on and the household water supply restored.

Fit another length of 15mm copper tubing into the outlet of the stop-cock. This must be sufficiently long to reach the point on the inside wall outside which you intend to fit the tap. Drill or cut a hole through the wall at this point, then connect a 15mm compression or capillary joint elbow. To this elbow connect another short length sufficient to pass through the wall and to bend over into the inlet of a wall plate elbow. Use the spring bending technique for this if necessary, but a capillary elbow will probably be better.

This wall plate elbow must be screwed to plugs in the wall. A bib tap, preferably provided with a hose connector outlet, can then be screwed into the threaded outlet of the elbow. In order to ensure a watertight joint, plastic thread sealing tape should be bound round the threaded tail of the tap before it is connected. Plastic thread sealing tape is available in rolls from any builders' merchant.

Fitting an outside tap

An internal stop-cock is fitted to enable the user to turn off the water and drain the pipe during the winter

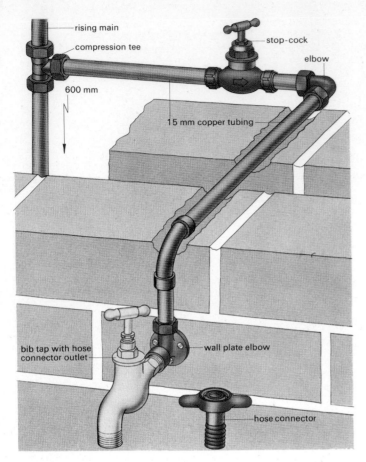

- rising main
- compression tee
- stop-cock
- elbow
- 600 mm
- 15 mm copper tubing
- bib tap with hose connector outlet
- wall plate elbow
- hose connector

When the tap is fitted and the wall made good, the stop-cock on the branch leading to the outside tap may be opened and the tap brought into use.

During frosty weather the branch stop-cock should be closed and the outside tap opened. This will permit the short branch pipe to drain and will eliminate the risk of frost damage.

Roof drainage

PVC roof drainage systems are lightweight, cannot corrode, need no decoration and are quite easily fitted. All manufacturers of PVC rainwater material supply detailed installation instructions.

Fixing the guttering

In fixing the rainwater guttering, the first point to establish is the position of the outlet. This will be immediately above the gully into which the downpipe is to discharge. Its position on the fascia board of the roof must be established with a plumb line.

Mark this point on the fascia board. Take a string line from it levelled by means of a spirit level to the end of the fascia board. Gutters are sometimes laid dead level but for good drainage it is better to arrange for a slight fall towards the outlet of 1 in 100. The farther end of the string line marking the run of the gutter should therefore be raised by 10mm for every metre of length.

Screw the gutter brackets to the fascia board using the string line to indicate their level. Brackets must be provided on either side of the outlet, in close proximity to a stop-end and on either side of an external or internal angle. They should also be provided to support straight runs of guttering with at least four to each standard 3m length. The guttering can now be fitted, working in each direction from the gutter outlet.

The notch at the end of the length of gutter is an essential part of the joint. After cutting a length of guttering with a fine tooth saw a notch must be made. The notch is 40mm long and 3mm deep and extends to within 10mm of the gutter end. There is a special tool available for making these notches quickly and easily but, if one isn't available, the job can be done with a file.

An offset must now be provided to bring the down-pipe back from the gutter outlet wall. This offset is made by solvent welding together with an offset socket, an offset spigot and a short length of down-pipe. After making the offset, leave for several minutes before fitting in position to enable the solvent welded joints to set properly.

Joints between lengths of rainwater down-pipe are not normally sealed but it is good practice to make a ring seal joint between the gutter outlet and the offset socket. The lower end of the offset is pushed into the socket of a length of down-pipe which must be secured to the wall by means of a pipe-clip.

The pipe-clip back-plate must be screwed to plugs which are hammered into holes drilled into the mortar joints in the brickwork. If the outlet of the offset does not coincide with a mortar joint it should be cut back so that the back-plate can be screwed to plugs fitted into the joint above.

The pipe clip is completed with a PVC ring that slips around the down-pipe socket and is connected to the back-plate with a nut and bolt. A pipe clip must be provided to support the socket of each length of down-pipe and the rainwater shoe at its base that discharges over the rainwater gully. When fitting the spigot of each length of down-pipe into the socket of the length below, a 10mm gap should be left to allow for expansion.

PLUMBING MAINTENANCE AND REPAIR

Refitting a tap washer

Rewashering a tap is a basic plumbing operation. A tap needs rewashering when it continues to drip after being turned off. The onset of washer failure is gradual like many other plumbing faults.

Fitting a new washer

Cut off the water supply to the tap. For the cold tap over the kitchen sink which is the one most likely to need rewashering, this means turning off the main stop-cock. For other taps it may mean tying up the float arm of the ball-valve supplying the main storage cistern and draining the cistern.

Unscrew and raise the easy-clean cover. It should be possible to do this by hand but if you cannot, use a wrench with its jaws padded to prevent damage to the chromium plating.

With a spanner or adjustable wrench, unscrew and remove the headgear of the tap by turning the hexagon nut immediately above the tap body.

You may find that the valve or jumper is resting on the valve seating in the body of the tap. Holding the valve with a

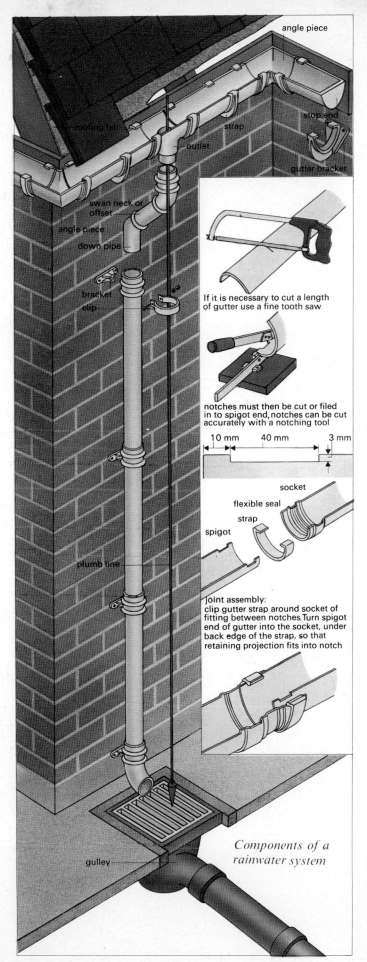

angle piece

stop end

roofing felt

strap

outlet

gutter bracket

swan neck or
offset

angle piece

down pipe

bracket

clip

plumb line

gulley

*Components of a
rainwater system*

If it is necessary to cut a length
of gutter use a fine tooth saw

notches must then be cut or filed
in to spigot end, notches can be cut
accurately with a notching tool

10 mm 40 mm 3 mm

socket

flexible seal

strap

spigot

Joint assembly:
clip gutter strap around socket of
fitting between notches. Turn spigot
end of gutter into the socket, under
back edge of the strap, so that
retaining projection fits into notch

pair of pliers or an adjustable wrench, turn the nut retaining the washer with a spanner. Having removed the retaining nut you can fit the new washer and reassemble. If the nut is difficult to remove you can simply replace the washer and jumper with a complete new one.

You may on the other hand find that the jumper is pegged in the headgear of the tap. It can be turned round and round but cannot be withdrawn. In this event make a really determined effort to remove the retaining nut. Apply a little penetrating oil if it seems immovable and try again after twenty minutes or so. If the nut *really* cannot be removed you can break the pegging by inserting a screwdriver blade as a lever between the base of the headgear and the jumper plate. When inserting a new jumper and washer complete, burr the stem of the jumper with a file to make it a tight fit in the headgear.

To replace a washer in a shrouded head tap first remove the shrouded head. The way in which this is done depends upon the make of the tap. In some cases the 'hot' or 'cold' indicator disc conceals a screw which, when unscrewed, permits the head to be removed. In other cases there is a small retaining grub screw fitted into the side of the head. With yet another make of tap the head can be pulled off after the tap has been fully opened.

Once the head has been removed you will find that the headgear and jumper of a tap of this kind differs very little from that of the more conventional bib or pillar tap.

Rewashering a Supatap is different and easier. There is no need to turn off the water supply to the tap. Unscrew the retaining nut at the top of the nozzle. Then turn the tap on and keep on turning. At first the flow of water will increase but it will then cease as the check valve falls into position. Another couple of turns and the nozzle of the tap will come off in your hand.

Tap the end of the nozzle on a hard surface and turn it upside down. The anti-splash device which also retains the jumper and washer will fall out. Replace with a new jumper and washer and reassemble. When screwing the nozzle back into position remember that it has a left-hand thread.

It sometimes happens that after rewashering, the tap continues to drip. This indicates that the valve seating has been scored and damaged by grit from the main.

Reseating a tap

It is possible to reseat a conventional tap with a special reseating tool made for that purpose. Generally, though, it is better to fit a nylon seating. Nylon seating and washer sets are available from most hardware stores.

The nylon seating is placed in position above the existing brass seating. The washer and jumper are fitted into the headgear of the tap and the headgear is then screwed down hard forcing the new seating into position on the old one. It may take a little while for the new seating to bed and to give an absolutely watertight result. A tool for reseating the valve of a Supatap can be hired from a builders' merchant.

Adjusting or renewing the gland of a tap

Leakage upwards past the spindle when the tap is turned on indicates that the gland or stuffing box needs attention. Another indication is that the tap turns on and off much too easily. This results in a sudden closing of the water way and is a common cause of water hammer.

Tap glands will fail eventually as the result of normal wear and tear but two situations cause rapid gland failure. One is back pressure within the tap that can arise from a connection

Tap washer-changing

Pad the grips to protect the chromium plating

With the tap full on a slim spanner will fit

Unscrew the headgear; it will retain the jumper

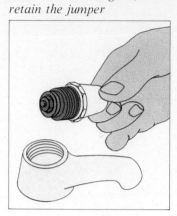

Unless pegged, the jumper can be pulled free

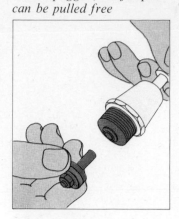

Hold the jumper and undo the washer-retaining nut

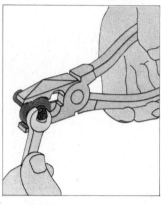

Remove the old washer and clean the jumper

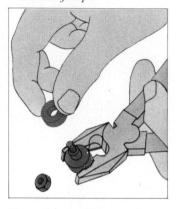

Fit a new washer and replace the retaining nut

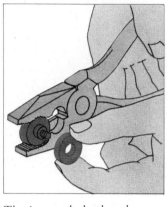

Replace the jumper and refit the headgear

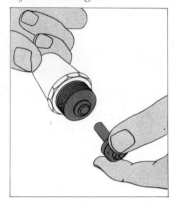

On a Supatap, release the retaining nut

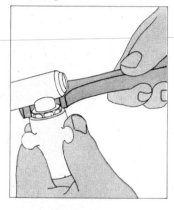

Turn the tap full on while holding the nut still

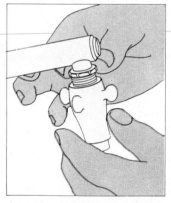

The internal check valve will cut off the water

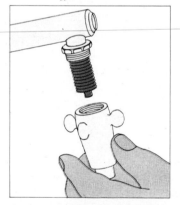

Press the nozzle to push out the jumper assembly

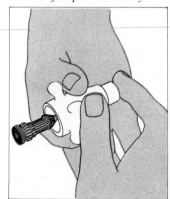

A coin will break the jumper/anti-splash joint

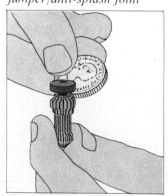

The jumper, complete with washer, now pulls free

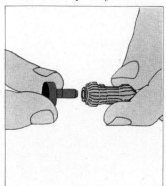

Put a new jumper assembly back on the anti-splash

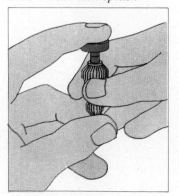

Fit the anti-splash into the tap nozzle and reassemble

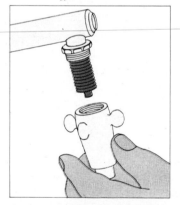

to a garden hose or washing machine. The other is detergent charged water running down the spindle into the tap body and washing the grease out of the gland.

It may be possible to correct the problem by giving the gland adjusting nut half a turn or so in a clockwise direction. This is the first nut through which the tap spindle passes. It should be possible to reach it without removing the tap handle by opening the tap to its fullest extent and raising the easy clean cover. But sooner or later all the adjustment in this nut will be taken up and the gland packing must be renewed.

To do this you must remove the tap head or handle. Unscrew and remove the tiny grub screw at the side that retains it. A sharp upward tap should now remove the handle. If you have difficulty in removing the handle in this way cut off the water supply to the tap, open it up fully, raise the easy clean cover and insert two pieces of wood—a spring clothes peg will do—between the body of the tap and the base of the easy clean cover. Then screw the tap down to close it.

The upward pressure of the easy clean cover will force the handle off the end of the spindle. Take off the easy clean cover and unscrew and remove the gland adjusting nut to reveal the stuffing box. With the point of a penknife blade, remove all remains of packing material within the stuffing box. Repack using knitting wool steeped in petroleum jelly. Replace the gland adjusting nut and screw down to a point at which the tap can be opened and closed easily—but not too easily. Replace the easy clean cover and the tap handle.

Some modern taps have a rubber O-ring seal instead of the conventional gland packing. With taps of this kind renewing the gland simply means removing the old worn-out O-ring and replacing it with a new one.

Stop-cocks

Stop-cocks are essentially bib taps set in a run of pipe. Their washers and glands fail in exactly the same way as those of taps and should be dealt with in the same way. In order to cut off the water supply to a main stop-cock to enable servicing to be carried out, it may be necessary to arrange for the water authority to turn off their stop-cock in the road outside.

Stop-cocks that are long disused are liable to jam open so that they cannot be closed in an emergency. To guard against this it is wise to close and open all stop-cocks about twice a year.

Refitting a washer in a ball-valve

When the overflow pipe of the cistern served by a ball-valve drips, the ball valve needs rewashering. Cut off the water supply to the valve. Then remove the split pin holding the float arm in position and put the float arm on one side and unscrew the cap, if any, at the end of the valve body.

Insert the blade of a screwdriver into the slot at the base of the valve body from which the end of the float arm has been removed and push the plug out of the end of the valve. Have your hand ready to catch it as it comes out. If you don't you'll have to plunge your arm into the icy water of the cistern to retrieve it.

The plug is in two parts, the main body of the plug and a screw-on cap that retains the washer. This cap can be quite difficult to remove. Hold the body of the plug in a vice and try turning the cap with a pair of pliers. If the cap is very stiff, don't risk damaging the plug in your efforts to remove it. Pick the old washer out from under the retaining cap with the point of a penknife and force the new one into position under

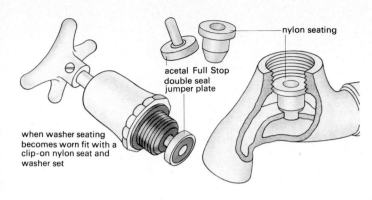

Grit in the water supply can damage the tap seat. Rather than recutting the seat, fit a seat/jumper kit

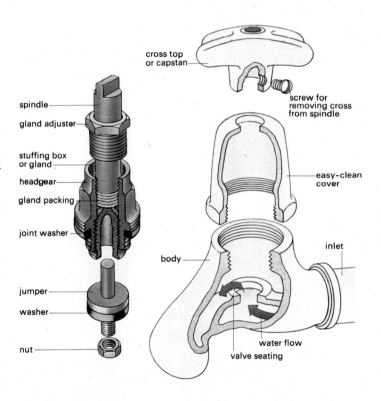

Water leakage past the tap spindle usually means the stuffing box needs readjustment or repacking

the cap making sure that it rests flat on its seating.

Before reassembling the valve, clean the plug with fine abrasive paper and lightly smear its surface with petroleum jelly. Bind a piece of abrasive paper around a pencil and clean the inside of the body of the plug in the same way.

The diaphragm valves rarely need attention. When the diaphragm does fail, the valve can be dismantled by turning the knurled retaining nut at the front of the valve by hand.

Persistent dripping from the overflow pipe after rewashering suggests that a low pressure ball-valve may have been fitted where a high pressure valve is required. Replace either with a high pressure valve or one of the types of equilibrium valve.

Inadequate flow through a ball-valve

If the valve is supplying a wc flushing cistern served by a main cold water storage cistern, check that a low pressure valve has been fitted. A wc cistern should fill within two minutes of use.

Another possible cause of poor flow through a ball valve is the plug sticking in the valve body as a result of scale formation. Dismantle and clean the plug and valve body as already explained.

Excessive ball-valve noise

Excessive noise is perhaps the commonest failing of ball-valves. There may be a sound of rushing water as the cistern fills or a vibrating, knocking or humming noise through the whole plumbing system. This noise emanates from the ball-valve and is due to ripple formation on the surface of the water in the cistern as water flows into it. These ripples shake the ball float up and down when the cistern is nearly full and cause noise by making the valve bounce on its seating.

You can buy a ball-valve stabiliser consisting of a plastic disc and an arm that is clipped to the float arm of the valve so that the disc is suspended a few inches below water level. This reduces the movement of the float and the consequent vibration.

Silencer tubes which are lengths of plastic tubing fitted into the ball-valve outlet so as to discharge incoming water below the level of water already in the cistern are now illegal. Modern diaphragm valves with an overhead outlet can be fitted with a kind of silencer that discharges the incoming water in a spray. Replacing the existing valve with a modern diaphragm or diaphragm/equilibrium valve will usually cure the trouble.

Ball-valve washer replacement is needed only rarely. The washer of this Portsmouth valve is in the piston

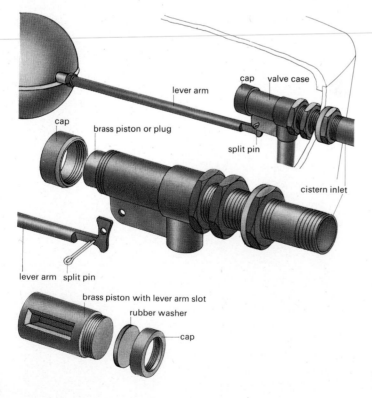

Make sure that the rising main in the roof space is securely fixed to the roof timbers. This is particularly important where a galvanised steel cistern has been replaced with a plastic one as plastic cisterns do not offer the same support to the rising main.

In difficult cases a cure can sometimes be effected by replacing the final 450mm or so of rising main with polythene tubing. This will not transmit and amplify vibration in the same way as copper tubing.

The flap valve is the only likely failure in a modern wc cistern. Replacement is fairly straightforward

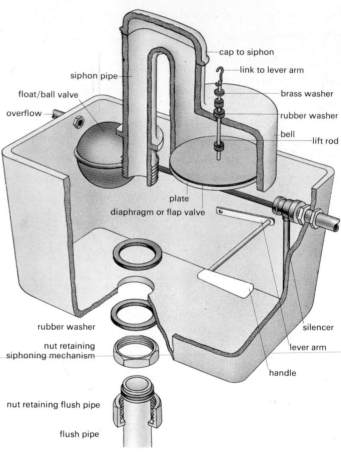

Flushing failure in cistern of wc

First remove cover of flushing cistern and check that the water level is correct. If there is no mark within the cistern indicating the correct level, then full water level should be about 12mm below the overflow outlet. Adjust the level by means provided if you have a modern ball-valve. If no means are provided, unscrew and remove the ball float. Then take the arm in both hands and gently but firmly bend the float end upwards to raise the water level.

If the water level is correct then the trouble with a modern direct action cistern is likely to be caused by failure of the diaphragm or flap valve within the dome of the siphon. To replace this diaphragm tie up the float arm to prevent more water from flowing into the cistern and flush to empty. Disconnect the flush pipe from the cistern.

Unscrew and remove the large nut immediately beneath the flushing cistern. Have a bowl handy because there will still be some water inside the cistern that will flow out as this nut is unscrewed. Once the nut has been removed the siphoning mechanism can be withdrawn from the cistern and access gained to the disc and to the diaphragm that rests on it.

You must, of course, obtain a new diaphragm before beginning this operation. If you do not know the correct size, get the largest size. It can be cut to the size required with a pair of scissors. The diaphragm should be large enough to cover the disc and just touch the walls of the siphon dome.

Although most cisterns can be dismantled, there are some types in which the siphoning mechanism is secured by bolts inside the cistern.

Continuing siphonage after flushing

This fault is most likely to occur with an old-fashioned bell cistern. Debris accumulates in the base of the cistern and reduces the gap between the base and the bottom of the bell. With a high pressure ball-valve, refilling may take place so quickly that air can never enter beneath the lip of the bell to break the siphonic action. The remedy is to clean out the cistern and, if necessary, reduce the flow by partially closing a stop-cock on the supply pipe feeding it.

Condensation on the flushing cistern

Condensation is most likely to occur where a cast iron or ceramic cistern is supplied direct from the main. The remedy lies in improved ventilation and a source of radiant heat – not warmth supplied by an unflued gas heater or an oil stove. An extractor fan fitted in the window of the wc compartment will help.

If the wc is situated in the bathroom, run an inch or so of cold water before turning on the bath hot tap. Refrain from the practice of drip-drying clothes over the bath.

Cast iron cisterns can be protected from condensation by painting externally with one or more coats of an anti-condensation paint. In severe cases it may be possible to insulate the cistern by lining it internally with strips of the kind of expanded polystyrene material that is used as insulation under wallpaper, affixed with an epoxy resin adhesive.

Failure of wc pan to clear

There can be several reasons for this fault. Check the level of water in the cistern to ensure that the pan is receiving the full flush. Then check that the flush pipe connects squarely to the flushing horn of the pan and that there is no obstruction at this point. The old-fashioned and unhygienic rag-and-putty joint between flush pipe and pan is frequently responsible for obstructions of this kind. Putty squeezes through into the wc inlet to obstruct the flow of water.

Be sure that the underside of the flushing rim is clear and free of obstructive hard water scale. You can check this with your fingers or with the aid of a mirror. Use a spirit level to check that the pan is set dead level. If it is not, introduce pieces of linoleum under the lower side to bring it level.

PROBLEMS IN THE PLUMBING SYSTEM

Air locks

A poor or intermittent flow of water from a hot water tap often accompanied by hissing and spluttering indicates that the supply pipe is obstructed by an air bubble or air lock. Air

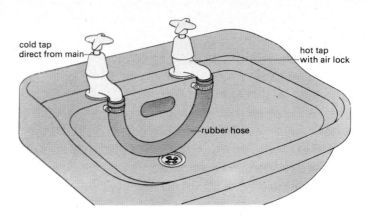

The high pressure from the mains, used like this, can cure an air lock in a hot water supply

cold tap direct from main

hot tap with air lock

rubber hose

locks can usually be cleared by connecting one end of a length of garden hose to the cold tap over the kitchen sink and the other end to the tap giving trouble. Turn both taps on fully and the pressure from the mains should force the air bubble out of the system.

Always seek the cause of recurring air locks. A common cause is having too small a cold water supply pipe from the cold water storage cistern to the hot water cylinder. If this pipe is only 15mm in diameter or has been effectively reduced to this diameter by a partially closed stop-valve, it will be insufficiently large to replace water drawn off from a 22mm bath tap. The water level will fall in the vent pipe until air is drawn into a horizontal length of pipe and causes a blockage. Horizontal runs of pipe taken from the vent pipe should always fall slightly away from this pipe to enable bubbles of air to escape. Other possible causes are too small a cold water storage cistern or a sluggish ball-valve feeding this cistern.

To reduce the risk of air locks forming when a hot water system is refilled after being drained, connect one end of a length of hose to the cold tap over the kitchen sink and the other end to the drain-cock beside the boiler. Open up both taps and the system will fill upwards, the rising water driving air in front of it.

Hard water scale

In hard water areas, hard water scale will form on the inside of boilers and on the surfaces of electric immersion heaters unless precautions are taken.

A boiler will be slow in heating up and will make hissing, bubbling and knocking noises if scale formations are present. Eventually, denied the cooling effect of the circulating water, boilers will burn through and immersion heaters will burn out.

Boilers may be descaled by partially draining the system and introducing an acid descaling fluid into the hot water system via the cold water storage cistern.

Scale formation can be prevented in several ways.

A direct hot water system can be replaced with an indirect one. Or a chemical scale inhibitor can be introduced into the cold water storage cistern. Alternatively a mains water softener can be provided.

Setting the thermostat of the electric immersion heater at 60 °C instead of 70 °C will also help to inhibit the formation of scale.

Corrosion in the cistern

Galvanised steel cold water storage cisterns are subject to internal corrosion and the almost universal use of copper pipes for plumbing services has increased this risk.

If a galvanised steel cistern is showing signs of rust it can be protected. Drain and dry the cistern and remove every trace of rust with a wire brush or abrasive paper. Fill in any deep pitmarks left by this process with an epoxy resin filler. When

Clearing a blocked sink can be a simple matter of using a sink plunger. Remember to block the overflow

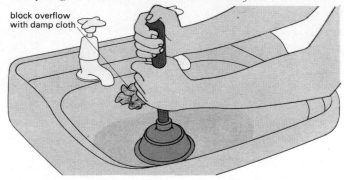

block overflow with damp cloth

On a normal U-trap, remove the drain plug with a rod

Use a piece of wire to probe for the obstruction

A flexible curtain wire is sometimes more successful

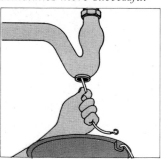

The trouble removed, replace the plug in the trap

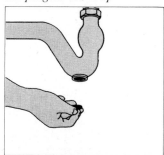

A bottle trap is easier. Unscrew the bottom by hand

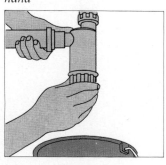

Use a suitable piece of wire to move the obstruction

the filler has set, apply two coats of a non-tainting bituminous paint. This treatment will afford protection for two or three years and may be repeated when required.

A cistern that is not yet showing signs of corrosion may be protected by installing a sacrificial anode. A lump of magnesium is introduced into the cistern and connected by means of a piece of copper wire to the cistern rim. The magnesium block will ensure that the cistern is protected. Unlike painting with bituminous paint, this method of protection can also be used with galvanised hot water tanks.

If a galvanised cistern is beyond restoration it should be replaced. Choose some form of plastic cistern, either a round polythene one or a rectangular glass fibre reinforced one. These cannot corrode and are tough, light and easily handled. The round polythene ones can be flexed through quite a small trap door into the roof space.

Installing a plastic cistern

The cistern must be placed on a flat level base, not just rested on the roof timbers. A piece of chipboard or two or three pieces of floor board are quite suitable. Pipes connected to the cistern must connect squarely so as not to strain the plastic walls. Two large size washers must be used on each side of the cistern wall between the wall and the nuts that hold the pipes in position. The plastic washer which has a metal washer behind it, is in direct contact with the wall of the cistern. No Boss White or other sealant must be used in direct contact with the plastic of the cistern.

Finally, make sure that the rising main serving the cistern is secured firmly to the roof timbers. Plastic cisterns do not give the same support as galvanised steel ones resulting in vibration noise.

Choked waste pipes

The indication of a choked waste pipe from a sink, basin or bath is that the water does not run out freely. Attempt to clear the blockage with a plunger which consists of a hemisphere of rubber or plastic, usually mounted on a wooden handle.

To use it place the hemisphere over the waste outlet. Hold a damp cloth firmly against the overflow outlet with one hand and plunge down sharply on the handle of the force cup with the other. If plunging doesn't clear the blockage, a solid object may be lodged in the trap. Place an empty bucket under the trap to collect the water. If you have a bottle trap unscrew the lower part of the trap to gain access to it. A conventional U trap will have an access cap at or near its base. Unscrew it and probe inside with a piece of wire. You will probably find that you can dislodge the obstruction.

If the pipe is still blocked try feeding a length of curtain wire into the waste pipe. This can be extremely effective in clearing stubborn blockages.

If a waste pipe appears to be partially blocked, try probing the grid of the outlet with a piece of wire such as a straightened out paper clip. You may find that debris is suspended from the grid and is partially blocking the outlet.

A build-up of grease is another cause of partial blockage. This can be cleared by the use of one of the proprietary drain clearing chemicals based on caustic soda. Use these with care and strictly in accordance with the makers' instructions.

Blocked drains

Water overflowing from a gully or manhole is one sign of a blocked drain. Another is water which rises and very slowly subsides when a wc is flushed.

Establish the site of the blockage by raising the drain manhole covers. If the manhole nearest to the bathroom is flooded while the one by the front gate is empty, the blockage must, therefore, lie in the length of drain between these two manholes.

You'll need a set of drain rods to clear the drain. Screw two or three rods together and insert the end into the flooded manhole. Feel for the half-channel at the base and push the rod into the drain in the direction of the blockage.

Screw on more rods as required until the blockage is encountered and dislodged. Various drain clearing tools that can be screwed on to the end of drain rods are available.

Turn the rods when pushing them into the drain or when pulling them out. Always twist in a clockwise direction. If you twist anticlockwise you will unscrew the rods and leave one or more lengths in the drain.

The intercepting trap is the most common site of drain blockage. To clear it, screw a 100mm drain plunger on to the end of the rods and push into the manhole. Feel for the half channel at the bottom and move the plunger along until you can feel the fall into the intercepting trap. Plunge down

sharply two or three times. There will be a gurgle of water and the level in the manhole will suddenly start to fall and the drain will clear itself.

After a drain has been cleared you should run the taps to flush it through and wash down the concrete benching and the walls of the manhole with hot water.

A particularly unpleasant partial blockage can arise at the intercepting trap. Sometimes, especially after heavy rain, pressure within the sewer may force the stoneware stopper of the rodding arm out of its socket. It will fall into the intercepting trap below where it will form a blockage. This may go unnoticed for a long time as the water level will rise in the intercepting manhole but will be able to escape down the rodding arm of the trap into the sewer. In the meantime the sewage in the base of the manhole will become steadily more and more foul. Where this occurs dispense with the stopper altogether and use a disc of slate or glass, lightly cemented in position in the socket of the rodding arm. If you should ever need to rod down the rodding arm to the sewer you can break this piece of slate or glass with an iron bar and replace it afterwards.

A basic knowledge of how the drainage system works can save a lot of worry. Here is a usual arrangement, together

with the equipment for clearing the blockage. When needed, this equipment can be hired

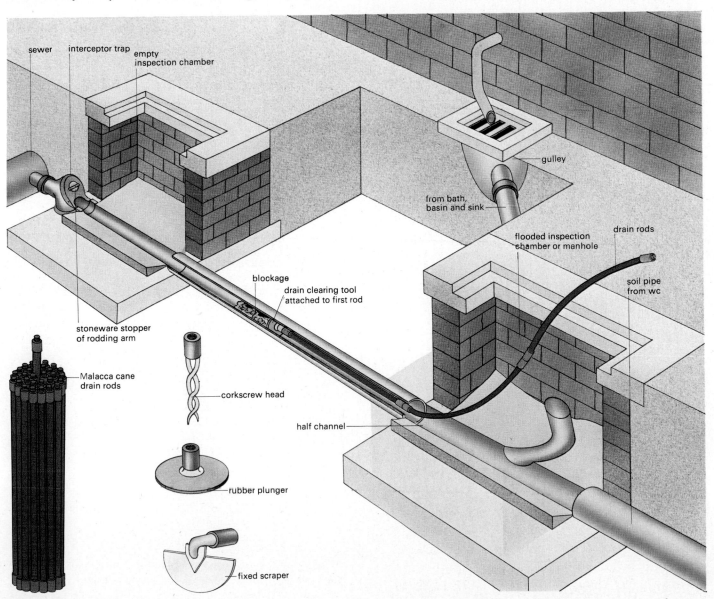

Quick guide to basic electrics

 ELECTRICAL INSTALLATIONS CAN, IF NOT PROPERLY EXECUTED AND MAINTAINED, LEAD TO FIRE AND ELECTRICAL SHOCK. ALL ELECTRICAL WORK MUST BE CARRIED OUT WITH GREAT CARE. A FEW SIMPLE SUBJECTS ARE DETAILED BELOW.

SAFETY FIRST

1 Turn off main switch before starting work on the electrical installation; remove the relevant circuit fuse and keep it in your pocket.
2 Pull out the plug of an electrical appliance before carrying out adjustments or repairs.
3 Turn off the light switch when replacing a dud bulb.
4 Never patch up a worn or damaged flex but replace it with a new length of the correct type and size.
5 To lengthen a flex use a purpose-made flex connector and observe the colour code. Watch out when joining old and new flexes with different code colours.
6 If an appliance is damaged, take it out of service even if it appears to be working.
7 Don't run appliances from light sockets (lampholders).
8 Don't attempt electrical work beyond your knowledge or capabilities.
9 Where an appliance has a provision for an earth wire connection it must always be utilised. Poor earth connections can result in serious electric shocks.

For quick emergency repairs, keep these items handy.

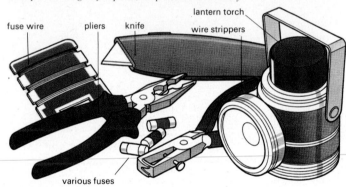

fuse wire   pliers   knife   lantern torch   wire strippers   various fuses

Wiring a 13 amp plug Most electrical appliances are fitted with three-core flex. If the appliance is new or was bought after 1970 the insulation around the cores will be brown (live); blue (neutral) and green and yellow stripes (earth). Appliances made before that date will have red (live), black (neutral) and green (earth) insulation.

When connecting a flex to a three-pin plug it is of the utmost importance that the wires are connected to their correct terminals. When you remove the plug cover to reveal the connections, you will note there are three terminals. The terminal at the top is the earth and is larger than the other two. This is marked E. The terminal on the right, next to the fuse, is the live terminal and marked L. The terminal on the left is the neutral terminal and is marked N.

When you connect the flex to the plug you connect the green-and-yellow (or green) wire to the E terminal; the brown (or red) wire to the L terminal; and the blue (or black) wire to the N terminal.

Cord grip At the bottom of the plug moulding is the cord grip which secures the flex so that any strain on it will not pull the wires free of the terminals.

On most plugs the cord grip is secured by two screws which, when tightened, cause the clamp to grip the flex. One make of plug—MK Safetyplug—has a screwless cord grip which increases its grip when any strain is placed on the flex. Unlike the conventional clamp, it does not distort when used with larger flexes.

Plug terminals There are two types of plug terminals; in the clamp version the wire is wound clockwise around a threaded post and is gripped by a special nut, usually slotted for a screwdriver blade. There is also a plain washer, either separate or captive to the nut. The post terminal has a hole for the wire which is pinched by a grub screw.

Flex preparation After removing the fuse, but before loosening the terminal screws, place the end of the flex against the plug and measure how much of the sheath (or braid) you need to trim. Remember that it is the sheath which is held by the cord grip. Allow about 10mm of bared wire for connection to the terminals. Remove the right length of sheath, taking care not to cut into the insulation around the wires. Place the flex end again on the plug to check the unsheathed ends for length. For most modern patterns of 13 amp plug, the three wires are cut to the same length. In some patterns the earth wire needs to be longer than the other two wires. With the wires now at the correct length, strip about 10mm of insulation from the end of each.

Thread the flex under the cord grip and lightly tighten the screws. Connect the green-and-yellow (or green) wire to the E terminal; the brown (or red) wire to the L terminal and the blue (or black) wire to the N terminal. Tighten the cord grip screws or press the flex into the screwless grip.

Position the wires neatly in the grooves of the moulding so that the cover can fit without pinching them. Check that all three terminal screws are tight, fit a fuse of correct rating, replace the cover and tighten the securing screws. When braided flexes are cut, the ends fray, so before cutting, bind near the cut position with PVC adhesive tape. Manufacturers often fit rubber sleeves on appliance flexes, leaving adequate insulated conductors for all patterns of 13-amp plug.

Fuse ratings There are two fuse sizes for 13-amp plugs; 3-amp, coloured red

On the left is a plug wired with old flex having red, black and green insulation. The modern brown, blue, green-and-yellow code is on the right.

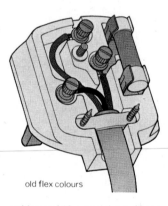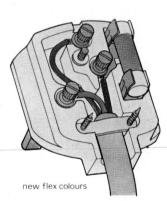

old flex colours   new flex colours

or blue and 13-amp coloured brown. For appliances up to 720 watts loading (not including electric motors), a 3-amp fuse should be used; other appliances need the 13-amp size. Ensure that the fuse makes good contact and is not loose.

Two-core flex Double-insulated appliances, such as some vacuum cleaners, electric drills, lawnmowers and devices with the double hollow square on the maker's label, are fitted with two-core flex. The plug is wired up in the same way as with three-core flex, but the earth terminal is left blank. The brown or red wire goes to the L terminal and the blue or black wire goes to the N terminal.

Reading a meter It is useful to know how to read your electricity meter. Not only will you be able to check consumption, bills and the meter readings, but you will be able to carry out a rough check on the accuracy of the meter.

There are two basic types of meter—one has figures rather like the odometer on a car, the other has a series of dials like those in the diagram. The White Meter, which measures off-peak and on-peak consumptions separately, has two sets of figures. Such a meter is usually of the digital type. There are six dials. The first one on the left registers the number of groups of 10,000 units consumed. The next dial measures the number of groups of 1,000 units consumed. Thus each dial reads one-tenth of the one to its left, right down to the sixth dial where each number represents one-tenth of a unit. So, by reading the dials from the left, the total number of units indicated can be written down. Two things to note. If a pointer is between two numbers, always take the lower of the two. And remember that the dials read alternately clockwise and anticlockwise, so care is needed! Of course, two readings are necessary to measure consumption. You subtract the first from the second and the result is the number of units (kWh) consumed between the two readings. Look at the diagram to see if you can read the dials and check your answer.

Checking your meter When electricity is being consumed, a disc on the meter revolves, the speed increasing with the rate of consumption. You can see only the edge of the disc and there is a black mark on it so that you can count how many times it revolves. As in the diagram, the number of revolutions for one unit of electricity consumed is marked on the meter. You can check this by switching everything off except, say, a 1kW electric fire. As this consumes one unit in one hour the meter disc in the example shown should turn 375 revolutions in one hour, or one revolution in about 10 seconds. With the aid of the second hand on your watch, you can count the number of revolutions and so check that the meter is recording accurately. You can also check the rate of consumption by the speed of the 1/10 dial. One complete revolution represents one unit of electricity. If the pointer takes half and hour to complete one revolution, the rate of consumption is two units per hour—which means 2,000 watts switched on.

Repairing a fuse The fuses in the consumer unit or fuseboard, usually located near the electricity meter under the stairs, are called circuit fuses. The modern consumer unit incorporates a main switch, while older installations may have a fuseboard with a separate switch or a number of main switch and fuse units. Before anything goes wrong it is as well to familiarise yourself with the various fuses, and label any which are not already labelled. Then when a fuse blows, you will be able to locate it immediately.

Why a fuse blows A fuse blows when an excessive current flows in a circuit. This excessive current can be caused by a fault or because the circuit is overloaded. When a number of lights or appliances fail to operate, the reason will usually be a blown fuse. When an appliance fails to operate it is likely to be the plug fuse which has blown. When a fuse blows, take a torch to the consumer unit, turn off the main switch and inspect the fuses. A blown rewirable fuse can be checked by examining the wire, but there is no visual means of telling when a cartridge fuse has blown. If you have no means of testing it, then replace the suspect cartridge by a new one.

Mending a rewirable fuse Having located the blown fuse, and removed it from this consumer unit, replace the fuse cover and turn on the main switch while you mend the fuse. To do this you need fuse wire of the right current rating, a small screwdriver and wire nippers (or a pair of scissors). Undo the terminal screw at each end of the fuse holder and take out the pieces of old fuse wire. Clean off any blobs of metal and insert the end of the new fuse wire into the ceramic or asbestos tube. Secure the end of the wire to the terminal. Cut the fuse wire to length leaving some slack to be taken up as the clamping screws are tightened and fix it to the other terminal.

Follow these colour codes and wire sizes for correct fuse ratings.

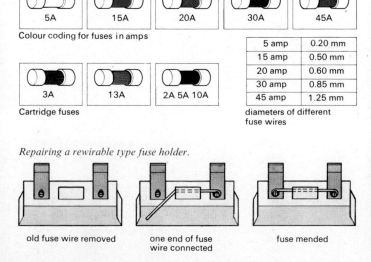

Colour coding for fuses in amps

| 5A | 15A | 20A | 30A | 45A |

Cartridge fuses

| 3A | 13A | 2A 5A 10A |

5 amp	0.20 mm
15 amp	0.50 mm
20 amp	0.60 mm
30 amp	0.85 mm
45 amp	1.25 mm

diameters of different fuse wires

Repairing a rewirable type fuse holder.

old fuse wire removed · one end of fuse wire connected · fuse mended

Now turn off everything in the circuit connected to the blown fuse. Turn off the main switch, replace the fuse holder and turn on the main switch.

Replacing a cartridge fuse The procedure is the same as for a rewirable fuse except for the actual replacement of the fuse element, which is the cartridge. With some patterns of fuseholder, the cartridge is removed by releasing a screw securing two halves of the moulding together. Upon releasing the screw, the cartridge falls out and is replaced by the new fuse, which must be of the same current rating—or it will not fit into the holder. With another pattern of cartridge fuseholder, the old cartridge is ejected when the new cartridge is pushed in.

Running costs Electricity consumption is registered on the meter in kWhs (kilowatt-hours) and is charged on your bill in units. One unit of electricity is equal to one kWh. A 1000-watt electric fire running for one hour consumes one unit of electricity.

There are many tariffs (means of charging for electricity), and when you calculate what various electrical appliances will cost to run, you have to find out the average cost per unit. If you are on the White Meter tariff, all electricity consumed during the eight hour night period can be reckoned as costing 25 per cent less than the standard daytime rate.

The amount of electricity consumed by an appliance or by an electric light bulb when switched on depends on its wattage. A 1000-watt (1kW) heater uses one unit of electricity ever hour it is switched on. More powerful appliances use more, lamps and low-power equipments use less.

In the table below the approximate amounts of electricity consumed in one hour by a selection of appliances commonly used in the home are listed. But remember that many are not switched on for a whole hour at a time. Although, for instance, a high-speed kettle will consume up to three units of electricity in one hour, to boil a kettle full of water from cold takes but a few minutes.

RATE OF ELECTRICAL CONSUMPTION BY ELECTRICAL APPLIANCES

40 watt bulb *25 hours 1 unit*
60 watt bulb *17 hours 1 unit*
electric blanket *10 hours 1 unit*
sewing machine *8 hours 1 unit*
colour television *6 hours 1 unit*
b/w television *10 hours 1 unit*
electric clock *negligible*
two-bar fire *2 units per hour*
one-bar infra-red fire $\frac{3}{4}$ *unit per hour*
coffee percolator $\frac{1}{2}$ *unit per hour*
immersion heater *3 units per hour*
hair dryer $\frac{1}{3}$ *unit per hour*
refrigerators and freezers *1 to 2 units per 24 hours*

dishwasher (heated) *3 units per hour*
washing machine (heated) *3 units per hour*
toaster *1 unit per hour*
kettle, standard *1 to 1$\frac{1}{2}$ units per hour*
kettle high speed *2$\frac{1}{2}$ to 3 units per hour*
cooker boiling rings *2 to 2$\frac{1}{2}$ units per hour*
grill of cooker *2 units per hour*
oven (max. setting) *2$\frac{1}{4}$ to 3 units per hour*
oven (min. setting) $\frac{1}{4}$ *to* $\frac{1}{2}$ *unit per hour*

This meter indicates 09629 units of electricity.

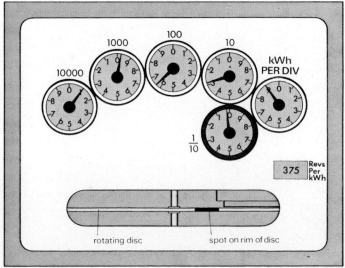

rotating disc · spot on rim of disc

Services to the Home
Central Heating systems and installation

HOME HEATING

Heating systems generally fall into one of four categories; partial, selective, background or full central heating. The various systems may be electric, solid fuel, gas or oil fired.

Partial heating describes a small system where one or two radiators are run from either an open fire back-boiler or small kitchen-located solid fuel boiler, or even a house where

Possible locations for central heating boilers

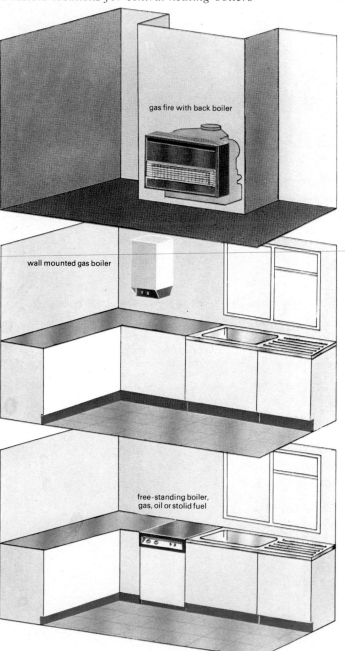

gas fire with back boiler

wall mounted gas boiler

free-standing boiler, gas, oil or stolid fuel

two or three electric night storage heaters are installed. A system of this type will heat only those rooms which contain the boiler, radiators or heaters. When additional heat is required, the system must be backed up with other independent appliances positioned in the various rooms of the house. The heat output capacity of the small boiler is strictly limited and it is not feasible to add extra radiators to extend this system. An electric system can be extended by installing further heaters if there is wiring capacity.

With a selective heating system, heat emitters are generally located in all rooms but the central heat source does not have the capacity to provide a constant comfortable temperature to all rooms at the same time. Controls fitted to the system allow parts to be shut down so that higher temperatures can be maintained in selected areas.

Background heating provides some warmth to all rooms, but must be backed up by other appliances in rooms where a comfortable temperature is required.

A full central heating system is designed to provide a specified internal air temperature, generally 21 °C, when the outside temperature is 0 °C. To maintain these temperatures, at least one heat emitter must be installed in every room, passageway and hall.

Choice of system

Before installing a heating system, the house should be well-insulated and draughtproofed. (See page 98.) Reducing the heat loss will improve the performance of the existing heating system which could possibly be kept simply by improving insulation. If this is not possible, improved insulation will nevertheless allow you to install a less powerful and therefore less expensive heating system.

When installing a completely new system, give careful thought to the wide range of types available. The most popular forms of central heating are based on a centrally located boiler. Heated water is circulated, usually under pressure from a small pump to radiators situated throughout the house. An equally effective type of heating is the warm air type. This system is more complicated to install in existing properties. A centrally located furnace is used to produce warm air which is distributed throughout the house via ducting.

There are other types of full heating systems such as individual gas heaters, fitted in each room. In these systems the heaters are not coupled to a central boiler or furnace. Each heater must be independently vented to the outside and must, therefore, be fitted to an external wall. Alternatively electric night storage, oil filled radiators or panel heaters can be fitted in each room; these do not rely on a central heat source.

Another full heating system is that of electric underfloor or overhead heating. Here purpose-made cables or mats are built into the structure of the floor or ceiling and connected to the mains electricity supply. No central heat source is required.

With both the night storage heaters and underfloor system, heating takes advantage of the special night time off-peak rates for electricity supply. The heat bank is built up during this period and is released throughout the day.

Boiler heat input must at least equal the losses

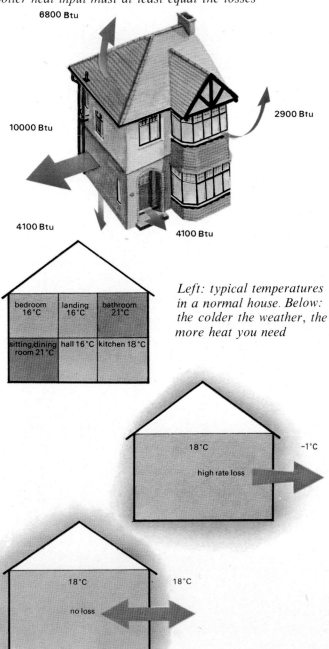

6800 Btu

10000 Btu

2900 Btu

4100 Btu

4100 Btu

bedroom 16°C	landing 16°C	bathroom 21°C
sitting/dining room 21°C	hall 16°C	kitchen 18°C

Left: typical temperatures in a normal house. Below: the colder the weather, the more heat you need

18°C

high rate loss

−1°C

18°C

no loss

18°C

Many factors must be considered in choosing the most appropriate type of heating system and fuel. Running costs are of prime importance but the cost of subsequent system maintenance is often overlooked. Oil- and to a lesser extent gas-fired boilers, require annual or even bi-annual servicing by a skilled engineer to ensure a constant performance. Electric systems such as night storage, underfloor and ceiling heating do not require regular maintenance and should run for many years without attention. Installation costs of electric systems are generally considerably less than for a comparable gas- or oil-fired system but electric systems cost more to run.

Most solid fuel systems require little in the way of skilled maintenance, but the fuel must be stored, transferred to the fire and then disposed of in the form of ash. Another disadvantage with solid fuel is that it does not provide an automatic on-off system because the fire must be kept alight whenever heating is required. Electric, gas and most oil fired systems on the other hand can be completely shut down and then restarted at a touch of a switch.

Central heating design

Heat is lost from a house when the internal and external air temperatures differ. The rate of loss is governed by the degree of difference. The various materials from which a house is built, the brick walls, plasterboard ceilings and glass areas all allow heat to pass at differing rates.

A heating system is designed to maintain the desired room temperature against a minimum outdoor temperature of −1°C. In colder parts of the country, or where the building is exposed to severe weather, the outdoor temperature should be taken as −5°C.

Heat is now measured in watts in the metric system rather than the British Thermal Units or Btus of the Imperial system. One kilowatt or kW equals 1000 watts. Although heating design is supposed to be completely metricated, many people will still refer to the Imperial system. Because of this situation, all figures which follow are in the metric system, but where watts are referred to, the equivalent in the more commonly used Btus/h is given. To convert Btus/hour to watts, multiply the number of Btus/h by 0·293. Thus a boiler that is rated at 30,000 Btus/h is equivalent to 30,000 × 0.293 = 8790 watts or 8·79kW.

The methods of estimating and calculating the various aspects of heating design are presented here in a simplified form, suitable for application to the average domestic installation. For the reader who wishes to investigate this further, a wide range of specialised textbooks and references are available.

To arrive at a suitable size for the heating installation, the total amount of heat lost through the various parts of the structure must be calculated and heaters equivalent to this loss installed.

Table 1a shows a list of the materials from which most buildings are constructed, with a U value for each. The U value represents the number of watts passing through a square metre of the material per hour per degree centigrade difference in temperature.

Another factor which must be taken into consideration is the volume of air and the optimum number of air changes per hour within the heated area.

The calculations for a heat loss figure are quite straightforward. In this example a simplified layout for a semi-detached house of conventional construction is used as a basis for calculating heat losses. The figures quoted apply regardless of the form of heating to be installed.

The calculations are to some extent based on estimated factors and, therefore, all interior doors, window and glazed door frames can safely be taken as part of the main adjoining area so far as U values are concerned.

Table 1a

U VALUES (based on modern materials and construction and average exposure)

External walls (brick plastered inside)	U value
230mm solid	2.4
280mm cavity ventilated	1.9
280mm cavity unventilated	1.7
280mm cavity with insulative infill	0.5

Internal walls (plastered both sides)	
115mm brick	2.5
230mm brick	2.1
75mm breeze block	2·4

Roofs (all plaster ceilings)	
Wood joists, tiles or slates on battens	3.2
as above, with 25mm glass fibre	1.8
Wood joists, tiles or slates on battens and felt	2.1
as above, with 25mm glass fibre	0.8
as above, with 75mm glass fibre	0.5

Floors	
Ventilated wood	
With lino or similar	1.7
With carpet	1.1
Solid	
With lino or similar	1.1
With carpet	1.1
With wood block or cork	0·8
Intermediate floors	
Plaster ceiling, wood floor over	1.6
Wood floor, plaster ceiling under	1.2
Windows and glazed doors	
Single glazed	5.6
Double glazed and sealed	2.8
Double glazed, non-sealed	3.9

Table 1b

Room	Temperature	Air changes per hour
Kitchen	18°	3
Hall	16°	1½
Landing	16°	1½
Bathroom	21°	2
Sitting/dining room	21°	2
Bedroom	16°	1½

Make the calculations in an orderly table as shown in the example. Refer to the tables for the U values for the various materials and for the recommended temperatures and air changes of each room.

As an example, consider wall 1 of the kitchen. The overall size of the wall is 2.4 × 2.4m = 5.76m². From this deduct the window area of 0.86m² to get the area of brick of 4.9m². The U value for the single glazed window is 5.6 and for the brick cavity wall is 1.7. The temperature in the kitchen should be 18°C which must be maintained against an outside temperature of −1°C. The temperature difference between the inside and outside of the wall is therefore 19°C, for both the window and the brickwork. Enter all these figures in the table and multiply the area, U value and temperature difference to get the heat loss. The window, for example, has a heat loss of 0.8 × 5.6 × 19 = 85 watts (290 Btus/h).

Different temperatures mean room-to-room heat movement

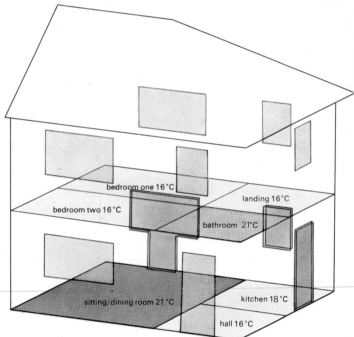

Dimensions of the kitchen in the worked example

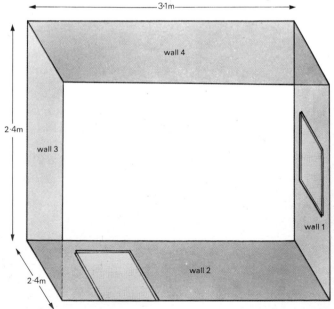

Kitchen Size: 3.1m × 2.4m × 2.4m ceiling   Air changes per hour: 3
Volume 17.85m³   Temperature: 18 °C

Reference	dimensions m × m	Area m²	U value	Temp. difference °C	heat loss watts (Btus/h)	heat gain watts (Btus/h)	total heat loss watts (Btus/h)
Wall 1							
total	2.4 × 2.4	5.76					
window	1.6 × 0.5	0.8	5.6	19	85 (290)		
brick		4.96	1.7	19	160 (546)		245 (836)
Wall 2							
total	3.1 × 2.4	7.44					
door	2.0 × 0.75	1.5	2.8	19	80 (273)		
brick		5.94	1.7	19	192 (655)		272 (928)
Wall 3							
brick	2.4 × 2.4	5.76	2.5	2	29 (99)		29 (99)
Wall 4							
brick	3.1 × 2.4	7.44	2.5	−3		−56 (−191)	−56 (−191)
Floor							
total	3.1 × 2.4	7.44	1.7	19	240 (819)		240 (819)
Ceiling							
total	3.1 × 2.4	7.44	1.6	2	24 (82)		24 (82)
	Ventilation			17.85 × 3 × 19 × 0.37 =	376 (1284)		376 (1284)
				total heat loss			1130 (3857)

Notice that there is a heat gain from the lounge/dining room.

To calculate the heat loss through ventilation, multiply the volume of the room, the number of air changes per hour, the temperature difference by the factor 0.37. Thus for the kitchen 17.85 × 3 × 19 × 0.37 = 376 watts (1284 Btus/h).

In the same way the heat loss is calculated, room by room, for the whole house. For this house the total figures were as follows.

	watts	Btus/h
Kitchen	1130	3857
Lounge/dining	2546	8690
Hall	747	2550
Bedroom 1	618	2110
Bedroom 2	724	2470
Landing	735	2510
Bathroom	1465	5000
Total	7965 watts	27187

Add approximately 10 % or 800 watts (2730 Btus/h) for the boiler. Therefore the boiler capacity required is 8765 watts or 8.77kW (29930 Btus/h) for central heating.

DOMESTIC HOT WATER SYSTEM

Water is heated in the boiler and then circulated by natural gravitation through a pipework coil within the hot water cylinder. Here the water heats up the domestic hot water supply contained separately within the cylinder. Circulation between boiler and hot water cylinder continues until switched off by a built-in thermostat once a certain temperature has been reached. With a solid fuel boiler, a thermostat automatically closes down the combustion air intake to reduce the heat output.

Cold water is supplied to the domestic hot water section of the hot water cylinder through the cold water storage tank. The storage tank level is automatically governed by a ball valve. Water supply to this tank is fed from the water main (see page 55). An outlet pipe is fitted to the top of the hot water cylinder and runs to all hot water taps in the house. This pipe is also continued upwards to terminate over the cold water tank as an open vent through which any air in the pipework can escape. The hot water cylinder is automatically topped up through the feed pipe when water is released through the taps.

The boiler is connected to the hot cylinder through the primary gravity circuit. In order to cope with the expansion of heated water and contraction of cooling water, a header tank is connected into the system through a feed and expansion pipe which, in effect, is an extension of the gravity return circuit. A constant level of water (supplied from the main) is maintained in the header tank through a ball valve. To allow any trapped air to escape and prevent any build-up of pressure within the system, a vent pipe is fitted as an extension of the gravity flow pipework.

Pipe sizing

With a gravity system, water circulation is maintained by temperature differential. Therefore pipework friction must be kept low—which requires relatively large pipework. The governing factors are height differential and horizontal distance between boiler and hot water cylinder. For the average domestic installation, 28mm pipe is suitable where measurements are within the limitations shown.

Where extra long or complicated pipe runs are involved, the circuit can be pumped and run in smaller bore pipe (see table 2). With either system of pipework, the hot water cylinder heat requirement must be added to the heating losses in order to arrive at a suitable figure for the boiler capacity. Where a 136 litre capacity hot water cylinder is specified, a 3kW (10000 Btus/h) allowance will provide for a three hour reheat cycle.

A suitable boiler rating, therefore, based on the heat losses shown would be 11.77kW (that is, 8.77kW central heating and 3kW domestic hot water).

Where a solid fuel boiler is to be installed, some part of the pipework must be run as a gravity circuit in order to provide a safety heat leak. Usually the domestic hot water primary circuit caters for this. Where pumped primaries are installed, at least one radiator must be served by a permanently open gravity circuit.

Heating circuit

The radiators are connected to the boiler through pipework positioned to best advantage round the house. Pipework can be either small bore or microbore. Small bore pipes are between 15 and 28mm diameter, whereas microbore pipes are between 6 and 10mm diameter. With a suspended ground floor the pipes can be run neatly under the floorboards with rises to the first floor taken where possible through built-in cupboards. With solid ground floors, the runs can be taken around the house at first floor level with drop feeds to the radiators. Pipe runs should be kept as short as possible. All underfloor pipework outside the house must be thoroughly insulated against heat loss. Pipework within the house contributes to the heating and therefore does not require insulating. The bathroom radiator is connected into the gravity circuit as a convenient means of providing heat to the bathroom when the main heating circuit is switched off.

Because of the complexity of the circuits serving the main

radiators, water will not circulate by natural gravitation alone. A pump must be installed to overcome friction in the pipework and ensure an adequate circulation of water between radiators and boiler. The dynamic head or pressure exerted by the pump must be equal to the frictional losses of the largest single circuit in the system. Although this can be determined by calculation, with modern pumps the output is adjustable within a relatively wide range and therefore precise matching is not necessary. Final adjustments can be made after installation.

Pipework circuits and sizing (pumped)

The diameter of the pipework carrying water to and from the various radiators must fall within certain limits. The governing factors are friction, pipe length and water velocity.

Table 2

Pipe size	Maximum circuit length	kW	Btus/h
15mm	24m	4.5	15358
22mm	33m	11·0	37543
28mm	45m	20.0	68260

The total heat load for the pumped radiator circuit of the example can be taken as under 8.77kW. Reference to Table 2 shows that this is outside the capacity of 15mm pipe but within the capacity of 22mm which can therefore be used as the main flow and return pipework from the boiler.

The various radiators throughout the house are, in effect, connected to one of three sub-circuits and as the total heating load on any one does not exceed the capacity of 15mm pipe, then all may be run in this size. In this example the radiator load of the circuit serving the hall, landing, bedroom 1 and the lounge/dining room radiator directly below amounts to 3.4kW (11600 Btus/h). The circuit serving bedroom 2, kitchen and lounge/dining room totals 3.2kW (11000 Btus/h) and the bathroom radiator circuit, 1.5kW (5000 Btus/h).

Radiators

Heat is given off to the various rooms of the house through heat emitters which are the simple steel panel type, skirting type, or electric fan-assisted convectors. All types are made

Left: direct hot-water-only system. Right: usual indirect system for central heating

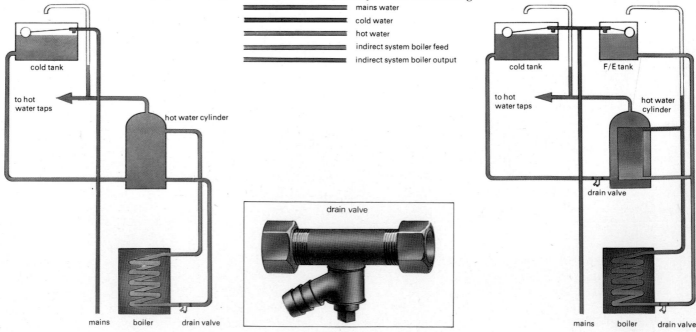

Domestic hot water plus central heating layout showing radiator outputs for each room

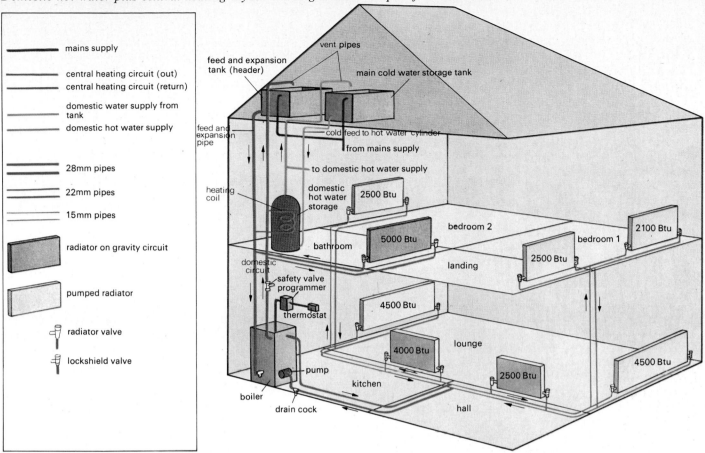

Legend:
- mains supply
- central heating circuit (out)
- central heating circuit (return)
- domestic water supply from tank
- domestic hot water supply
- 28mm pipes
- 22mm pipes
- 15mm pipes
- radiator on gravity circuit
- pumped radiator
- radiator valve
- lockshield valve

vent pipes
feed and expansion tank (header)
main cold water storage tank
feed and expansion pipe
cold feed to hot water cylinder
from mains supply
to domestic hot water supply
heating coil
domestic hot water storage
2500 Btu
bedroom 2
bedroom 1
2100 Btu
5000 Btu
bathroom
2500 Btu
landing
domestic circuit
safety valve
programmer
thermostat
4500 Btu
4000 Btu
lounge
2500 Btu
4500 Btu
pump
boiler
kitchen
hall
drain cock

Physical limitations for efficient operation of a gravity primary circuit

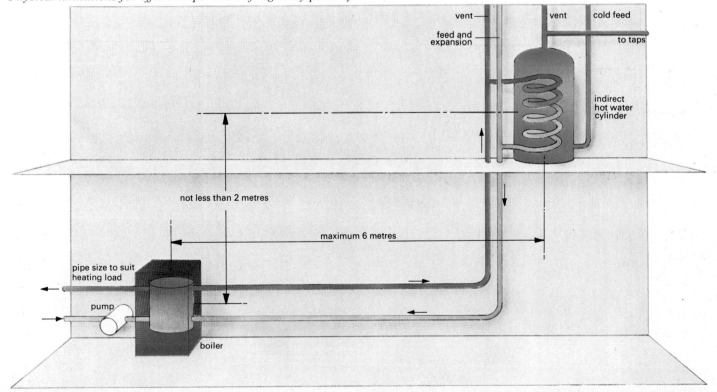

vent
vent
cold feed
feed and expansion
to taps
indirect hot water cylinder
not less than 2 metres
maximum 6 metres
pipe size to suit heating load
pump
boiler

with a wide range of heat outputs and one matching the requirement for the room should be chosen.

Panel type radiators are supplied with metal wall fixing brackets which must be securely anchored using an appropriate wall plug or patent fixing. The radiators should be positioned in the coldest part of the room. This generally means under a window or on an external wall. Each radiator must be fitted with a valve to both the flow and return connections. One valve is used simply as a manual on-off and the second is used to make fixed adjustments to the flow of water through the radiator during the course of balancing the system. Each radiator is also fitted with a key operated valve used to bleed air from the system on initial filling.

System control

Some form of control over the central heating system is essential if comfortable temperatures are to be maintained and running costs kept within reasonable proportions. Basic essential controls consist of an electrically operated programmer which can be adjusted to give the boiler two on and two off sessions per 24-hour period. A system of this type ensures automatic reheating of the hot water cylinder when the boiler is switched on. Most programmers also incorporate some form of switch to control the radiator circulating pump. This is wired through an air thermostat switch located in either the lounge or the hall. The thermostat is intended to switch the pump on or off as and when temperature fluctuates above or below the setting.

The design running temperature for the boiler is 80 °C and it follows that the stored domestic hot water would be at boiler temperature which is excessively high for normal use. Various types of controls are available to shut down the domestic hot water circuit when a preset temperature is reached. Such controls are not generally suitable for use with a solid fuel boiler because with most installations this circuit must be open at all times as a safety heat leak.

Thermostatically controlled radiator valves, fitted in place of the hand control are most useful where a secondary form of heating is occasionally used. Here the thermostat controlling the pump should be located in the hall and therefore away from the influence of the secondary heater. The automatic radiator valve can then be set to control the individual radiator independently from the rest of the heating system to prevent the room being overheated.

Motorised valves situated in the pipework of the system and activated by either a time switch or thermostat can be used to control a particular zone within the system. Valves of this type can also be used to give either the domestic hot water circuit or radiator circuit priority when both call for heat. Other types of control allow mixing of the flow and return water in order to obtain optimum comfort and running costs. All should be considered at the design stage so that a suitable system can be integrated to suit individual needs.

Full wiring instructions included with all electrical controls must be carefully followed during installation.

Boiler

Complete instructions for boiler installation will be supplied by the manufacturer. Particular attention must be paid to combustion air supply, fuel connections, hearth construction and proximity to combustible materials. When a gas- or oil-fired unit is installed, a qualified engineer should be present on initial firing to check over the fuel connections and adjust the fuel/air mixture for optimum combustion efficiency.

Pump

This is normally fitted to the return pipework adjacent to the boiler, flow direction being indicated by an arrow cast into the casing. Valves should be fitted to either side of the pump in order to facilitate removal in the event of maintenance or breakdown.

Filling and balancing

The heating system is filled with water via the header tank and then completely drained through flexible hose temporarily fitted to the drain-cocks in order to remove any debris. All joints and fitting must be checked for leaks and all valves left fully open.

The domestic hot water supply is fed through the main cold water storage tank and therefore filled independently from the heating circuit.

A fan convector is small and gives rapid heating. A skirting heater is unobtrusive

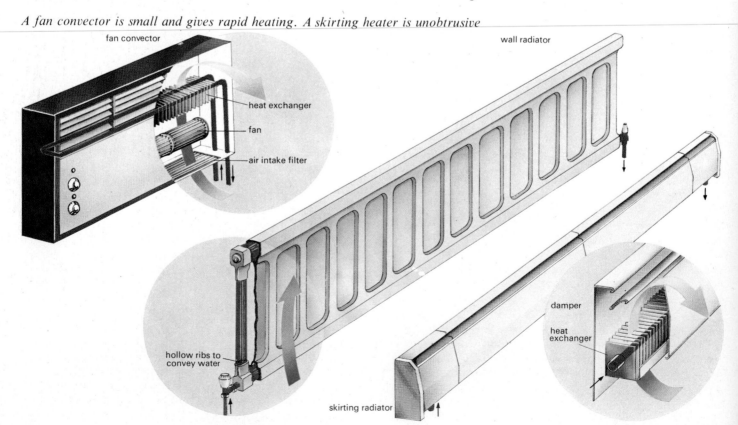

fan convector
heat exchanger
fan
air intake filter
wall radiator
hollow ribs to convey water
damper
heat exchanger
skirting radiator

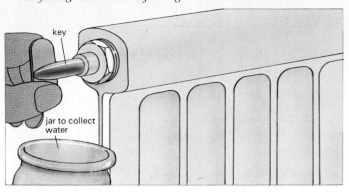

Bleeding air from a radiator—it should be necessary only when filling. Bottom: adjusting a lockshield valve

key

jar to collect water

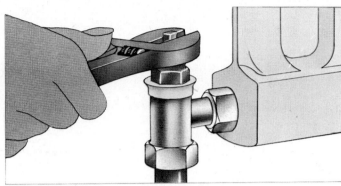

With the system completely filled and the pump switched off, air must be bled from all radiators starting at the bottom and working up. The boiler can then be fired and the circulating pump which is set at the lowest setting can be started. Inevitably with all valves fully open the temperature of the radiators will vary throughout the system and it is for this purpose that a balancing lockshield valve is included on each radiator. Approximate balancing can be carried out by touch with the lockshield valves on the warmest radiators being progressively closed in order to increase the flow through the colder radiators. For accurate balancing, two purpose-made clip-on thermometers are attached to the flow and return pipework of each sub-circuit and radiator. The temperature drop should be approximately 6°C in accordance with the design figures. If, after complete balancing, the overall temperature is not achieved, the pump setting should be progressively increased.

Introduce a chemical inhibitor to the heating circuits with the final filling in order to minimise corrosion problems in the radiators and pipework. The inhibitor is simply poured into the header tank as filling takes place. Four litres is sufficient for the average system.

Microbore systems

Microbore heating systems are similar to small bore so far as the boiler and radiators are concerned. Many systems include a traditional gravity domestic hot water circuit.

The real difference lies in the pipework arrangement to the radiators where either nylon or soft temper copper tubing is used in measurements of 6mm, 8mm and 10mm diameter. Each radiator is served by an individual pipework circuit, connected to a centrally located multi-connection manifold which distributes the hot water, supplied by a main feed pipe, to each separate radiator circuit. Table 3 offers a guide to the heat carrying capacities of microbore tubing as applied to the

average domestic installation.

In many ways a microbore system is simpler to install than small bore because the more flexible copper tubing is easier to handle. Far fewer fittings are required and this means fewer joints and less likelihood of a leak. Connection to the radiators is made through a double entry valve which incorporates both hand and lockshield valves in one fitting. Water distribution within the radiator is achieved by a simple injection tube fitted to the valve during the course of assembly to the radiator.

Table 3

Guide to heat carrying capacities of copper tube as applied to average usage.

Pipe runs	Tube diameter					
	6mm		8mm		10mm	
	kW	Btus/h	kW	Btus/h	kW	Btus/h
6m	0.88	3000	2.2	7500	4.4	15000
9m	0.7	2400	1.76	6000	3.5	11950
12m	0·59	2000	1.5	5100	3.0	10250
15m	0.54	1850	1.3	4450	2.6	9000

INSTALLING A WATER/RADIATOR CENTRAL HEATING SYSTEM

The small bore and microbore systems are installed in the same way. The installation will of course vary considerably with the make and type of equipment chosen and with the construction and layout of the house. These instructions are therefore fairly general.

Tools and materials

Once planning and design of the system is completed all necessary materials, equipment and tools should be assembled. If the items are supplied as a complete kit, the delivery note should be checked and each part examined for good condition.

To list the pipework and fittings necessary with a non-kit installation, prepare a drawing and after pipe sizes have been marked, take the number, type and size of fittings directly from the drawing by reference to a fitting manufacturer's list. Gauge approximate lengths for pipe runs by measurements taken directly from the building.

In addition to the usual plumbing tools and fittings, other materials will be required during the installation:

Sand, cement and plaster filler – for general making good and for bricklaying;
Concrete – for foundations for oil tank piers and boiler hearth;
Fire cement and asbestos rope – for flue and chimney gasket seals;
Woodscrews, wall plugs and fittings – for attaching radiators and other wall fixed items, pipe clips;
Electrical cable – for connecting the various electrical parts and fittings;
Pipe sealing compound – for screwed joints (oil and water);
Chimney liner, cap and fittings – where specified or required.

In addition to plumbing tools the following tools are required for the carpentry and building necessary in arranging underfloor and through-wall pipe runs:

89

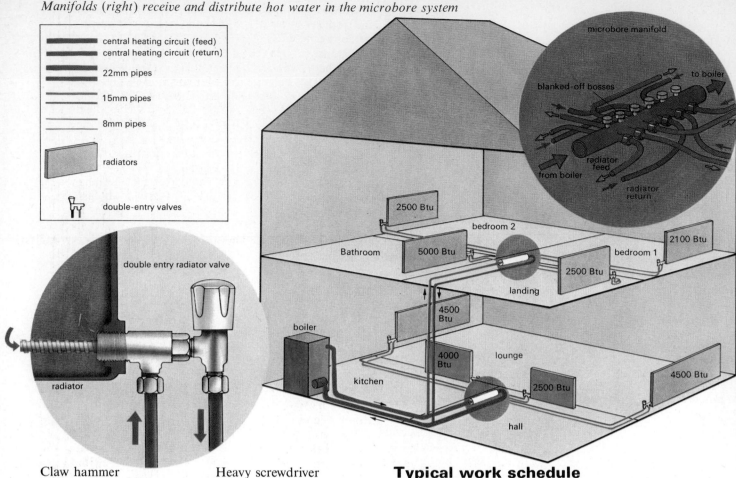

Manifolds (right) receive and distribute hot water in the microbore system

central heating circuit (feed)
central heating circuit (return)
22mm pipes
15mm pipes
8mm pipes
radiators
double-entry valves

microbore manifold
blanked-off bosses
to boiler
radiator feed
from boiler
radiator return

double entry radiator valve
radiator

2500 Btu
Bathroom
5000 Btu
bedroom 2
2100 Btu
bedroom 1
2500 Btu
landing
boiler
4500 Btu
kitchen
4000 Btu
lounge
2500 Btu
4500 Btu
hall

Claw hammer
Crow bar
General purpose saw
Carpenter's brace and bits
Woodworking chisels

Heavy screwdriver
Club hammer
Cold chisel
Electric drill with
masonry bits

Additional plumbing equipment

Pipe bending vice (may be hired)
Radiator key
Asbestos mat

Many suppliers now run a specialised service offering a complete design and advisory service for installing central heating. Complete kits of materials and equipment are offered. The system is then installed by the customer to the supplier's design and instructions. Dealing with a specialised supplier can greatly simplify the design problems.

Order of work

To a large extent the order of work will be governed by the type of system being installed, the layout of the premises, whether or not it is occupied, if some existing equipment is to be re-used and so on. Often installation must be carried out with the house occupied and therefore the work must be planned so as to cause the least disruption. In particular the water system must be kept out of action for the shortest possible period. A great deal of work can be carried out before the water supply is shut down. With an oil-fired installation, for example, the storage tank could be installed and the supply run to the planned boiler location before any internal work is started. This will avoid the delay of the tank being installed after the heating system. Similarly once runs have been planned, all radiators and much of the pipework can be installed without interfering with the water supply.

Typical work schedule

1 Install oil tank and oil line.
2 Make up and install radiators.
3 Run main heating pipework.
4 Remove old system.
5 Fit boiler.
6 Fit flue liner and connect to boiler.
7 Fit hot water cylinder and cold tanks.
8 Fit all pipework associated with boiler, cylinder and tanks.
9 Connect heating pipework to boiler and fit pump.
10 Arrange electrical supply and wire controls.
11 Connect fuel supply to boiler.
12 Fill system with water.
13 Fire boiler.

Conversion unit for a direct hot-water cylinder

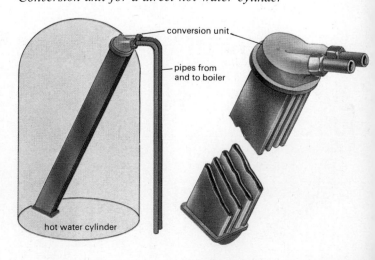

conversion unit
pipes from and to boiler
hot water cylinder

Removal of old plumbing

Often parts of old plumbing will have to be removed either before or during the course of the work. In some cases the existing components may be re-used. Copper pipe and fittings can be used again, although size compatibility between Imperial and metric sizes may cause a problem. Special adaptors are available to overcome this difficulty. Re-use the main cold water supply tank or the modern indirect hot water cylinder and associated feed and expansion tank and pipework if they are in good condition. If a copper direct cylinder is fitted, this can be re-used by fitting a conversion element into the immersion heater tapping. (See plumbing, page 78 for instructions on replacing the cold water tank.)

Pipework

Joints in old iron pipework may be dismantled using a Stilson wrench but if serious rusting or corrosion is present it will probably be more expedient simply to cut through the pipes with a hacksaw. Even with the system drained, it is possible that pockets of water may still be present in the pipework so be prepared for some leakage during the course of the work.

With copper pipe, threaded joints are generally simple to dismantle using a spanner. Soldered joints may be heated and pulled apart or cut through with a hacksaw.

Boiler installation

Modern boilers are available in a wide range from the standard free standing types to wall-mounted mini-boilers and, of course, installation instructions vary accordingly. All manufacturers supply a complete manual with their product and it is important that all aspects of installation be properly and strictly carried out. Certain aspects of boiler installation are covered by the Building Regulations, namely the hearth, flue, chimney, proximity of combustible materials and supply of combustion air and this part of the work should be approved by the local authority surveyor.

Under the regulations, domestic appliances are divided into two groups. Oil and solid fuel form one group and gas another. Generally oil and solid fuel appliances must be positioned on a 125mm thick concrete hearth with a 150mm projection to the sides and a 300mm projection to the front and any flue pipe serving the appliance must be of either cast iron or sheet steel construction with a minimum wall thickness of 4.75mm.

The regulations regarding gas-fired appliances are less stringent because there is no danger from falling fuel and here a sheet of 12mm thick asbestos may be used with 150mm projections to the sides and back and a 225mm projection to the front. A flue pipe may be of the asbestos cement type or vitreous enamelled steel type.

The main boiler connection fittings to the water jacket should be installed before the unit is finally located as access at this stage will generally be easier. The manufacturers' instructions should also be consulted as to the removal of any internal packaging or assembly necessary before the boiler is positioned on the hearth or fixed to a wall. With the boiler located, levels should be checked and packing used as and where necessary to ensure that the boiler is level.

Water and flue pipe connections should be made after levelling and with the boiler solidly located. Sealing of the flue/boiler connection is generally carried out using fire cement applied over an asbestos rope gasket but the procedure will vary with the make and type of boiler and whether the flue is conventional or of the balanced wall terminal type.

Chimney and flue

If a high rated gas- or oil-fired appliance is to be connected to a conventional brick chimney, it will probably require lining to prevent the products of combustion from cooling too rapidly and condensing within the chimney. If this occurs, the mortar construction can quickly break down, leading to possible staining of the internal house walls and damp patches forming on plastered areas. In addition, the rapid cooling of exhaust gases within an oversized and uninsulated chimney can lead to poor combustion and rapid boiler corrosion.

Lining the chimney is a relatively simple operation carried out by installing a purpose-made metal tube. Often the major problem involved is that of access to chimney discharge point, usually situated above the roof of the building. Safe access in the form of a roof ladder or scaffolding is necessary for this job.

The liner is quite light in weight and is supplied in a coil complete with necessary fittings consisting of a wooden or plastic tapered plug with a length of strong cord attached. This is fitted to the liner to facilitate travel through the chimney. The procedure for fitting a liner starts with removal of the existing chimney pot and surrounding cement flaunching. Sweep the chimney in order to remove all soot and rubble which may interfere with the lining work.

With the chimney clear take the tapered plug to the roof. The loose end of the cord is then weighted and lowered through the chimney to a helper below. Lower the plug on a

Flexible flue liner with removable bullet nosepiece

Fitting the liner, from stack to fireplace

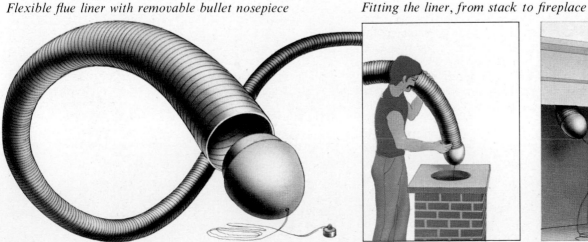

second piece of cord from above and feed it through the chimney to check clearance for the main liner. Having established that the chimney is clear, fix the bullet to one end of the liner usually by simply nailing it in position. Take it to the roof where the loose end of the cord is again weighted and passed through the chimney to a helper. Then enter the liner and feed carefully into position with a gentle pull from below.

The lower end of the liner must be attached to the flue pipe running to the boiler and the joint sealed with an asbestos rope gasket and fire cement and the liner/chimney cavity sealed.

A purpose-made clamp plate is supplied with the liner for supporting it at the chimney top. Before this is fitted, a lightweight granular insulating material such as is used for roof insulation, can be poured into the liner/chimney cavity to improve chimney performance. Insulating the flue gases in this way will reduce still further the possibility of condensation forming within the chimney. If condensation is expected a condensation drain should be fitted.

After the clamp plate is fitted, the chimney top should be neatly weathered all round with new cement flaunchings. An appropriate terminal, suitable for the appliance is then fitted. If an existing chimney is not available, a purpose-made prefabricated type may be used.

Combustion air supply

With conventionally-flued appliances a free flow of combustion air to the appliance must be arranged through a ventilator to the outside. The vent should have a free area of at least twice the cross-sectional area of the flue as follows:

Flue	Ventilator
100mm	157cm^2
125mm	245cm^2
150mm	354cm^2

So far as is possible the necessary ventilator should be fitted close to the boiler in order to eliminate draughts which occur when boiler and vent are at opposite ends of a room. If a suspended floor is fitted, a purpose-made ventilator may be fitted through the floor, taking combustion air from underfloor.

Arranging adequate combustion air ventilation is a vital aspect of boiler installation and if incorrectly carried out it can cause poor combustion within the appliance leading to sooted or corroded flueways and high running costs. There is also the added possibility of flue gases being sucked back into the house thus creating a possible health hazard.

Balanced flues

Many gas- and some oil-fired appliances are fitted with a balanced flue arrangement in place of the conventional flue/chimney layout. A flue of this type completely eliminates the need for a conventional chimney but the appliance must be fitted to an outside wall with free air access.

The balanced flue arrangement fitted to a gas-fired appliance contains two separate ducts at the wall terminal, one for combustion air inlet and the second for flue gases to be vented to the outside. An advantage with this type of flue is that siting generally is much more flexible than with a conventionally flued appliance. Since it is room sealed, the

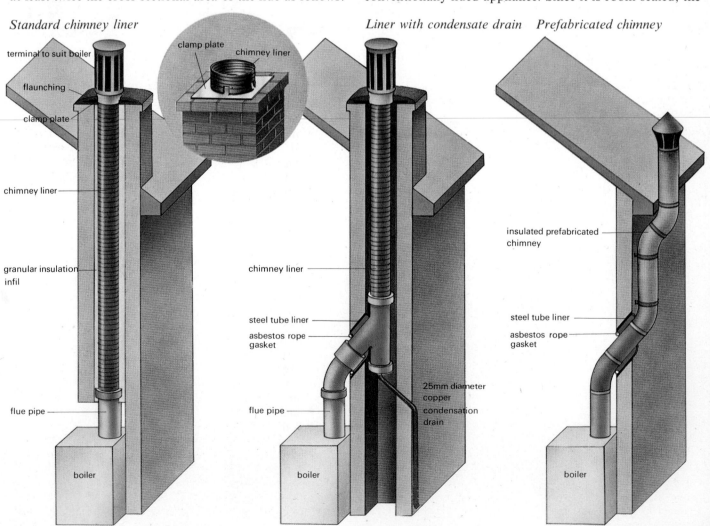

Standard chimney liner

terminal to suit boiler

flaunching

clamp plate

chimney liner

granular insulation infil

flue pipe

boiler

clamp plate

chimney liner

Liner with condensate drain   *Prefabricated chimney*

chimney liner

steel tube liner

asbestos rope gasket

flue pipe

boiler

25mm diameter copper condensation drain

insulated prefabricated chimney

steel tube liner

asbestos rope gasket

boiler

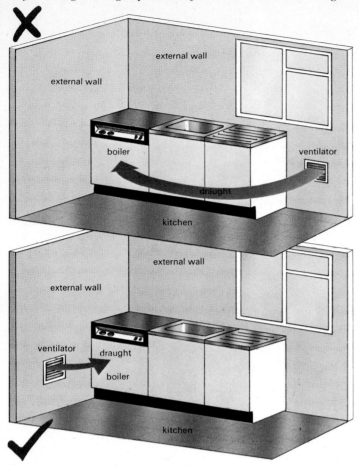

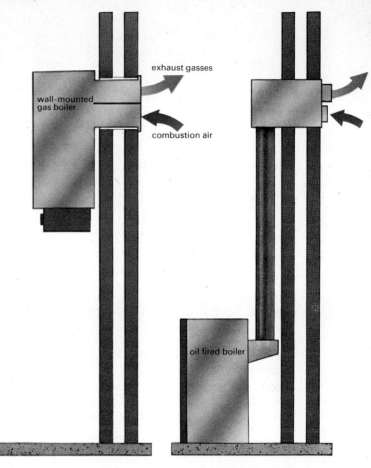

burner does not create internal draughts to satisfy combustion air demand.

The layout of a balanced flue used for an oil-fired appliance is somewhat different from gas. The principle remains the same in that both combustion air and flue gases are fed to and from the boiler, through separate ducts connected to the outside through a wall terminal.

Radiators

Each radiator will have four threaded tappings, one to each corner and these can be used for the necessary fittings to suit the pipework runs. Normally one of the top tappings will not be required and therefore will be simply blanked off with the appropriate fitting. The second top tapping is fitted with an air bleed valve while the two bottom tappings are used for a manual or thermostatic control valve and a balancing lockshield valve. All threaded joints must be sealed with either a purpose-made compound or ptfe tape. The compound is normally used in conjunction with a few strands of hemp which are wound tightly into the thread. The compound is smeared over the threads both before and after hemp application. With ptfe tape no compound is used. For installing the radiator air bleed and plug fitting a purpose-made square shank internal spanner will be required.

For neatness, the radiator brackets must be aligned accurately so that when the radiator is fitted it will be square and level. Radiator wall fixing brackets generally consist of a piece of angled steel with hooks to match slots in brackets welded to the rear face of the radiator.

To mark the bracket locations, start by striking a vertical centre line under the window shelf. Measure the distance between the fixing lugs on the back of the radiator and mark two more vertical lines on the wall at this distance and equally spaced on either side of the centre line. Stand the radiator in position but with the fixing lugs facing into the room and hang a wall fixing bracket on to one of the lugs. Measure vertically from floor to bracket top and then use this measurement plus 150mm for floor clearance to mark the top horizontal location of one bracket. Hold the bracket in position and mark the wall for fixing screw locations. Drill and insert appropriate wall fixings and fit the bracket. Use a spirit level and straight edge positioned on top of the fixed bracket to locate a second bracket. With both brackets securely fixed, the radiator is simply hung in position by mating wall brackets and radiator lugs. At this stage the radiator valve bodies should be connected hand tight only to the fixed tails. Although radiator fixings vary, the described method of setting out the wall bracket locations can easily be adapted to suit all types.

Pipework small bore

Important factors to bear in mind when installing pipework are that runs should be as short as possible and as unobtrusive and neat as possible. Bends and rises which could form air pockets must be avoided. Where this is not possible fit either a manual or automatic air vent. All major components such as boiler, hot water cylinder, tanks and radiators, must be sited before pipe runs are set out.

In a typical pipework layout both underfloor and through-wall runs are involved. After all routing has been planned, the necessary floorboards must be lifted and joists notched. If tongued and grooved floorboards are fitted, a purpose-made circular cutter will assist in cutting neatly through the tongue to prevent splitting when the board is levered up. The cutter

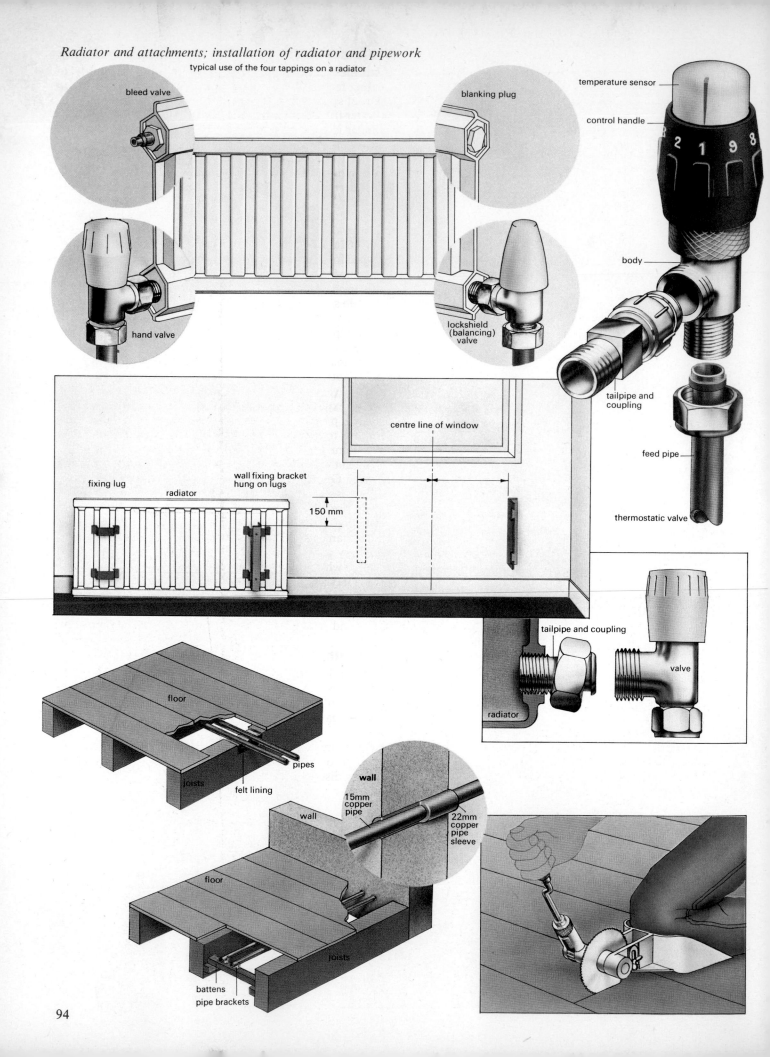

Radiator and attachments; installation of radiator and pipework

typical use of the four tappings on a radiator

bleed valve

blanking plug

hand valve

lockshield (balancing) valve

temperature sensor

control handle

body

tailpipe and coupling

feed pipe

thermostatic valve

centre line of window

fixing lug

radiator

wall fixing bracket hung on lugs

150 mm

tailpipe and coupling

valve

radiator

floor

joists

felt lining

pipes

wall

15mm copper pipe

22mm copper pipe sleeve

wall

floor

joists

battens

pipe brackets

can also be used to cross-cut where a trap is required. If pipe runs are across the joists, cut notches and line them with carpet felt or similar material to allow the pipes to move with the expansion and contraction of heating and cooling. If the pipes run with the joists, provide support in the form of cross battens.

Table 4 – Spacing of pipe supports

Pipe diameter	Horizontal run	Vertical run
under 15mm	1m	1.5m
15mm	1.2m	2m
22mm	2m	2.5m
28mm	2.5m	3m

Remember to provide ample clearance between floorboards and pipes. Drill holes through the walls with an appropriate size masonry drill or cut them with a cold chisel and hammer. Make allowance for pipe movement in holes through walls. Line the hole with a short length of pipe slightly larger than the outside diameter of the heating pipe.

For vertical pipe runs or wall-fixed horizontal runs, use specially designed brackets. (See plumbing page 59 for instruction on cutting and joining pipes.)

Copper pipe up to 22mm in diameter may be bent with the aid of a bending spring. This is inserted in the pipe where the bend is to be made. The pipe is then pulled carefully to shape over a knee or mandrel. Larger diameters of pipe should be bent with the aid of a bending vice.

Check underfloor pipe runs for possible joint leaks after the system has been filled. Do not fix floorboards or other coverings until after filling and testing has been completed.

Pipework – microbore

Soft temper copper tubing used for microbore installations is available in coils and is much easier to handle than the pipes used for small bore systems. The tube may be bent by hand around a large radius. If a sharp bend is required, a simple hand bending tool is used. Because the tube is easier to bend, few fittings are required and runs can be completed in one continuous length. Runs may be taken underfloor in much the same way as already described for small bore with padding used at contact points with joists or floorboards. The tube may be clipped using simple plastic U fasteners which are supplied complete with hardened masonry pins suitable for wall fixing or fixing to timber.

Because of the higher water velocities used with microbore systems, pipe runs are less critical than with small bore. If necessary the tube may be taken around an obstruction to avoid disturbing a solid floor.

Cold supply tanks and hot water cylinder

With the typical heating layout the cold water supply and heating feed and expansion tanks are conveniently sited in the roof space where the height provides the necessary head of water for effective operation of the system. The hot water cylinder is usually located in a bathroom airing cupboard. The cylinder could be fitted in the kitchen or elsewhere provided that the gravity pipework circuit is within the measurements shown.

Modern cold storage tanks are generally either glass fibre or plastic and holes for fittings may be cut using a saw or drill attachment. With plastic tanks, jointing compound between fitting and tank should not be used unless specified by the tank manufacturers. Nylon washers are usually recommended for this job. Tanks must be supported firmly on a flat base consisting of 25mm thick timber or 18mm blockboard of sufficient size to cover the whole base area. The capacity of the main supply tank should be approximately 275 litres but some water authorities insist on larger capacities. If the tank is to be replaced, make enquiries to check the acceptable size.

Capacity of the feed and expansion tank should be approximately 23 litres with the ball valve set so that the water depth is kept at about 125mm. This will allow ample space to accommodate additional water as the system content expands with heating. Both tanks together with all exposed pipework in the loft space must be effectively insulated to prevent freezing. This work should be done after the system has been filled and all joints tested for leakage.

The hot water cylinder must be located on a firm base and set level. Gravity pipe runs between boiler and cylinder must be kept as short as possible and be either horizontal or have a steady rise. Avoid dips, as air locks will inevitably develop restricting water flow and reducing efficiency. Bend fittings rather than elbows should be used and if a right-angle bend is necessary at a high point, a bleed valve should be fitted through which an air lock could be released.

A safety valve must be incorporated in the main gravity flow so that in the event of undue pressure building up in the system it will be released safely through the valve. Drain valves and gate valves should be included in the pipework.

The pump

Many modern pumps are supplied complete with valves and couplings which are included in order to facilitate removal in the event of a breakdown. If such valves are not supplied, standard gate valves should be installed on either side of the pump.

The pump should be wired into the electrical control system through a standard 13 amp electrical plug and socket for easy disconnection.

Bending microbore tubing

Using a pipe-bending spring

Clips for securing pipework

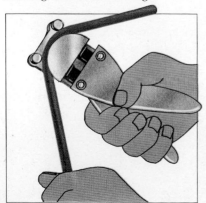

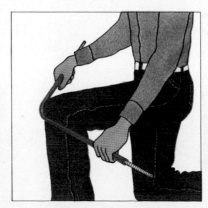

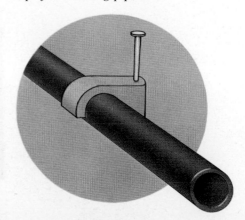

Electricity supply

Mains electrical power for the system should be arranged through a fused supply. From here it usually runs to the controlling time switch or programmer. All manufacturers supply comprehensive installation instructions with their products and these should be carefully followed.

Basic components of an indirect domestic hot water central heating system. The enlarged components in circles

Gas connections

With a gas appliance, the final connection of mains to appliance is best left to a qualified gas authority engineer, who should check and test the installation before use. The procedure for setting up and checking the installed boiler must be carefully carried out to the manufacturers'

correspond with outlines in small circles on the main diagram

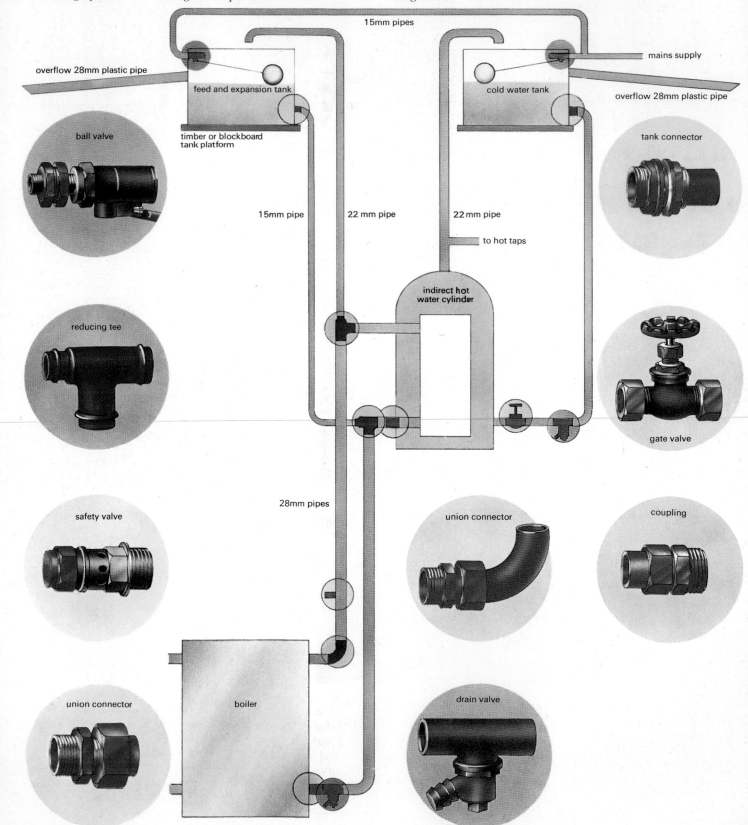

15mm pipes

overflow 28mm plastic pipe

mains supply

feed and expansion tank

cold water tank

overflow 28mm plastic pipe

ball valve

timber or blockboard tank platform

tank connector

15mm pipe

22 mm pipe

22 mm pipe

to hot taps

reducing tee

indirect hot water cylinder

gate valve

28mm pipes

safety valve

union connector

coupling

union connector

boiler

drain valve

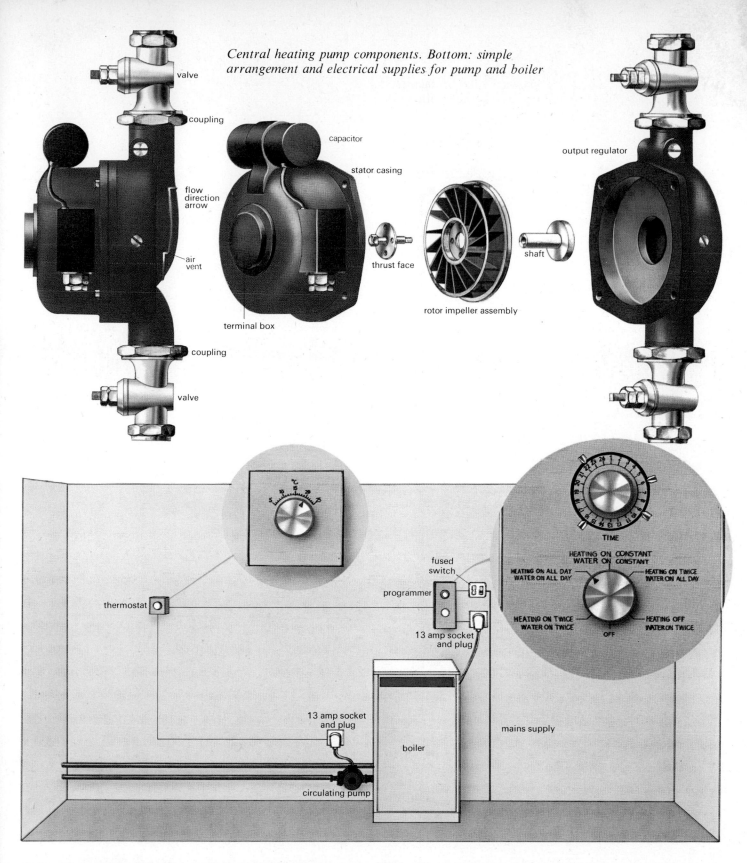

Central heating pump components. Bottom: simple arrangement and electrical supplies for pump and boiler

valve

coupling

capacitor

stator casing

output regulator

flow direction arrow

air vent

thrust face

rotor impeller assembly

shaft

terminal box

coupling

valve

fused switch

programmer

HEATING ON CONSTANT
WATER ON CONSTANT

HEATING ON ALL DAY
WATER ON ALL DAY

HEATING ON TWICE
WATER ON ALL DAY

thermostat

13 amp socket
and plug

HEATING ON TWICE
WATER ON TWICE

HEATING OFF
WATER ON TWICE

OFF

TIME

13 amp socket
and plug

mains supply

boiler

circulating pump

instructions, with all built-in safety and flame-failure test procedures checked.

Oil connections

Before the boiler is connected to the oil line, all air should be purged by opening the service valve and draining at least one litre of oil into a suitable receptacle. The valve is then shut down and the boiler connected. Purging the final length of

line will depend on the type of burner involved and manufacturers' instructions should be checked on this point. Adjustment and setting up of an oil burner requires specialised equipment to measure the flue gas temperature, composition of flue gases and chimney draught. It is therefore vital that a skilled engineer undertakes this work. Incorrect settings will result in inefficient combustion, frequent breakdowns and high running costs.

Services to the Home
Keeping the house warm

It is well-known that insulating a house saves fuel and money. There are other benefits from a fully insulated home which tend to be overlooked. Life becomes more comfortable. There are no more chilly corners, so all parts of a room can be enjoyed with complete freedom from cold draughts. Cold walls are eliminated and this combined with a warmer atmosphere helps to make condensation less of a problem.

If you intend to install central heating or are changing from one heating system to another, insulation will save a great deal of money because a less powerful system will be required. It has been shown that it is possible to reduce the area of radiators by almost half and reduce the boiler size by a third by fully insulating a house.

Good insulation also reduces the period when heating is necessary. In a really well-insulated house, about six weeks' heating can be saved each year. The heat that is created just by living in the house, body heat, heat from cooking, water heating and electrical appliances is enough to warm the house. A fully insulated house is easier to sell, as its value is increased.

Before dealing with full insulation it is useful to know where heat escapes from a house and how much heat is lost. These figures vary from house to house depending on the type and design of the house, materials of construction, aspect and exposure to winds. It can be assumed, however, that in a typical uninsulated house three-quarters of the heat that is generated inside is lost through the walls, roof, floor, windows and doors. Of the heat that is lost, approximately one third escapes through the walls, one quarter through the roof, one quarter through windows and doors and one sixth through the floor.

These losses can be greatly reduced by insulating the house. The more thorough the insulation the more heat is saved. It is impossible to eliminate heat losses but it has been shown that by fully insulating roof, walls and windows plus draughtproofing, heat losses can be reduced by as much as a half.

INSULATING THE LOFT

The first place to insulate is the roof space. A large proportion of expensive heat escapes here and good insulation can cut this loss by 85%. It does not take long to install the insulation and the cost is not high, so in terms of heat saved the insulation should pay for itself in three to four years.

Where the heat goes

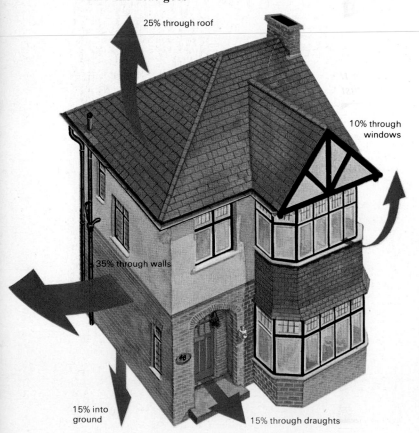

25% through roof

10% through windows

35% through walls

15% into ground

15% through draughts

In this house, when uninsulated, about three-quarters of the heat produced for keeping the occupants and structure warm actually escapes through the walls, roof, floor, windows and doors. As the diagram shows, 35% goes through the walls; by filling the cavities between the leaves (assuming this is the method of construction), this loss can be cut by two-thirds. And the cost of the job is usually recovered in terms of fuel savings in about five years.

The second largest loss is through the roof. Insulating the loft is an easy job and relatively cheap – the cost of materials can be recovered in about two to three years.

Draughts, apart from being extremely uncomfortable, waste a tremendous amount of heat – 15%. All normal joinery gaps in an average house are equivalent to a hole made by 23 bricks missing out of your living room wall! The low cost of the materials for this job is recovered in a matter of months rather than years.

The losses into the ground are taken care of to a large extent by normal floorcoverings and draughtstopping. But the 10% lost through windows is a costly business to stop – if comfort is your aim, double glaze, but don't expect to save money by this job. Fitting double glazing can be a complicated job as well. Heavy, lined curtains can make a difference, as long as they do not cover the radiators if these are placed under the windows.

98

Loft insulation in a normal roof and one where the roof forms part of the room ceiling

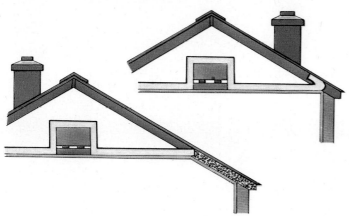

Expanded polystyrene on the ceiling helps. On the left is *the roll form while on the right are ceiling tiles*

When working in a loft with insulation materials, wear a simple breathing mask. Glass fibre materials irritate the skin, so wear gloves and old clothes

The 1974 Building Regulations specify 50mm of insulation material laid on the floor of the loft area over bedroom ceilings. It is now generally agreed that this is insufficient and 75mm should be the minimum. The electricity industry recommends 100mm and a 175mm layer is used in Scandinavia.

There are various materials for loft insulation which all work on the principle that the best insulator is a layer of still air trapped just above the upper floor ceilings. Glass fibre, mineral wool, expanded polystyrene, vermiculite and cork are all suitable loft insulating materials containing a high proportion of air trapped in relatively little solid matter. Aluminium foil is also used for insulation. Loft insulation material is available in rolls or sheets or as granules for pouring between joists. Rolls of glass fibre or mineral wool blankets are supplied ready for laying between the ceiling joists in 50mm, 75mm and 100mm thicknesses. The 50mm size is intended for laying over existing 25mm insulation to bring it up to the required standard. Sticking expanded polystyrene, cork or fibre board tiles to the ceiling of the rooms below the loft will create valuable additional insulation.

Laying insulating blanket

Be careful to walk only on the ceiling joists in the loft. It is best to lay two or three planks over the joists and work only from these. Wear a dust mask and start by clearing the worst of the dirt from between the joists. In a fairly new house you can use a dustpan and brush on the smooth plasterboard ceilings, but in older houses with lath and plaster ceilings, brushing will knock off many of the plaster nibs and weaken the ceiling. In this case, it is best to clean up as best you can using a cylinder vacuum cleaner.

To lay the insulation, unroll the material between the joists, starting at the eaves and tucking the end of the roll well

Clean up the working area with a dustpan and brush

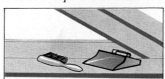

Start at the eaves and work towards the middle

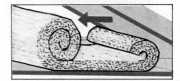

Push well into the eaves with a T-shape tool or stick

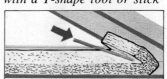

Fill neatly between joists or turn into a U-shape

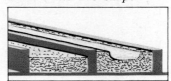

Cut strips and rejoin underneath loft pipework

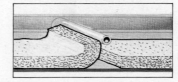

Don't forget the hatch – cut a piece to fit and tack on

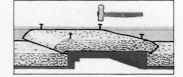

into the corner formed by roof and ceiling. Wear thick rubber gloves and a dust mask for protection especially if working with glass fibre.

Rolls of insulation are normally wide enough to allow the material to be tucked between the joists with the edges turned up the sides of the joists. Keep a careful watch for signs of active woodworm and if any is found take remedial action before proceeding further with the insulation.

Insulating blankets can be laid safely over water pipes and electric cables that run close to the ceiling. If the blanket has to be cut to clear an obstruction, overlap the ends by about 50mm to ensure there are no breaks in the insulation.

Insulate all parts of the loft space, including narrow gaps between walls and joists and tack a square of insulation loosely over the trap door.

If there is already some form of loft insulation and the thickness is being increased, lay the matting across the joists. In this way the small amount of heat that passes through the joists will be reduced.

Single-sided, non-reinforced aluminium foil can also be laid across joists to increase insulation. It should be tacked in place and the joints sealed with tape.

Laying polystyrene slabs

Expanded polystyrene slabs come in various thicknesses and are useful for loft insulation. Expanded polystyrene is a slightly better insulator than glass fibre or mineral wool of the same thickness. Install the sheets by cutting into panels which fit between the joists as neatly as possible.

Loose fill

Loose fill insulating granules made from expanded polystyrene, vermiculite, loose or pelleted mineral wool or cork are very easy to lay and can be fitted without waste between irregularly spaced joists and awkward corners. They can also be used to insulate attic rooms by simply pouring the granules between the sloping ceiling and rafters.

Clean the loft and make a T-shape spreader so that the arms rest on the joists and the middle piece will just fit between the joists leaving a space the thickness of the insulation between the base of the spreader and the ceiling.

Pour the insulation between the joists and rake to an even depth with the spreader. Awkward to reach places can be levelled by hand. It is best to start at the eaves and take the granules towards the middle of the loft. If cavity walls are exposed under the eaves or if holes for pipes or electric cables have been made in ceilings, these openings should first be sealed with polythene, cardboard, paper, wood or plaster.

Loose mineral wool fibres are very difficult to spread evenly and are unpleasant to handle. If this type of insulation is required it is as well to consider fibre insulation installed by a specialist contractor. The insulation is delivered by van and is pumped into the loft space through a flexible hose.

Insulating the roof

If the loft needs to be kept warm, clean and dry, insulation should be fixed directly under the roof rafters.

The coldest and dirtiest attics are found in older houses where roofing felt or boards have not been attached under the

Money spent on insulating the loft can be recovered in a very short time in terms of savings in heat losses and, consequently, fuel bills. When insulating a loft floor, attention should be given to filling even the smallest gaps, especially when there is no roof underfelt. This is where loose fill insulation, such as vermiculite, is useful, but if the loft is very draughty, loose fill can blow about. Vermiculite is also useful for filling inaccessible cavities

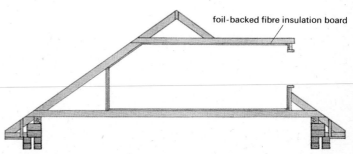

Expanded polystyrene is available in thick slabs. Cut it with a sharp knife to fit between joists

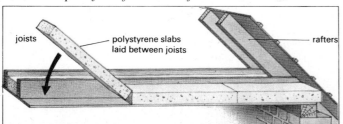

Above: dormers need careful attention. Below: glass-fibre blanket fixed to rafters with battens and clout nails

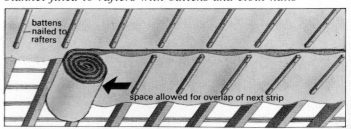

Loose fill is especially useful when joist spacing is non-standard. Right: a loft with living space

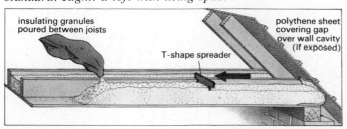

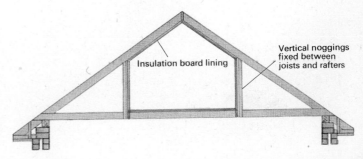

roof tiles. The cheapest way to stop draughts is to fix waterproof building paper to the undersides of the rafters. Attach it horizontally across the rafters starting at the ridge. Overlap each strip by 75mm and finish at the eaves so that water or snow that penetrates will not run into the loft space and spoil the ceilings of rooms below.

Reinforced aluminium foil, foil-backed building paper, roofing felt or roofing felt with glass fibre or mineral wool mat bonded to one side provides better insulation.

The roofing felt/insulation sandwich is fixed with the felt next to the tiles and the insulation exposed. To prevent tearing of these strips fix them to the rafters with laths. Pin the felt lengthwise between the rafters tucking the end into the gutter at the eaves.

Converting the loft

Before converting the loft into a room or for use as a storage space, have an expert check the strength of the ceiling joists which will support the new floor. If they are strong enough proceed by insulating the loft. Don't forget that if you do intend to carry out the conversion, you will need to have plans passed by the local council and they will have to comply with the Building Regulations.

A good finish can be obtained by nailing foil-backed fibre insulation board or foil-backed plasterboard to the undersides of the rafters. For even higher standards of insulation, panels of expanded polystyrene, glass fibre or mineral wool can first be fitted between the rafters. The insulation can be held in place temporarily with thread or

For living in
When the loft is used for living accommodation, insulation is doubly important, but more difficult because it has to be put, not on the floor, but on the roof structure. It is desirable that there is felt under the tiles, or slates, not only to reduce cold air entering, but to allow insulating materials such as glass-fibre matting, to be put between the rafters. When fixing material to rafters, use a lightweight hammer, because heavy hammering may dislodge tiles

nylon fishing line fixed to the rafters with drawing pins or tacks until the boards are fixed.

To build the short walls which close off the low sloping spaces along the sides of the loft, fix vertical 75 × 50mm timbers between rafters and ceiling joists. For wallcovering, remember to select a convenient width and length of foil-backed wall board which will pass through the hatchway. Use galvanised clout nails to fix the boards to the rafters and vertical timbers.

The brick gable ends can be lined if necessary using the method described for the dry lining of walls. Make a floor from new or secondhand floorboards or from 19mm thick chipboard.

DRAUGHTPROOFING

In many houses the fuel bill could be cut by 10% by draughtproofing. Draughtproofing is best done after insulating the loft. The idea is to reduce to a minimum the amount of air leakage into a room, but not to the extent that fumes are prevented from escaping.

Doors and windows

The first essential is to fit doors and windows as well as possible. Make sure hinges are not worn and check screws for tightness.

If the screws cannot be tightened, remove them and add wall plugs to the holes. Wide gaps between the door or window and frame can usually be cured by gluing and

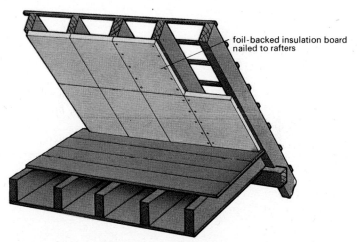

foil-backed insulation board nailed to rafters

Where headroom is a limiting factor, insulation board can be fixed flush with the face of the rafters

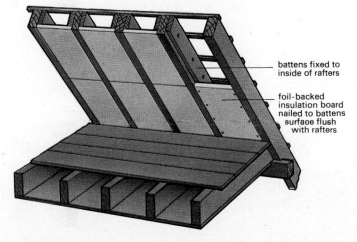

battens fixed to inside of rafters

foil-backed insulation board nailed to battens surface flush with rafters

nailing plasterboard to rafters ▶

insulation board   glass fibre matting

use glass fibre matting only if roof is lined with felt or timber boards

rafters

slate/tile battens

floorboards

ceiling joists

Draughtproofing doors
*Left: the cheapest draughtproofing, self-adhesive foam
strip. Middle: an expensive, but efficient, proprietary
system. Right: spring strip which causes painting problems*

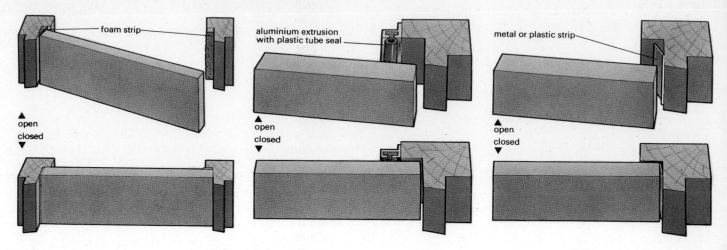

*Left: fitting foam strip is easy provided the rebate is
clean. Middle: a rubber draught strip. Right: a plastic
spring strip which comes with a metal guide clip*

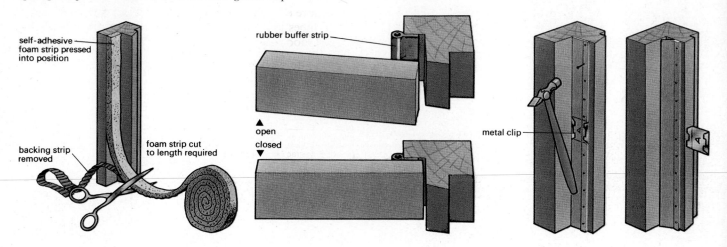

cramping a timber batten to the uneven edge. When the glue
has hardened the batten can be planed to make it a really
good fit.

Metal windows sometimes become distorted due to an
accumulation of paint on the closing surface. If this is
removed and the surface is repainted, the gap may disappear
and draught excluder may not be needed.

Self-adhesive foam strip available in several thicknesses is
the cheapest and easiest draught excluder to fit to timber and
metal windows and doors. It should not be used where it can
get wet or on surfaces that slide together. It will need
replacing after a year or so or when redecorating. Wipe the
frame and allow it to dry before removing the backing from
the strip.

Fit the foam strip to the frame so the door or window
closes on to it. Be careful not to stretch the strip as it is
pressed into place.

If there is a considerable gap and water gets in, use a rubber
buffer strip. This is held in place with tacks and is fitted to the
frame so the door or window closes on to it.

There are several types of sprung, hard plastic and metal

draught excluders for sealing around timber window and door
frames. These types have a working edge that springs away
from the frame forming a draughtproof seal when the door or
window is closed. They are durable and unaffected by wet and
are easily cleaned and painted if necessary. This type can be
used on surfaces that slide together which is useful when
draughtproofing sash windows.

Most sprung draught excluders are fitted into place by
tacking to the frame at regular intervals. The plastic type has
a useful clip temporarily to hold the strip in place leaving
both hands free for fixing. After fixing, run your fingers
behind the flange of the strip, flexing it away from the frame
along its entire length.

Self-adhesive plastic foam strip will draughtproof metal
windows cheaply but it is better to use proprietary
aluminium strips which simply snap over the outside frame.

Under-door draughts
Small draughts at the top of a door ensure there are sufficient
air changes in the room. But draughts under doors can create
problems.

Threshold draught excluders are fitted to the floor under doors so that a strip of plastic or rubber touches the bottom of the door when it is closed. This type is easy to fit and is unobtrusive when the door is closed, but is easily tripped over when the door is opened.

Draught excluders that fit to the back of the door close to the floor are safer but less attractive. The simplest type to fit are self-adhesive plastic strips incorporating a felt ribbon which presses against the floor or threshold when the door is closed. Some types screw to the bottom of the door. They consist of strips of flexible rubber, plastic, foam or bristles that press against the floor and seal the gap when the door is closed. The bristle type can also be used for sliding doors.

A carpet may make it difficult to open a door fitted with a draught excluder. In this case a sprung type should be used. The seal is held off the floor while the door is open and when the door is closed, a spring mechanism lets the seal drop to the floor to close the gap. This type is quite easy to fit. It is cut to the width of the door and screwed in place. There is usually a screw adjustment to ensure that the seal closes the gap properly.

Floors

Draughts in houses with timber floors are often caused by cold air coming up through the floor. Underfloor ventilation is essential to prevent timber decay so do not try to cure the draught by blocking up air bricks. The best, although most expensive solution is to lay fitted carpets with thick felt underlays. These will stop draughts and give insulation too.

Under-door seals
Left: a seal strip fitted to a door. Right: fitted to the threshold. Bottom left: a bristle seal accommodates unevenness. Bottom right: seal for carpeted areas

However, in terms of heat saved it will take many years to repay the cost of the carpets. When the floorboards are to be retained as a decorative feature the gaps must be sealed.

A frequent cause of troublesome draughts is the gap between floor and skirting boards. Small cracks can be sealed with a wood filler, but fitting a timber moulding at the intersection of the floor and skirting is a better method. The moulding should be mitred at corners and glued and pinned to the floor so that if there is any further movement between floorboards and skirting a new gap will not appear.

Fireplaces

If a solid fuel fire will not draw properly unless a door or window is opened, an adjustable ventilator should be fixed to the floor on each side of the hearth. With a solid floor, fit a ventilator over the door leading to the hall. Disused fireplaces create draughts and waste a lot of heat. They can be bricked up and plastered over or more simply sealed by fitting a screen into the opening. Whichever method is chosen, it is important to leave a hole approximately 50mm by 75mm to allow some ventilation in the chimney and prevent it from becoming damp.

INSULATING THE PLUMBING SYSTEM

The more efficient the loft insulation, the greater the risk of burst pipes and split cold water storage cisterns after a cold spell. Good insulation over the loft floor means that the loft

Skirting to floor gaps
Gaps at the junction of the floor and skirting appear as a result of movement throughout the life of the building. Here are two ways of dealing with it

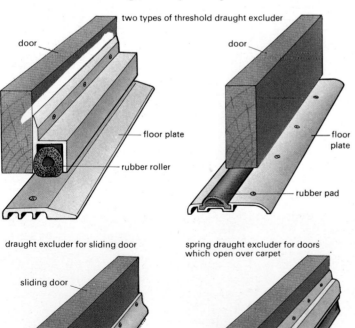

two types of threshold draught excluder

door — floor plate — rubber roller

door — floor plate — rubber pad

draught excluder for sliding door

sliding door — bristle seal

spring draught excluder for doors which open over carpet

carpet

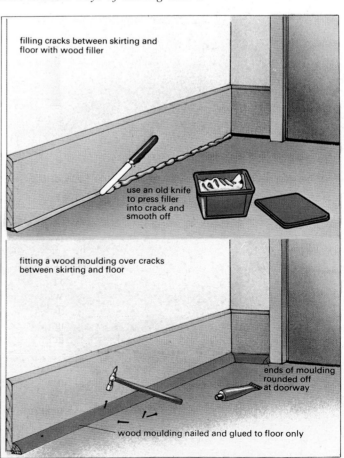

filling cracks between skirting and floor with wood filler

use an old knife to press filler into crack and smooth off

fitting a wood moulding over cracks between skirting and floor

ends of moulding rounded off at doorway

wood moulding nailed and glued to floor only

103

space is colder than before. If you confine insulation to rafters then the entire loft space will benefit from the heat that rises from the bedrooms and insulation of pipes and cisterns should not be necessary. It is still best to lag them, especially as this can be done quickly and inexpensively. The hard-to-get-at pipes close to the eaves where conditions are coldest are in most danger so be especially careful to insulate these thoroughly.

Pipework

There are two methods of insulating pipes; pipe bandage and moulded sections. Pipe bandages are cheaper than sections but take a little more time and trouble to fit. Efficient insulating bandages are usually made of felt, mineral wool or glass fibre and have a waterproof paper or PVC backing. They are available in rolls 75mm wide and 3.6m long.

Bandages are suitable for cold and hot water pipes and are installed simply by wrapping spirally around the pipework. Start at the cistern or where pipework passes through the floor of the loft. Put two full turns of lagging around the pipe and tie with a loop of string. Any backing strip should be on the outside of the lagging, away from the pipe. Wrap the bandage spirally around the pipe so the edges just overlap. Do not bind the lagging tightly.

Finish off each section by binding with string and overlap the next bandage by one full turn before continuing. Make sure that no section of pipe is left exposed and put a full turn around the stem of any stop-cock. Remember to lag overflow pipes as these can freeze during cold weather.

It may be impossible to wrap lagging around pipes that run close to the floor of the loft. In this case cover the pipes with glass fibre blanket or other loft insulation material.

Moulded sections provide a neater and quicker way to insulate pipework. The sections may be made of flexible foam plastic, rigid expanded polystyrene or rigid mineral wool. The sections are split longitudinally to enable them to be slipped over the pipe and secured with tape. Flexible sections can be used around bends, but rigid sections can be used only for straight runs. In the latter case bends must be insulated with pipe bandage or flexible sections.

When ordering sections, specify the diameter of the pipe to be insulated. Sections are made in different sizes and it is important they fit the pipe exactly. Also state whether they are to be used for hot or cold water pipes.

Sections should butt together with no gaps where they touch the cistern or pass through the loft floor or wall. To make doubly sure there are no air gaps, seal joins with tape.

Cold water cisterns

There are three methods of insulating cold water storage cisterns; with glass fibre jackets, expanded polystyrene slabs or granular insulation.

Fitting a lagging jacket

Glass fibre jackets are available in a variety of sizes for rectangular and round storage cisterns. The jackets consist of a glass fibre blanket sandwiched between thin plastic covers. Before fitting the insulation, make sure the cistern is fitted with a water-resistant cover. This is important because water will form on the underside of the cover. The cover must *not* be airtight. Specially moulded plastic lids are available for a number of cisterns or you can make a cover from expanded polystyrene sheet, plastic sheet, asbestos-cement or a sheet of corrosion resistant metal.

Wrap-around insulation

When binding bandage around pipes, secure it with adhesive tape or string

Along the length of the pipe, wrap neatly to eliminate gaps – but not too tightly

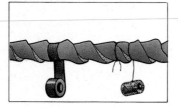

At stop cocks, bring the insulation right up to the spindle or it may freeze up

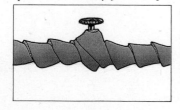

At cisterns, start with a turn secured to the pipe to hold the end in place

When the bandage runs out along the pipe, overlap the new length and tie

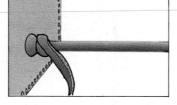

Where pipes pass through walls, be sure to make a good seal to stop draughts

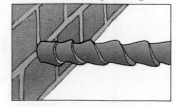

Moulded sections

Neat and quick are moulded flexible or rigid sections to fit various pipe sizes

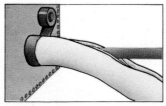

Secure moulded insulation with plastic adhesive tape. Start at the cistern

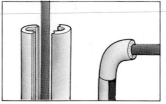

Where mouldings join along a length of pipe, seal the joint with tape

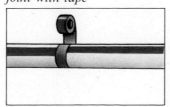

One-piece flexible moulding is simply opened up and slipped over the pipe

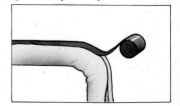

Use the tape to seal the joint where the moulding is split – especially at elbows

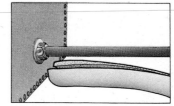

At walls, ensure the insulation goes right up close to prevent draughts

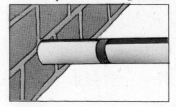

Circular cisterns
Insulation of a circular cold water cistern using purpose made tank wrap and loose matting

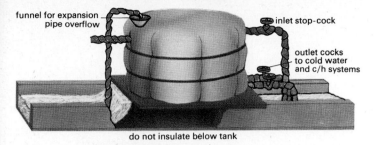

funnel for expansion pipe overflow

inlet stop-cock

outlet cocks to cold water and c/h systems

do not insulate below tank

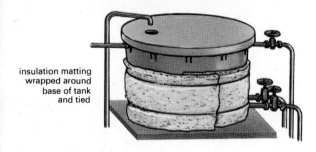

insulation matting wrapped around base of tank and tied

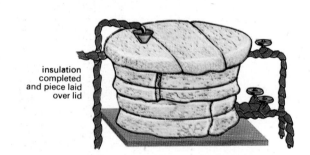

insulation completed and piece laid over lid

Square cisterns
Although loose wrap can be used here, an excellent material is expanded polystyrene slabs

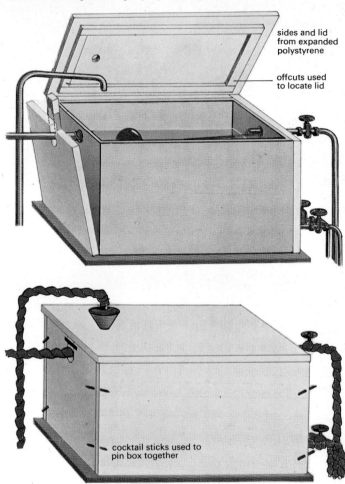

sides and lid from expanded polystyrene

offcuts used to locate lid

cocktail sticks used to pin box together

The glass fibre jacket should be fluffed up like a pillow and laid over the cistern so the insulation hangs around the sides. The insulation is then lightly secured with plastic tape which is usually supplied with the jacket. Check that there are no gaps in the lagging through which the cistern can be seen. The insulation must not be tucked under the cistern no matter which form of cistern insulation is used. The small amount of heat that comes up from the room below will help to avoid freezing in cold spells.

Lengths of glass fibre cut from a roll of loft insulation can be used to make a lagging jacket. Lay lengths over the cistern so they hang down and entirely cover the sides. Loop strings loosely around the cistern to hold the lagging neatly in position.

Using paper-backed glass fibre insulation causes less skin irritation but it is best to wear thick rubber gloves when handling this material.

Polystyrene insulation box

Expanded polystyrene is available in sheets up to about 75mm thick. It can be made into an excellent insulating box for a rectangular cistern using a minimum thickness of 25mm. Buy enough polystyrene to make four sides and a cover which can be fitted loosely on the cistern.

Trim the polystyrene to size with a sharp knife or saw and cut slots to allow the sides to be fitted round pipes. The sides can be glued together with polystyrene tile cement or pinned together by pushing in wooden cocktail sticks as nails. When the box is finished replace the pieces cut from the pipe slots and fix with tile cement or tape. Ceiling tiles fixed beneath the lid will ensure that the lid fits exactly over the sides. Do not worry if there are a few small gaps here and there. It is important that the box is not airtight or water will not flow freely when the taps are opened.

Loose fill

Granular loft insulation materials can also be used to insulate a cistern. Make a box to contain the granules around the tank in a layer at least 50mm thick. Before starting work on the box, ensure that the cistern is standing on a board so that the granules will not trickle under the cistern.

Make the box from whatever sheet is most convenient. Hardboard is suitable but it will need to be tacked to a 50mm by 25mm timber batten framework. Asbestos-cement sheets also need to be mounted on a framework. If a thicker sheet material is used a framework will be unnecessary. Insulating fibre board is ideal as it is itself a good insulator. Chipboard and blockboard both make a very strong but expensive box.

Make the box at least 100mm larger than the cistern dimensions to allow sufficient space for the layer of insulating granules around the cistern. Cut slots to enable the sides to be fitted around pipes. When the box is finished, seal the slots by sticking scraps of hardboard or wood over them. Make a lid that will rest on top of the tank with a 50mm high lip all round to hold the granules that are spread over the surface.

If an expansion pipe discharges above the cistern, drill a hole in the lid and fit a plastic funnel to catch any water that comes from the pipe.

When construction work is finished, carefully pour the insulating granules into the gap between the cistern and sides of the box. Fit the lid and spread a layer of granules over the top.

Hot water cylinders

Check the insulation of the hot water cylinder and hot water pipes which should be insulated to prevent heat wastage. If there is only a thin jacket on the cylinder, put a thicker one over it. Measure the height and diameter of the cylinder to be sure of getting a jacket that fits.

Jackets are usually made in segments which clip around the pipe at the top of the cylinder and hang down the sides where they are secured with plastic tape.

INSULATING WALLS

There are basically two types of house walls; cavity walls and solid walls. Since the 1920s most houses have been built with cavity walls. The inner plastered wall and the outer exposed wall are separated by an air gap about 50mm wide. With a cavity wall, the bricks on the outer wall are laid in stretcher bond with only the full length of the bricks showing. If headers or half bricks show, the wall is probably solid.

Cavity infill

The great advantage of cavity walls is that damp cannot cross the air gap to reach the inner wall. But the air gap is ventilated allowing a constant stream of cold air to move through the cavity and cool the inner wall. The principle of cavity wall insulation is to seal the air in the cavity.

There are two forms of cavity infill. Urea formaldehyde foam is injected into the wall cavity or mineral wool is blown in.

Neither job is for a home handyman and should be carried out only by approved contractors. Before work is started

Another method for square cisterns – box in and fill the gap with vermiculite

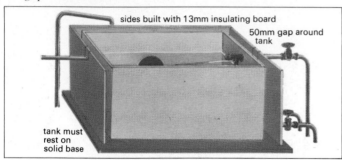

Hot water tank losses can be enormous – wrap up well with a minimum 75mm jacket

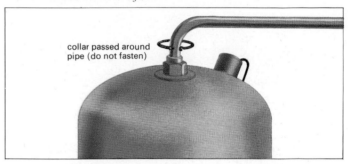

Usual gap size is about 50mm. Don't neglect to fill in where pipes pass through

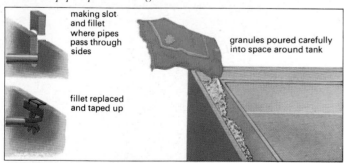

Plump up the jacket before fitting the segments evenly around the tank

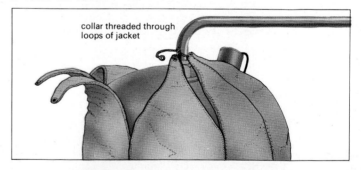

The lid is made like a box filled with granules. Vents are led into funnels

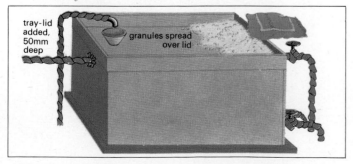

Secure without gaps but do not do up too tightly and flatten the insulation

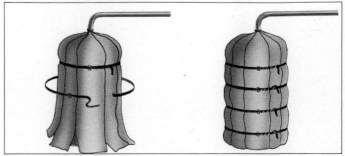

make sure you have approval for the work from the local authority.

One of the main objections to insulating cavity walls with foam was the possibility of it causing damp to enter the building because the work was not carried out by a competent contractor and the foam was not properly mixed. As long as the contractor belongs to an accredited body and is on the list of approved installers compiled by the Government's Agrément Board, then Building Regulation approval should be a formality. To be safe, make sure the installer gives a written guarantee to cover his workmanship.

Most installers will apply for local authority approval on your behalf and you should ask for a copy of the approval notice for your records.

Foam is considerably cheaper to install than mineral wool which is dry and arrives ready to use. It will not shrink or settle, is impervious to the movement of water and is completely fireproof.

Whichever method is chosen for cavity infill, the installation is similar. Holes are drilled into the cavity through the outside wall at about one metre staggered centres. Liquid foam made on site is injected into the cavity where it sets or mineral wool is blown into the cavity and packed to a uniform density. After installation the holes are filled with colour matched mortar. All the work is done outside the house and is likely to be completed in a day.

Solid walls

Solid walls are much more difficult to insulate than cavity walls, but the householder can do the work himself. A lining of insulation is applied either to the inside or outside of exterior walls.

It is probably best to insulate the inside wall surfaces because the work can be carried out under cover and completed in stages spread over a period of time.

Wrapping the outside of the house with insulation means that the insulation material must be covered with a waterproof skin. The appearance of the house is altered as it is clad with tiles, weatherboarding or even bricks. Before starting work of this nature contact the local authority.

Cavity wall insulation is high on the list of priorities – but how do you decide if your walls have cavities? The way the bricks are laid is a good guide

The filling process – done by specialist companies – comprises drilling, pumping in insulation and filling the holes. This usually takes only a day

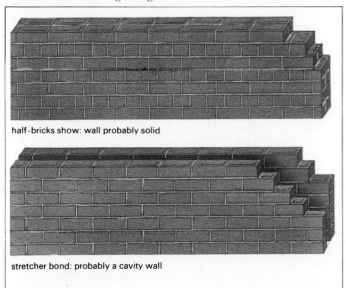

half-bricks show: wall probably solid

stretcher bond: probably a cavity wall

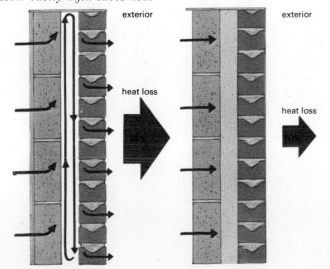

How cavity infill saves heat

exterior

exterior

heat loss

heat loss

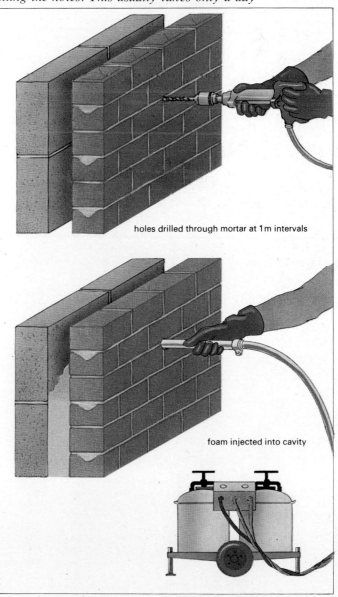

holes drilled through mortar at 1m intervals

foam injected into cavity

107

Insulating behind radiators

The simplest way to insulate walls is to reduce the heat lost through the wall at the hot points just behind radiators. If self-adhesive heat reflecting radiator foil is affixed, over 90% of the heat that would otherwise be lost will be reflected back into the room.

This radiator foil is plastic coated to prevent tarnishing for at least five years and is reinforced with glass fibre to make it easier to handle. It can be fitted without removing radiators, but first turn them off and allow them and the wall to cool.

The foil is supplied in a roll with a long handle applicator bar. Wrap a duster around the applicator and use it to clean behind the radiator. Cut the radiator foil slightly smaller than the radiator.

To make the job of fitting easier, it is best to cut the foil into three sections, a centre piece, and two end pieces with slots to go around the radiator brackets. Remove the backing paper and lower the foil behind the radiator. Position it against the wall and smooth down with the applicator rod. The end pieces can be fitted in the same way and the radiators turned on.

Polystyrene lining

Another simple method for insulating solid walls is to apply expanded polystyrene veneer available in rolls in thicknesses from 2mm to 5mm. Paint the wall with heavy duty wallpaper paste containing a fungicide, then apply the polystyrene as you would wallpaper.

The majority of straight edges can be butt jointed, but when this is not possible, allow the edges to overlap and cut along the overlap with a sharp knife. Pull away the surplus edges, apply more paste to the wall and roll the edges together.

For decoration, wallpaper can be hung over the polystyrene. If the paper is heavy it is best to first put lining paper horizontally across the veneer. A 5mm thick wall veneer will reduce heat loss through the walls by about 4%. Thicker veneers will give better figures.

Moulded expanded polystyrene wall panels and tiles are equally easy to fix and reduce heat loss by 10%. These are available up to 25mm thick in a range of decorative finishes, such as stone or brick. Plain panels can be painted with emulsion or special fire retarding paints after fixing with polystyrene tile adhesive.

Decorative cork wall tiles have an insulating effect and are easily stuck to the wall with a general purpose flooring adhesive or contact adhesive. All these materials are soft and are easily dented by furniture or accidental knocks but they are warm surfaces that will probably overcome many condensation problems.

It is important to remember, however, that they will not stop damp from coming through a wall and they should not be used to hide damp patches which will only get worse.

Dry lining

Dry lining is the most effective method of insulating exterior solid walls. The inside surface of the wall is lined with a suitable insulating material which may be covered with plasterboard. If this work is properly carried out, considerable savings in heat loss will be achieved. The work is time consuming, fairly expensive and slightly reduces the floor area. Do not tackle it unless you are very keen. Check with your local council first to see if you need permission.

In older houses it may be difficult to make a neat join where the lining meets the decorative cornice around the ceiling. One way to overcome this is to stop the dry lining at picture rail level and give a neat finish to the lining by making a narrow shelf that extends around the room. This can be used for decorative pieces.

There are many methods of dry lining. It is best to use a system of light timber battens, treated with wood preservative and fixed to the walls with screws and wall plugs or simply

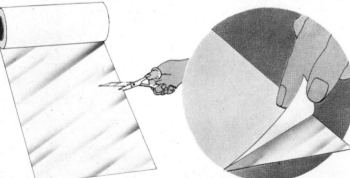

Radiator backing foil can be cut with scissors

Shaping complete, the foil release paper is pulled off

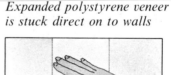

Expanded polystyrene veneer is stuck direct on to walls

At some joins the strips are overlapped and cut through

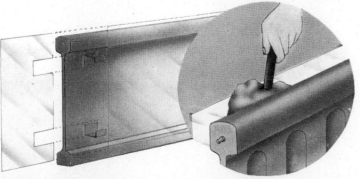

Cut-outs are made to fit around radiator brackets

A padded stick is used to smooth the foil to the wall

The strips are pulled back and the offcuts removed

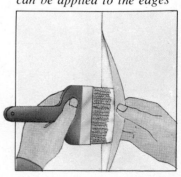

If necessary, extra adhesive can be applied to the edges

Dry lining

Carrying out a dry lining on a straight, flat wall is relatively easy; where corners, radiators, windows, doors, socket outlets and switches are involved, it can be *extremely trying. Here is the basic build-up of components for a really good standard of insulation. This is not a job to be tackled lightly*

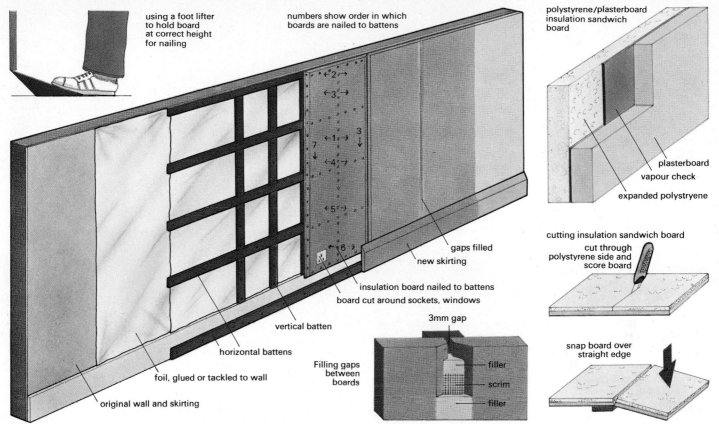

using a foot lifter to hold board at correct height for nailing

numbers show order in which boards are nailed to battens

polystyrene/plasterboard insulation sandwich board

plasterboard

vapour check

expanded polystryene

cutting insulation sandwich board
cut through polystyrene side and score board

snap board over straight edge

gaps filled

new skirting

insulation board nailed to battens
board cut around sockets, windows

3mm gap

filler

scrim

filler

Filling gaps between boards

vertical batten

horizontal battens

foil, glued or tackled to wall

original wall and skirting

---

with masonry nails. Insulating board is then nailed to the battens or insulating material is placed between the battens and plasterboard nailed over the surface. The first step is to remove skirtings, door and window trims and picture rails, and then remount electrical accessories.

Lining with insulation boards

Covering a solid brick wall with aluminium foil and 13mm thick insulation board affixed to a timber frame will provide more than adequate thermal insulation. Insulation boards are usually 1220mm wide and 10mm and 25mm thick in heights which vary to suit standard wall heights found in domestic premises.

Start by gluing or tacking foil-backed building paper to the wall with the foil facing inwards. Construct the timber frame to support the insulation boards providing intermediate supports and cross bracing as required. The main frame is made of 50mm × 25mm timber, but supports and cross pieces can be 38mm × 25mm.

Fix uprights vertically at each side of the room and check plumb and level. Fix cross pieces horizontally at top and bottom and add other verticals and cross braces.

When the framework is complete, put the insulating boards in place pressing them up to the ceiling. Fix with galvanised clout nails starting at board centres and working outwards.

Be sure to leave a 3mm gap between boards which is filled later with cellulose filler reinforced with jointing scrim.

Finally fix skirting and door and window trims. Use plaster or expanded polystyrene cove to finish the ceiling/wall joint. Paint the boards with hardboard primer to seal the surface

and prevent subsequent water entry. Wallpaper can then be hung as normal.

Polystyrene/plasterboard lining

A plasterboard/expanded polystyrene laminate is also available for insulating. These tapered edge boards have a built-in vapour check and are simply nailed to a timber framework. They are ready for decoration as soon as the joints are filled. Independent expanded polystyrene slabs also can be used to insulate a solid wall with ordinary plasterboard as a surface finish. Foil is not essential. Make the timber framework as described for insulating boards and cut 25mm thick panels of expanded polystyrene and wedge these between the battens. Cover with polythene sheet to prevent condensation from affecting battens. Then fix plasterboard in the same manner as insulating board. If aluminium-backed plasterboard is used, the polythene vapour barrier will not be required. Finish joints with filler reinforced with plasterboard joint tape. Use reinforced corner tape around doorways. Finish with plaster or polystyrene cove between wall and ceiling.

Glass fibre/plasterboard lining

Glass fibre loft insulation can be used behind plasterboard. Polythene-faced flanged building roll is ideal as this is easy to staple to the battens and forms a vapour barrier in one operation. It is available 50mm, 75mm and 100mm thick. The battens of the framework must be increased to accommodate the thickness of the insulation used. The problem is that the thicker the dry lining, the smaller the room area becomes.

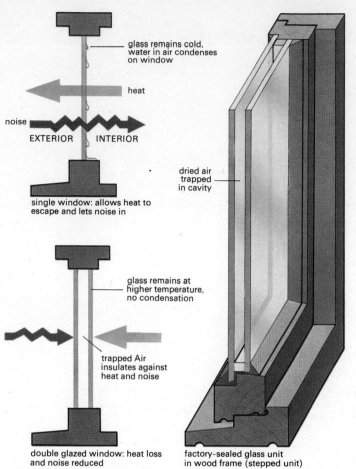

glass remains cold, water in air condenses on window

heat

noise

EXTERIOR INTERIOR

single window: allows heat to escape and lets noise in

glass remains at higher temperature, no condensation

trapped Air insulates against heat and noise

double glazed window: heat loss and noise reduced

dried air trapped in cavity

factory-sealed glass unit in wood frame (stepped unit)

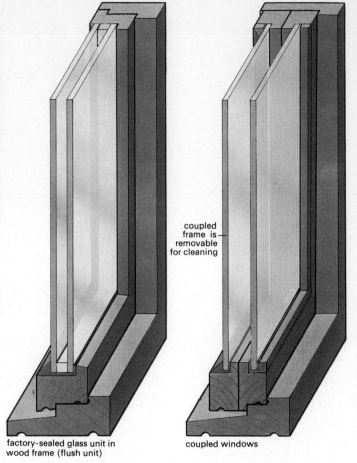

coupled frame is removable for cleaning

factory-sealed glass unit in wood frame (flush unit)

coupled windows

Mineral wool/plasterboard lining

Mineral wool can be obtained in slabs 600mm wide and 30mm to 100mm thick. The thicker the slab, the better the insulation. The battens must be as thick as the slabs used. Set them 600mm apart and wedge the slabs between them. If necessary the slabs can be cut with a bread knife. Cover with a polythene sheet before facing with plasterboard, or use aluminium-backed plasterboard.

INSULATING WINDOWS

Double glazing

For a permanent reduction in heat loss through glass, double glazing is required. Double glazing involves adding a second sheet of glass to a window so that an insulating layer of still air is trapped between the two sheets. Some double glazing systems are very expensive to buy and it can take a very long time for savings in the heating bills to pay for the cost of the double glazing.

The cost of the double glazing and the amount of heat saved depends on the area of glass, the exposure of the windows, whether the house is continually or intermittently occupied, whether there is full or background heating, the type of fuel used for heating, the standard of draught exclusion and the amount of roof, floor and wall insulation. Fuel savings of 10% to 15% are possible and even greater savings can be made if the glass area exceeds 15 square metres.

Apart from fuel saving, double glazing makes a great deal

of difference to the comfort of a room. It should lessen the incidence of condensation, reduce some window draughts and improve sound insulation.

For thermal insulation the glass thickness has no significant effect on the amount of heat lost through the glass. The air space is the critical factor. A 3mm air space gives substantial thermal insulation and this increases progressively up to an air space of 20mm. Above 20mm thermal insulation is not improved.

The three basic methods of double glazing use factory sealed insulating glass, coupled windows and secondary sashes. Secondary sashes are the type most often fitted by the home handyman. To improve the efficiency of all types, it is important to draughtproof the frames before double glazing is fitted.

Sealed units

Sealed units are the most efficient method of double glazing. A unit consists of two pieces of glass hermetically sealed in a factory with a metal or plastic spacer all around the edges. These units are indistinguishable from a single pane of glass and because they are sealed under carefully controlled conditions, condensation will not form between the panes. These units are suitable for installation in new buildings and can be used for conversion of existing window frames, although it may be necessary to enlarge the rebates to take the extra depth of glass. The units are available in a range of standard window sizes or can be purpose-made.

If it is difficult to alter the depth of the rebate of the frame,

a cold area close to windows and stopping draughts is well worth while. Here are some methods in common use, from *the hermetically sealed, factory made glass unit to the cheapest – and most unsightly – method, plastic sheet*

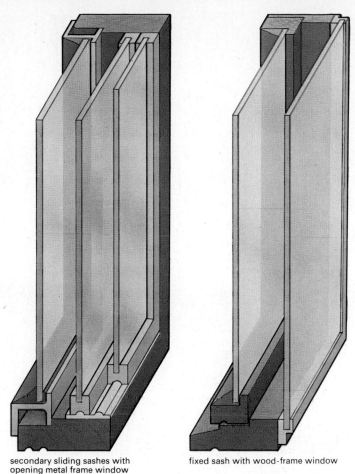

secondary sliding sashes with opening metal frame window

fixed sash with wood-frame window

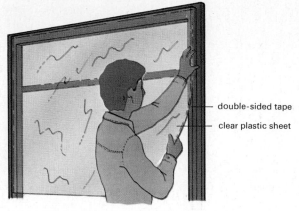

cheap method of double glazing with clear plastic sheet

double-sided tape
clear plastic sheet

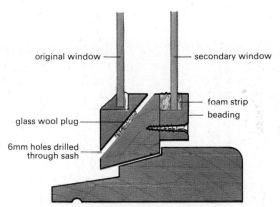

original window
secondary window
foam strip
beading
glass wool plug
6mm holes drilled through sash

do-it-yourself method of double glazing, showing method of draining condensation

special stepped units are available. These are modified versions of standard sealed units and have one pane bigger all round than the other. Units of this type are usually purpose-made.

Coupled windows

A coupled window consists of a single glazed window with a second window coupled to it so that both open together. The second frame is fastened to the first so the frames can be separated for cleaning. Coupled windows are usually used in conversion work where the entire frame is replaced, although they can be used in existing frames if each frame is strengthened to take the strain imposed by the weight of the second piece of glass.

Secondary sashes

The secondary sash system allows a second pane of glass to be fitted within the existing window opening. The second frame works independently of the other one and can be fixed, hinged or sliding. These systems are made-to-measure and some are fitted by the supplier while others are fitted by the customer. There are many hinged and sliding systems consisting of plastic or aluminium extrusions which can be cut to length and fitted with corner pieces to hold the opening frames together.

A fixed system using flexible plastic channels and clips to hold the second pane of glass is a cheaper method. Alternatively wood, plastic or metal beads can be screwed to the frame to hold the second pane of glass. After loosening

the clips or screws, the frames can be removed for cleaning or for storing during summer.

The cheapest method of double glazing is to fix sheets of transparent flexible plastic to a light timber frame or direct to the window frame with double-sided adhesive tape. Clear polythene can be used but transparent plastic is less obtrusive. This method is not as efficient as using glass, but is useful when dealing with a large window. Large windows are expensive to double glaze and the size and weight of the sheet of glass can cause problems in making up a sufficiently strong frame. The main difficulty with plastic sheet is getting the sheet taut and wrinkle-free.

Condensation on windows

Condensation is a problem in many houses which is reduced by double glazing. With hermetically sealed insulating glass condensation should not occur within the cavity. But with secondary sash systems some condensation may occur. This is annoying and is the result of moist air entering the cavity from the room or the surrounding wall and condensing on the cold glass of the window.

Bags of silica gel crystals are sometimes used to keep the air dry between the panes, but they quickly become saturated and ineffective. They only postpone condensation unless frequently renewed or reactivated. A more effective way to cure this type of condensation is to drill 6mm breather holes top and bottom to connect the cavity to the outside air. Push a plug of glass wool into each hole to exclude dirt and insects. Drill two holes for every square metre of glass area.

111

Basic hand tool woodworking kit

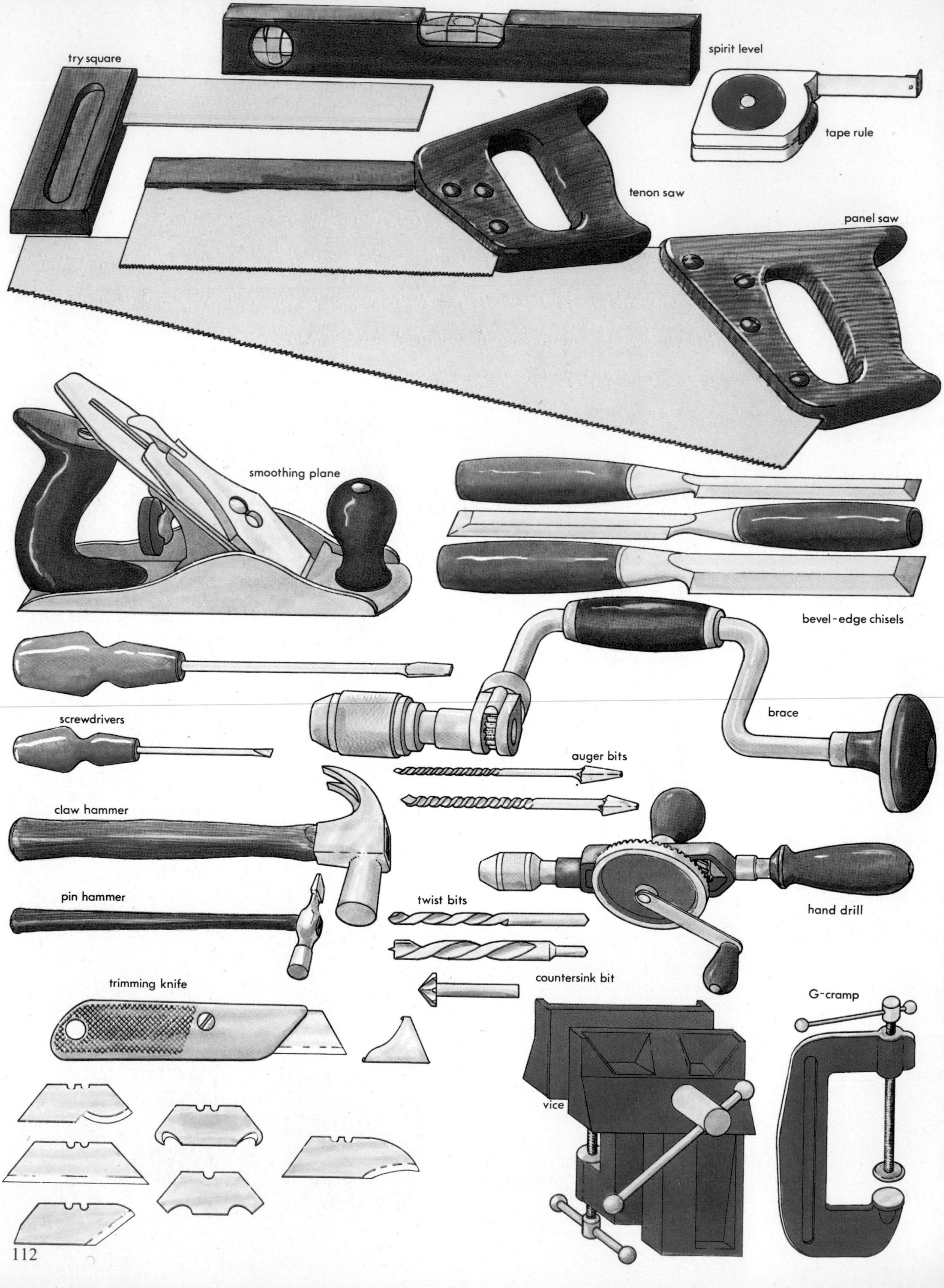

try square

spirit level

tape rule

tenon saw

panel saw

smoothing plane

bevel-edge chisels

brace

screwdrivers

auger bits

claw hammer

pin hammer

twist bits

hand drill

countersink bit

trimming knife

G-cramp

vice

Introduction

Building your own furniture and fittings does not have to involve complicated and old-fashioned joinery like dovetails and mortise and tenons. You can join wood just as firmly and much more easily using the many clever connectors available in do-it-yourself shops. And sheet materials like plywood, chipboard and blockboard make it easy to build large surfaces without any worry of warping and cracking. It is very important to consider the standard sizes of both softwood boards and of sheet materials and doors when planning your projects. For larger projects like fitted cupboards or kitchen cabinets, get a free catalogue from a timber merchant showing the various products he stocks. To avoid working with large sheets, prepare a cutting list and have a local timber merchant cut it up accurately into easily transported pieces.

A permanent workshop is a luxury and most of us have to make do with a temporary bench in the garage, basement or hallway. A portable workbench which folds up after use is very useful. It has a vice which holds wood securely for any kind of work like sawing or planing and can be adapted to hold large sheets as well. The price of such an item will be repaid many times over.

MATERIALS

Timber and sheet materials

Wood is either softwood or hardwood. Softwood, which in some cases is very hard, is from evergreen trees whereas hardwood is from deciduous trees. Softwood grows much faster in large uniform forests and is therefore much cheaper than hardwood. Most timber merchants stock only softwood since hardwoods, like mahogany, oak or teak are now used almost exclusively for expensive furniture and special projects.

Buying wood

Softwood is available in boards of various sizes and in mouldings and other special shapes. The most common sizes are from 12 to 50mm thick and from 25 to 200mm wide. It is important to remember that wood sizes, such as 50 × 100mm are the sawn sizes. You can buy sawn wood but it is very rough and used mostly for structural work. To make furniture and cupboards you will need the more common planed wood, referred to as planed all round or P.A.R. This is still referred to by the sawn size even though 3 to 5mm have been removed in planing it smooth. Thus 50 × 100mm P.A.R. softwood is actually 47 × 95mm. This may cause slight problems in planning projects where precise dimensions are important.

Softwood is now sold in metric sizes so bear this in mind when making up a cutting list. If you were working in Imperial units, for example, and needed several 4ft lengths, you may find that the nearest metric length converts to either 7ft 9in or 9ft 9in. In either case there would be too much costly waste in cutting the board into 4ft lengths.

Most timber merchants also stock a range of standard mouldings for skirting boards, architrave, and for covering up edges and joins in woodwork. These mouldings should not be confused with picture-frame mouldings which have a special shape to hold the picture and glass.

A few merchants stock a limited range of hardwoods such as oak, mahogany and beech, usually only in sawn planks. Hardwood is very expensive but it may be worth using for a special project where a durable and luxurious finish is required. The larger timber merchants will usually plane it to the required thickness for an extra charge.

The most common way of using hardwood today is as veneers, which are very thin slices of the hardwood which are glued on to cheaper wood to give a surface of hardwood. You can buy veneers of various exotic species from specialist stockists but it is easier to buy blockboard or chipboard with the veneer already glued on.

Defects in wood

Wood should be sold only after it has been dried, either in the open air or in kilns, to a moisture content of about 20%. Above this moisture content wood is more vulnerable to attack by various fungi. (See page 46.) But no matter how carefully it is dried, wood absorbs moisture from the atmosphere when it stands in open sheds. When it is brought into a dry room it will tend to warp. Avoid buying timber which feels wet. It is always best to store new timber for a week or two in a dry environment similar to that where it will be used. Store it flat adding spacers at short intervals between boards. Put weights on to hold it flat if necessary. Generally avoid buying timber with knots, splits or discolorations.

Sheet materials

Manufactured sheets of various types, thicknesses and sizes are readily available from most timber merchants. They include plywood, blockboard, chipboard and hardboard. They are usually sold in 1220 × 2440mm sheets but can also be bought in other sizes.

The Workmate, when folded, left, takes up little space. Right is the dual-height model in its working position

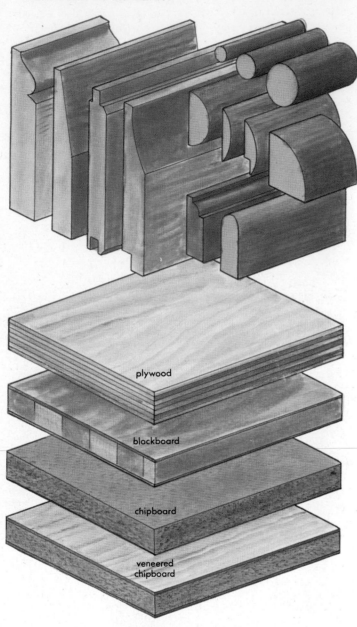

plywood

blockboard

chipboard

veneered chipboard

An electric iron is used to fix edging strip coated with heat-sensitive glue. Brown paper, omitted here for clarity, is placed between the iron and strip

Plywood is made by gluing layer upon layer of thin veneers together. The outside layer is usually a better quality veneer than the inner core. The most common plywoods are made from Douglas fir, birch, beech and gaboon in thickness from 3mm to 25mm.

Blockboard has a similar surface to plywood, but it is constructed of timber blocks laminated together to form the core. The core is then sandwiched between layers of veneer. These surface veneers can be birch, gaboon, parana pine or various other species.

Both plywood and blockboard are also available with special decorative surface veneers such as oak, teak or afrormosia.

Plain chipboard

Chipboard consists of chips of wood coated with a resin or binder and then formed into a sheet under heat and pressure. The resultant board is strong and rigid, but does not possess the high strength of plywood and blockboard. Because of the make-up of the board, it does not grip edge-driven nails or screws as well as plywood or blockboard. This can, however, be overcome by using one of the many connectors designed specifically for chipboard.

The material can be worked with standard woodworking tools but the adhesive in chipboard tends to dull cutting edges of tools rather quickly.

Chipboard is available in standard sheet sizes 1220mm × 2440mm and is cheaper than plywood or blockboard.

Veneered chipboard

Ready-veneered chipboard sheet finished in a range of wood, plastic and other decorative materials has become a popular furniture building material. The sheets are available in a range of widths, generally in 75mm increments from 150mm to 1220mm wide. Most manufacturers issue a list of stock sizes. Consult this list at design stage so that standard size panels can be utilised. The tedious and often wasteful process of rip sawing a board can thus be eliminated. Cut non-standard widths out of a wider piece so that it leaves a useful-size offcut for some other project.

Veneered chipboard can be worked with standard woodworking tools but because the surfaces are ready-finished, extra care must be taken especially when cutting. The sheet must be adequately supported on either side of the cut so that there is no danger of the last 50mm or so of uncut material breaking away near the unsupported end. It is also important that the saw blade be sharp.

Most veneered chipboard manufacturers market a flexible edge trim, usually about 18mm wide to match the various surface finishes. The edge trim is supplied in rolls, ready coated with a heat sensitive adhesive backing. The trim is carefully laid on the chipboard edge and the adhesive activated by passing a warm electric iron over the top surface. A piece of brown paper between iron and trim will prevent heat from damaging the finished face.

Hardboard

Hardboard is made of wood fibres, which are processed and formed into sheets under pressure and heat. The quality of the board depends largely upon the density of the fibres.

Hardboard is generally available in 2440mm × 1220mm sheets and some suppliers also stock smaller sizes. Stock thicknesses are usually 3mm or 6mm.

In addition to the standard plain material, hardboard is also available with a range of ready-finished surfaces which, although intended primarily for wall cladding, can also be adapted for use in furniture building.

Plastic laminate veneer

Plastic laminate veneer is an excellent finishing material for household work surfaces and is particularly suited to kitchens where an easily cleaned and decorative surface is required. The material is manufactured in a wide range of patterns and colours. If properly applied it will give years of maintenance-free service.

Manufacturing processes for all types is basically the same. The laminate is fabricated from specially processed papers impregnated with phenolic and melamine resins. The treated papers are brought together in a press where the surface melamine layer is faced to a mirror finished stainless steel sheet. The papers are then passed through a high temperature oven where heat and pressure fuse the layers into a homogeneous solid panel. The sheets are then trimmed and the surface is finished.

Sheet laminate veneer is available in standard 1220mm × 2440mm sheets. Some suppliers also stock other sheet sizes or will cut to size.

Plastic laminate veneer is designed to be bonded to a solid backing such as plywood, chipboard or blockboard. Special contact adhesives are recommended for bonding. If the finished work will be subject to considerable heat or moisture a waterproof adhesive must be used to ensure a permanent fixing.

Hardware

Besides the usual nails and screws there is an ever increasing number of special connectors, hinges, catches and knock-down fittings which make it quick and easy to make furniture yourself.

Nails

Although nails are not generally used in fine furniture making, they are very convenient for making fitted furniture. Nails come in a variety of shapes and sizes but the types most frequently used in woodwork are generally round or oval wire nails and panel pins. These nails are interchangeable but the oval type are less likely to split the wood. Lengths are generally from 12 to 150mm in increasing thicknesses. Panel pins are between 12 and 50mm long. They have small heads which can be hidden in the wood.

Nails are sold in small boxed quantities in local shops but can be bought less expensively by the kilo from larger merchants.

Screws

Whereas nails hold wood by friction, screws form a stronger mechanical fixing. Wood screws are either countersunk, round head or raised head. Countersunk screws are generally used to fix wood or hardware to other wood, round head screws are used to fix hardware or sheet metal to wood and raised head screws are used for fixing decorative hardware.

Brass or steel screw cups match the screws and give the screws a more workmanlike finish.

Screws are bought by the length and by the diameter or gauge. Screws of a particular length, say 38mm, come in various gauges, in this case from gauge 6 to gauge 14 screws. The higher the gauge or number, the heavier the screw. The most common sizes are 12 to 50mm long and between 4 and 10 gauge.

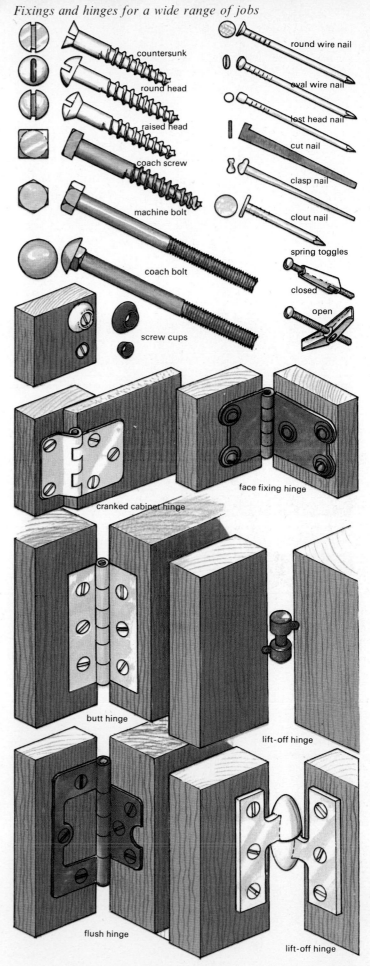

Fixings and hinges for a wide range of jobs

countersunk
round head
raised head
coach screw
machine bolt
coach bolt
screw cups
round wire nail
oval wire nail
lost head nail
cut nail
clasp nail
clout nail
spring toggles
closed
open
cranked cabinet hinge
face fixing hinge
butt hinge
lift-off hinge
flush hinge
lift-off hinge

Nuts and bolts

Screws are used more frequently than bolts in woodworking, but bolts are useful for special applications. Besides the heavy machine and coach bolts, which are used mainly for structural work, smaller machine screws are useful in woodworking, particularly for fixing two thin pieces of wood together.

Machine-thread screws are available from 6 to 50mm long and from 4 to 50mm in diameter, complete with nuts and washers. Use machine screws with special toggles or anchors to fix to hollow walls or to plaster ceilings.

Hinges

You can buy hinges in a bewildering variety of shapes and finishes. The most common are butt hinges for heavy doors, flush, face-fixing, cranked or lift-off hinges for light doors and continuous hinges for lids and doors. They are available in sizes ranging from 25mm to about 150mm measured from top to bottom. It is best to seek the advice of an ironmonger while planning the work. He can usually recommend the correct type and size to be used.

Catches and latches

The most frequently used hardware for holding cabinet doors closed are magnetic catches. There are several types and they are all easy to fix and practically unbreakable. There are also various designs of mechanical catches made of brass or nylon.

Knock-down fittings

Knock-down fittings have many general applications. Because they are strong, easy-to-fix connectors they are particularly useful for the home handyman. And they are very useful in making furniture which you may eventually want to take apart for storing or moving.

Flush mount fittings have many applications such as hanging fittings flush against the wall. The half which is screwed to the fitting simply slips over the other half which is screwed to the support.

The most common knock-down fitting is the two-piece block joint, which is frequently used with chipboard. The two halves are first screwed to the separate components and then bolted firmly together.

The cross dowel fitting which is extensively used in the furniture trade, is more sophisticated. It is for use with sheet material which is at least 18mm thick.

Some knock-down fittings may be difficult to find. As a substitute use ordinary wood screws fixed into holes filled with fibre wall plugs. To take apart, undo the screw and use a drill to remove the plug. To reassemble, simply screw back together using a new wall plug.

Shelf fittings

There are many ways to support shelves. Probably the easiest and most efficient way is to use one of the many metal brackets which lock into a metal channel screwed to the wall. For movable supports in bookcases use either plastic shelf studs and sockets or bookcase strip with clips.

The plastic sockets are tapped into tight-fitting holes. The studs which are pushed into the sockets can be relocated easily.

The aluminium or bronzed bookcase strip is screwed to the side of the case. Small studs fix on to the strips to support the shelf.

In addition to conventional methods of putting up shelves, there is a wide range of shelf fittings on the market. Here are three fairly common types

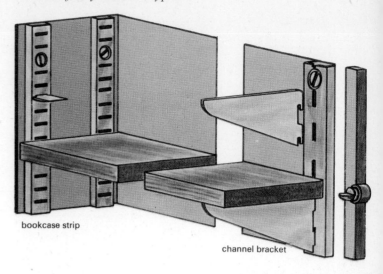

bookcase strip

channel bracket

Castors

Castors and gliders have many applications. Use them to support under-bed storage boxes, children's toy boxes or any movable furniture such as tea trolleys. The most common variety screws to the underside of the fitting. Others push into a socket or simply screws into a previously drilled hole.

Glue

Modern adhesives are so strong that they are often stronger than the materials they bond. It is useful to know the difference between a few of the common glues so that you can use the right one for the right job.

For most interior jobs the white PVA woodworking glue, which usually comes in a plastic bottle, is excellent. It requires cramping to set properly but it sets in about 15 to 20 minutes. However, it is not totally water resistant.

For areas which are damp use casein glues which come in powder form and are mixed with water.

For very moist areas, urea formaldehyde is excellent. Powdered glue and hardener are mixed with water and the glue sets in about four hours.

Contact adhesives are not usually used in woodworking. They are used mainly for fixing laminates to work or counter tops. The glue is applied to both surfaces and left until touch-dry and the surfaces are then brought together.

FINISHING MATERIALS

Polyurethane varnish

One of the most useful finishing materials is polyurethane varnish. It is easy to apply with a brush and it dries to a very hard finish.

It is available clear in either a matt or a gloss finish and should be applied in two or three coats over well-prepared wood. Between each coat smooth with a very fine sandpaper. After the final coat, rub in a coat of wax for a really luxurious finish.

These varnishes are also available already mixed with either wood-tone or brightly coloured stains. Apply two or three coats as for clear tones to build up a rich colour. For some applications, such as where a degree of movement is expected and for exterior work, yacht varnish is superior.

Polyurethane paints are very tough and are safe to use on children's furniture. Apply two or three coats, sanding lightly between coats.

Oil finish

You can buy several proprietary oils such as teak oil which when rubbed well into any hardwood surface will give a nice rich texture with moderate resistance to moisture and stains. It should be renewed every six months or whenever it looks dull or stained.

For cutting boards and wooden bowls use light coats of olive oil to protect the wood and prevent it from cracking.

Wax polish

Modern prepared furniture waxes are excellent as a final finish to almost any varnish.

Staining

It is important to test a wood stain on a piece of spare wood before starting a job. Stains are easy to apply but it is difficult to achieve a natural looking surface. Many stains, particularly water-base stains, tend to blotch on plywoods and blockboards. Oil-base stains are more uniform but give off a strong chemical smell during application. It is probably best to use a stain already mixed with polyurethane varnish, otherwise apply stains carefully with a cloth, wiping along the grain. Choose a light tone if possible. After staining, apply one or two coats of varnish.

TECHNIQUES

Measuring and marking

A steel tape is best for most measuring jobs. Most makes incorporate a special sliding hook at the end which automatically adjusts for both internal and external measurements. The tape case is usually 50 or 75mm long so that internal measurements can be made merely by adding 50 or 75 to the indicated length.

To mark a square line across a board, hold the stock of the try-square firmly against the side of the work and mark with a marking knife or sharp pencil. It is essential that you use the try-square to mark a board whenever you have to cut it. Boards which do not have square ends are very difficult to work with.

The engineer's square can be used as a try-square to mark 90° lines or to mark 45° lines. The steel rule can be removed for separate use.

To mark cutting lines for traditional joints, use a marking gauge. Loosen the screw to set the pin the exact distance from the stock, then tighten the screw again. Hold the stock firmly against the side of the wood and push it away from you at a slight angle. The pin makes a starting groove for the chisel.

To check for both horizontal and for vertical or plumb, use a spirit level. These are available in various lengths but for most interior work the 600mm length is adequate. Hold the spirit level against the work and adjust it until the bubble is perfectly centred between the guide marks.

For inside measurements, the tape rule case is included. The try-square gives right-angles; the engineer's square also gives 45° angles. A spirit level can check verticals and horizontals. When hand sawing, keep the width of saw cut on the waste side of the line. A power saw makes working so much easier

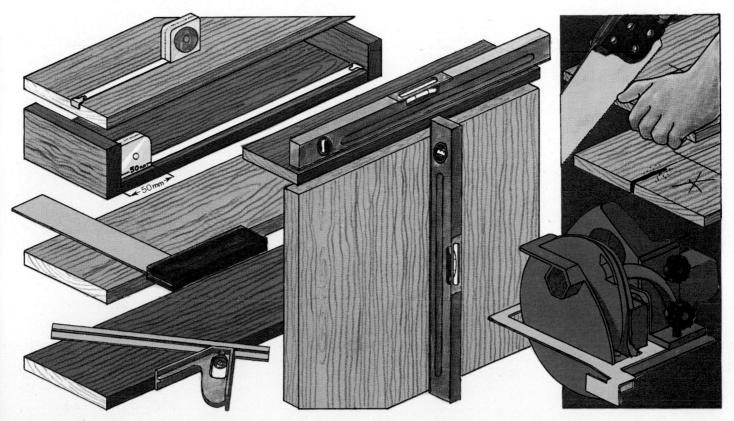

Cutting timber

*Clamp a straight-edge to
the work to act as a guide*

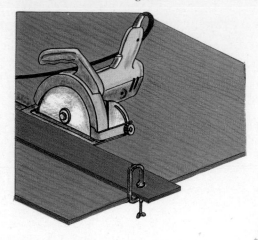

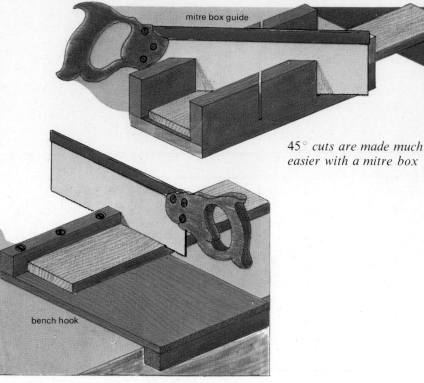

mitre box guide

*45° cuts are made much
easier with a mitre box*

*A simple bench hook makes
for accurate, easy cutting*

bench hook

Sawing

The most important part of sawing is to use a sharp saw and to support the work properly. Don't force the saw and use firm, smooth strokes for straight cutting.

You can saw either across the grain—cross-cutting—or along the grain—ripping. General purpose handsaws with about 8 teeth or points per inch will do both jobs well but special rip and cross-cut saws are available.

Remember that a saw cut has width, caused by the thickness of the blade and the set of the teeth. When cutting accurately to a finished size, learn to cut on the waste side of the marked line so that the saw cut doesn't encroach on the finished workpiece.

When cutting a board, remember to support the loose end so that it won't break off before you finish sawing. It is hard work to cut up large sheets with a handsaw. Hold the saw at a lower angle when cutting a very thin sheet. For a neater and quicker job use a portable power saw.

A small portable power saw is indispensable for making quick, straight cuts in sheet materials. Some manufacturers sell saw attachments which fix on to their electric drills.

Portable power saws are perfectly safe if used according to instructions. The saw blade is always protected by a guard which automatically covers the blade when the saw is removed from the work. Always adjust the blade so that it just cuts through the material.

Here is a good tip for straight cuts. Don't use the rip guide provided by the saw maker. Clamp a true straight-edge (such as a machine-cut strip of chipboard) to the workpiece against which the edge of the saw soleplate can run. You will have to make a trial cut on a piece of scrap wood first, to find the distance between the edge of the soleplate and the edge of the cut. Don't forget the width of the cut!

The best way to cut up a large sheet of manufactured board is to lay it on the floor, but held about 10mm clear by scrap battens. Provided the circular saw blade is set to just cut through the board, you will make successful, accurate cuts.

No room to lay it flat? Slightly more difficult, but certainly practical, is to cut the board while it is leaning against a convenient wall.

Whatever you do, don't try to cut board on trestles—they do not give sufficient support, particularly when nearing the end of a cut.

A tenon saw with 12 to 14 points is used for finer, more accurate cuts. The top of the blade is stiffened to keep it straight. It is best to hold the wood in a vice but for small, quick cuts a bench hook is very convenient. Make a bench hook out of a 200 × 300mm piece of plywood and two 250mm lengths of 25 × 50mm timber. To use it, hold the work firmly against the top guide with the bottom guide against the workbench or table.

To make accurate mitre (45°) cuts use a mitre box with the tenon saw. Mark the wood carefully, then hold it firmly against the side of the box while sawing gently.

A coping saw is useful for cutting curves in wood. Loosen the handle to insert the blade, which can be rotated to face the direction of the cut.

Using a hammer

Almost everyone knows how to use a hammer – but they don't! Don't strangle the poor thing – always hold it near the end of the handle away from the head and use the hammer with an easy, swinging action. For rough work and large nails use a claw hammer of a comfortable weight. Pull out nails with the claw, keeping a piece of scrap wood under the head if you wish to protect the surface. For finer work use a light pin hammer to drive nails or panel pins.

To hide panel pins below the surface of the wood, drive the nail until just the head is exposed. Finish driving it below the surface with a nail punch the shank of which is no bigger than the nail head. Then fill the hole with wood filler of a matching colour.

Drilling holes

There are three ways of drilling holes. You can use a hand drill, a hand brace or an electric drill.

A hand drill uses twist bits for holes between 1mm and 7mm in diameter. Insert the twist bit into the end and tighten the chuck while keeping the handle from moving. To use the hand drill, hold the handle and apply pressure with the left hand while turning the handle with the right hand.

Use a hand brace to bore holes between 7mm and 25mm. Insert the auger bit into the chuck and tighten the chuck. Use a centre punch or a nail to mark the centre of the hole then, holding the brace upright, turn the handle while applying pressure from the top with the other hand. Don't drill all the way through the board. To prevent splitting the wood, drill far enough for the drill point to stick through, then turn the wood over and finish the hole from the other side.

To drill larger holes with the brace use a special expansive bit which can be adjusted to bore holes between 12mm and 62mm in diameter.

The simplest and quickest way of drilling holes is to use an electric drill. These are well worth the investment even if only for the occasional job of putting up shelves. With the electric drill, use the twist drills for small holes and special flat bits for large ones.

Using a screwdriver

A screwdriver is a simple tool, but it is easy to mangle screw heads unless you use a screwdriver which fits the screw slot properly.

Always use the correct size of screwdriver for the screw being driven. Safest type of screw and screwdriver to match is the Pozidriv. Do not confuse this with continental and American cross-slot screws.

A ratchet screwdriver saves the effort of letting go of the handle each time you reach the limit of your wrist turning action. It has three operating positions: ratchet right, ratchet left and locked solid – like an ordinary screwdriver.

The spiral ratchet – sometimes called pump – screwdriver has a ratchet action with a telescopic shaft which drives screws merely by pushing the handle back and forth. An extremely useful tool, but it must be used with great care, for the shaft is spring-loaded and can shoot out with considerable speed and force.

Using a chisel

Chisels are used extensively in joinery to cut grooves and slots in woodworking joints. But chisels are necessary even in the

Choose a hammer type and weight to suit the job in hand – here are three examples. An electric drill saves

effort – a good all-rounder is a two-speed model with a 10mm chuck. Bits for drill and brace are necessary extras

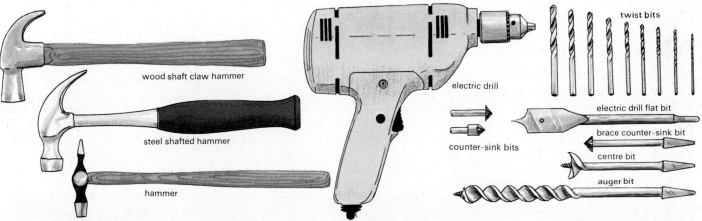

wood shaft claw hammer

steel shafted hammer

hammer

electric drill

twist bits

electric drill flat bit

brace counter-sink bit

counter-sink bits

centre bit

auger bit

Use a pad to protect the work; deep-driving with a nail punch; using a brace and auger bit; work from both sides

to avoid splintering; countersinking with an electric drill; spiral-ratchet screwdrivers save time and effort

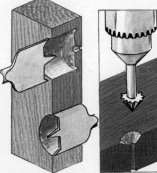

relatively rough carpentry involved in building cupboards and fittings.

When using a chisel, mark the area to be removed with fine lines, preferably with a marking knife, to form a starting groove. Support the wood well and work carefully, tapping with a mallet if necessary. Remove a little wood at a time. Keep chisels razor sharp by honing frequently on an oilstone.

A half-lap joint is useful for frameworks in building fitted cupboards or kitchen cabinets. Saw along the marks to the required depth, then chisel out a little at a time until all the wood is removed. Mortises, if necessary, are marked and started by drilling out most of the wood with a twist bit smaller than the width of the mortise.

Start the chisel near the middle, tapping with the mallet. Work towards the ends, deeper and deeper. If the mortise goes right through the wood, mark both sides and work towards the middle. When planning mortises, try to make the mortise exactly the same width as one of your chisels. Then you will take out precisely the right amount of timber – preferably with a mortise chisel – and not have laborious work clearing out the sides of the mortise.

Planing

Old-fashioned joinery involves planing with a variety of special purpose planes. Today, wood is usually bought to a required thickness already planed. But a general purpose plane such as a 230mm smoothing plane is still useful to smooth down rough, sawn edges of plywood or to remove a few shavings from a sticking door. Support the wood firmly on a bench or in a vice. Adjust the blade by sighting along the bottom and turning the knob to give a fine, even cut. Then hold the front knob in the left hand to guide the plane and push with the other hand on the handle with smooth, easy strokes.

JOINING WOOD
Traditional joints

The craftsman who enjoys spending a great deal of time building furniture still uses the traditional joints. These joints have been used for centuries and have undoubtedly proved their soundness. But they require considerable skill and effort. For the handyman without an extensive range of tools and a proper workbench, it is much easier to use one or two simple joints when necessary but to rely on the modern mechanical fixings which are quicker and easier to make.

Screwed joints

To fix two pieces of wood together with a screw, first mark and drill a hole in the top piece the same diameter as the shank of the screw. Countersink the hole if required. Then hold the two pieces together and use a nail or screw to mark the hole location in the bottom piece. Use a smaller drill to make a hole in the bottom piece to the depth of the screw. The first hole is a clearance hole, the second is called a pilot, or thread, hole. The size of the pilot hole depends on the gauge of the screw and the density of the timber into which it is being driven.

For most work, up to gauge 8 screws a 1 to 2mm diameter hole is about right (use a bradawl). Between gauge 8 and gauge 12 – the largest most people normally work with – a 3mm hole is needed.

Don't screw directly into the end grain, which splits very easily. If necessary, drill a larger hole in the end grain and fit a masonry wall plug before fixing the screw.

Screwed butt joints are used for joining sheet materials, particularly veneered chipboard. The easiest consist of two or three screws simply screwed into drilled holes in the upright and the shelf. This joint is made stronger by first

Chopping out a mortise. A: *marked-out half-lap joint.* B: *saw cuts on waste side of lines.* C: *work from both sides.*

D: *the finished joint.* E: *many saw cuts ease chisel work.* F: *use a drill or brace to remove the bulk of the waste*

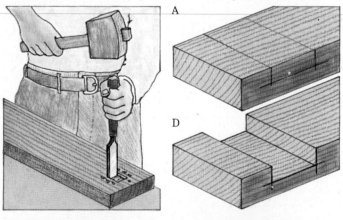
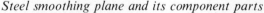

Steel smoothing plane and its component parts

wedge lever
wedge iron
cap iron
blade
screw
centre screw
adjustment lever
knurled knob

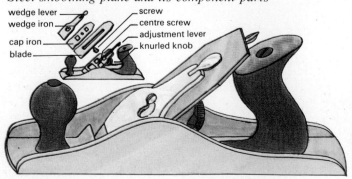

One plane grip for edge

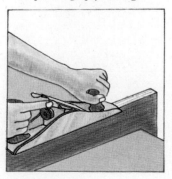

The forefinger adds control

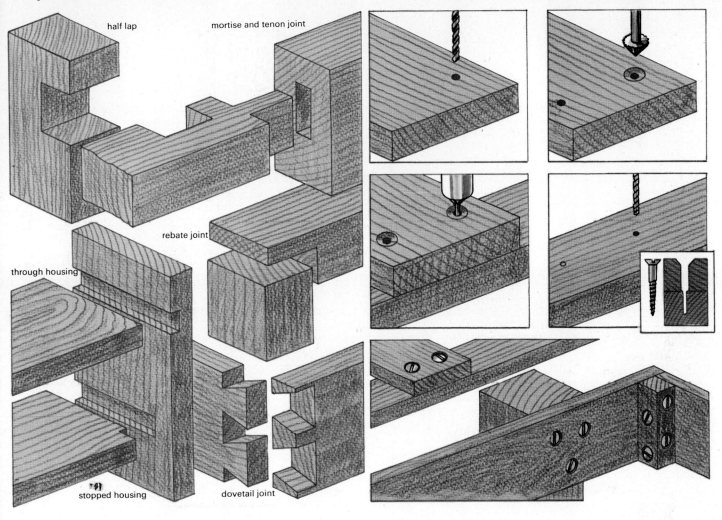

For those who like joints, here is a selection – but for most purposes dowels are neater, stronger and easier for the inexperienced woodworker to make

Two sizes of drill and a countersink bit can be used to produce the correct screw hole (inset). Alternatively, use a special bit. Bottom: screwed joints in common use

half lap

mortise and tenon joint

rebate joint

through housing

stopped housing

dovetail joint

adding masonry type plugs into the ends of the shelves. To make the exposed screw heads more attractive, use brass cup washers with brass screws.

For a stronger butt or corner joint, screw and glue a batten, say 25 × 25mm or 38 × 38mm, to both pieces. If you want to take them apart again, omit the glue.

Nailed joints

Nailed joints are very useful in rough carpentry. They can also be used very effectively in conjunction with glue to hold battens on to sheet materials for use in fitted furniture. Spread glue along the batten, then nail the sheet to it every 100 to 150mm. The nails actually act as a cramp holding the surfaces tightly together until the glue sets.

Dowel joints

Use a dowelling jig to make the holes in the two members to be joined. You can cut short lengths of dowel yourself but it's easier and quicker to buy them ready made.

Exceptionally strong are the serrated dowels. These allow glue to penetrate every part of the joint and the crushing action when the dowels are forced home makes a very secure job.

FIXING SHELVES

With an electric drill and a screwdriver it is very simple to put up shelves. The neatest shelf support is the metal bracket fixed to the wall track, but for an alcove it is much cheaper to screw battens to the walls.

The shelves can be either laminate covered chipboard or painted or varnished 25mm thick solid timber. Buy the shelves to the correct width and length. Most bookshelves are between 200 and 250mm wide but for extra wide books or record players and loudspeakers, make them as wide as required. Place intermediate supports as necessary for adequate strength.

Fixing the metal upright is straightforward. Hold the upright vertically on the wall against a spirit level, and mark the fixing holes on the wall with a pencil or nail. Make sure to mark every hole. Remove the wall track and drill the holes for the wall fixings. Use wall plugs for fixing the uprights to solid walls. Think very carefully before putting shelves on hollow walls as they are not usually strong enough to carry the weight. If you are confident on this point, use spring or gravity toggle bolts – although this can prove expensive for a long run of shelves.

121

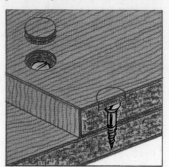
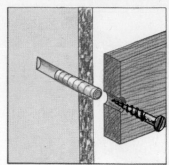

Ways of using nails – and hiding them. Don't use two in line along the grain

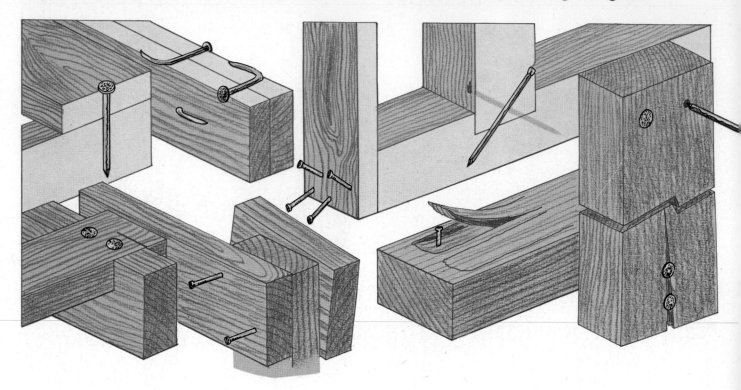

One important point. When fixing the second (or third) upright, accurately line up the fixing holes along a horizontal line with those in the first upright. Failure to do so will mean shelves which can never be levelled!

In alcoves, screw battens to the walls. First drill two holes in the battens for gauge 10 screws. Hold the battens against the wall and check with a spirit level before marking the wall through the two holes. Drill the holes, insert the wall plugs and fix the battens. Finally cover the screw heads with filler, and paint the batten to match the wall before placing the shelf.

Fixing a wall plug

Wall plugs are made in a bewildering variety with many claims made for both the fibre and various designs of plastic types.

In general, wall plugs are sold by screw gauge – as are the masonry drill bits to match them. However, some plastic types are sold with the claimed advantage of accepting a range of screw sizes.

The disadvantages here are that larger masonry drill bits are needed and you cannot make the hole in the wall and insert the plug while the batten or other fixture remains in position.

Weigh up these points before deciding which types to use for a given project.

The actual fixing is fairly easy. Use a proper masonry drill bit; while drilling always keep the bit cutting – never let it rotate without biting into the wall.

If the wall is very hard, or you are drilling into concrete, use either a hammer drill or a hammer attachment. When using these, however, do use masonry bits made for the purpose as ordinary types will not stand up to the hammer action. Such special bits are usually called double duty.

The hole you make should be deep enough for the length of screw which will need to go into the wall and for the wall plug used.

When the hole is made, tap the plug into it and take care to ensure that the screw goes into the middle of the plug and not to one side of it.

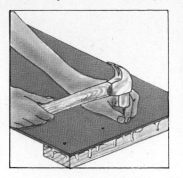
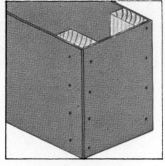
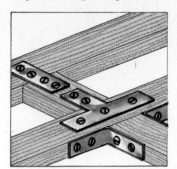
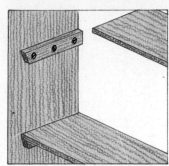

Dowels – for joints and supports

Methods of shelf-fixing

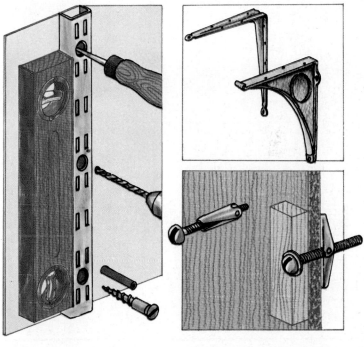

FREE-STANDING SHELF UNIT

This basic shelf unit can be made in an afternoon from almost any sheet material such as plain or veneered chipboard or plywood. You can have the pieces cut up by your timber merchant or use the white melamine faced boards cut to the appropriate lengths. Don't be afraid of altering the dimensions to suit your own needs. Make it taller, narrower or deeper, but don't increase the width without using thicker shelves.

Materials

Chipboard or plywood 19mm thick:
Uprights: 2 pieces 400 × 1400mm
Shelves: 2 pieces 325 × 1000mm
           3 pieces 250 × 1000mm
Hardboard or plywood: 3mm thick
Back: 1 piece 1220 × 1038mm
20 gauge 8 screws, 30mm long.
Finishing cup washers, optional.
24 panel pins, 19mm long.

Assembly

Using a rule and try-square, measure and mark off the shelf locations identically on both uprights. Then fix the shelves with two 30mm panel pins at each end as a temporary fixing, which can later be punched below the surface with a nail punch and filled over.

Make sure the back edges of the shelves are flush with the back of the uprights. Although the pins will produce only a temporary fixing, this should, with careful handling, be sufficient to hold the unit together while the necessary screw holes are drilled.

An ideal tool for drilling the hole in one operation is the combination screw bit, which may be used either in a power or hand drill.

After fixing all the shelves with the screws, nail the backing board to the uprights and to the shelves with the 19mm panel pins.

Screw heads may be covered with a disc of iron-on edge trim which can be cut to shape using a pair of sturdy scissors or a wad punch. Where a painted finish is to be applied, the holes may be filled with plastic wood and then sanded

Several arrangements are possible for the shelf unit and room divider; modify dimensions and components to suit

space and needs. A disc of veneer (bottom left) can cover screw heads – or leave polished screws exposed

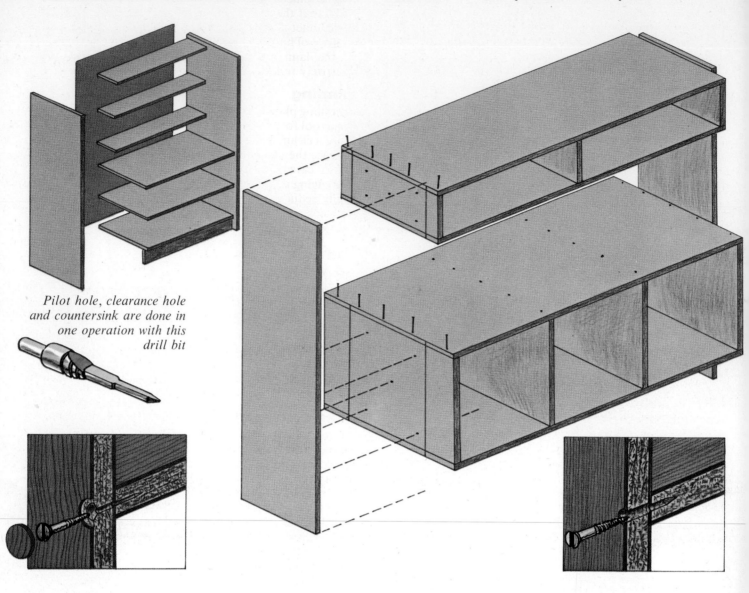

Pilot hole, clearance hole and countersink are done in one operation with this drill bit

smooth after the filler has dried. Alternatively, you can make a feature of the screws by using brass screws with matching cup washers.

Room divider

It is quite straightforward to extend the techniques used for the shelf unit to make a larger, but equally simple storage unit. Use chipboard or blockboard with hardboard or plywood backing for the bottom unit. The top and bottom units are made as simple boxes with nailed or screwed corner joints. These are then screwed to the two uprights. Make the unit about 1·5m high and 1·8m long.

FIXING A NEW PLASTIC LAMINATE COUNTER TOP

Whether you are building new kitchen units or renewing old ones, brightly coloured and easy-to-clean plastic laminate is the ideal material for all counter tops. For a small job, have the laminate cut to size when buying it. For larger jobs plan the cutting carefully so that you get the maximum out of the standard sheet with a minimum of waste.

Cutting

The simplest method of cutting laminate is to use a purpose-made scoring tool. Lay the laminate sheet on the ground, preferably on a sheet of hardboard or plywood. Mark the line to be cut and use a straight-edge consisting of a 150mm wide strip of hardboard to guide the tool. Pull the scoring tool along the straight edge with just sufficient pressure to cut into the face side of the laminate. Having established an accurate score line, make further passes with the tool well into the laminate backing. With the straight edge still held firmly in position lift the free side of the laminate steadily upward until it snaps free cleanly along the cut line. If it is difficult to break, use the scoring tool again to deepen the cut. Experience quickly shows the optimum cutting depth.

To cut a curve use the tool freehand along a pencilled mark

or use a shaped hardboard templet as a guide. With a curve, the groove must be cut deeper to assist with final snapping. To cut a square angle, cut one leg right through with the scoring tool and take care that the two points of the cut meet.

Generally it is better to cut laminate to shape, allowing about 2mm trim oversize all round, before bonding, but in some cases, such as a sink unit top where a bowl is to be installed, the hole is best cut after bonding.

Bonding

A contact adhesive is the usual method of fixing. Many types of contact adhesive allow no margin for error because a firm joint is made immediately, but some types are claimed to allow a restricted degree of slip after light contact has been made.

Contact adhesives provide an excellent bond provided the manufacturer's instructions are carefully followed. Spread the adhesive thinly and evenly to both mating surfaces and then leave it to set for a specified period depending on the temperature. Warmth will reduce setting time while cold or damp will delay it. The important point is that both coated surfaces must be touch dry *before* contact is made. Poor bonding is generally the result of contact being made too quickly while the adhesive is still wet. When in doubt always delay for a few extra minutes. Be sure that no blobs of adhesive are left on either surface to create an area of poor adhesion which often shows on the surface as an unsightly bubble.

Edge bonding

Most laminate manufacturers market a matching edge trim and this is generally thinner and more flexible than the sheet material. Edge trim is best applied after the main surface veneer has been bonded and trimmed. But if you use a strip of the standard sheet material as edging, apply and trim it before fixing the main surface.

Score the laminate surface with a special knife blade

Lift the laminate with the straight-edge still in place

Strips of wood hold the prepared surfaces apart

Bring the surfaces together as the strips are removed

Trim sharp edges flush with a fine file or plane

Edge strip, when fitted, can be trimmed similarly

Application

Because contact adhesives allow little or no adjustment, it is essential that the veneer and backing be accurately aligned before contact takes place. A simple method is to use some clean strips of hardboard placed between the mating surfaces while the laminate is being positioned. The strips are progressively removed as firm contact is being made.

Trimming

A smoothing plane, particularly the replaceable blade type, is an ideal tool for trimming straight edges. A sharp plane will produce a clean, square edge ready for mating with the edge trim. Once the laminate edge has been trimmed in this way, take great care because the trimmed edge will be razor sharp. Where edging is not to be applied, the sharp edge should be carefully reduced with fine glasspaper wrapped around a wood block and applied at a 45° angle. Use a file to trim the thinner edge trim.

Three simple projects from solid wood

1. LAMINATED BREAD/CHOPPING BOARD

Materials

12 lengths 50 × 25mm softwood or hardwood, 350mm long
Waterproof wood glue
About 40 brass or plated panel pins, 30mm long
4 rubber-headed nails.

For this chopping board you can use offcuts of softwood but for the most durable board try to use hardwood, mixing light and dark strips for interest. Construct the board by using a staggered nailing system with the strips being progressively pinned and glued together to build up a suitable width. Try to keep the top surface smooth and even as you add the strips. The sizes given are intended as a guide only and can be amended if desired. With the final timber strip fixed, all exposed nails should be punched down and filled with plastic wood. After the glue has thoroughly dried, sand the top first with rough then with finer glasspaper to get an even surface. If the top is very uneven it may be necessary to plane it down slightly.

As an alternative method of construction, cramps may be used instead of pins to hold the laminations steady while the glue dries.

2. TOWEL RAIL

Materials

2 pieces 25 × 150mm softwood, 460mm long
3 pieces 18mm diameter dowel, 600mm long
4 mirror plate brackets with 18mm screws
4 gauge 10 woodscrews, 25mm long
4 gauge 10 wall plugs
6 40mm panel pins.

This useful kitchen or bathroom fitting is both practical and attractive. And it is very simple to make. It should not take more than an hour or two.

Cut the two side members to the sizes shown, rounding and smoothing after making all straight cuts. Use a woodworking drill bit matched to the size of the dowels and drill the necessary holes with the two sides cramped firmly together. To ensure a clean hole, cramp a piece of scrap timber to the underside of the lower piece. Trim notches in the rear edges to accommodate the mounting brackets.

Cut the dowels to length and press the sides into position after applying woodworking glue to the joints. Fix the dowels with panel pins as shown.

3. WINDOW BOX

Materials

25 × 150mm softwood approximately 2.2m long cut into five pieces:

    2 pieces 600mm long
    1 piece 555mm long
    2 pieces 200mm long
18 gauge 8 woodscrews, 45mm long.

The window box uses standard 150 × 25mm planed softwood. All the pieces are simply cut from a standard width plank about 2.2m long. If the box is to be used outdoors, drain holes must be included in the bottom member part 'B'. To use the box indoors fit an aluminium foil one-piece liner to prevent contact between earth and woodwork. Cut all pieces to length.

Check all parts for fit and then temporarily pin together with a few panel pins. Counterbore for all screws and then drill shank clearance and pilot holes before driving the screws home. Screw heads may be hidden using either wood plugs or wood filler. Sand smooth, paying particular attention to all exposed end grain.

If the box is to be located outdoors, a thorough soaking in horticultural type wood preservative will be necessary. For

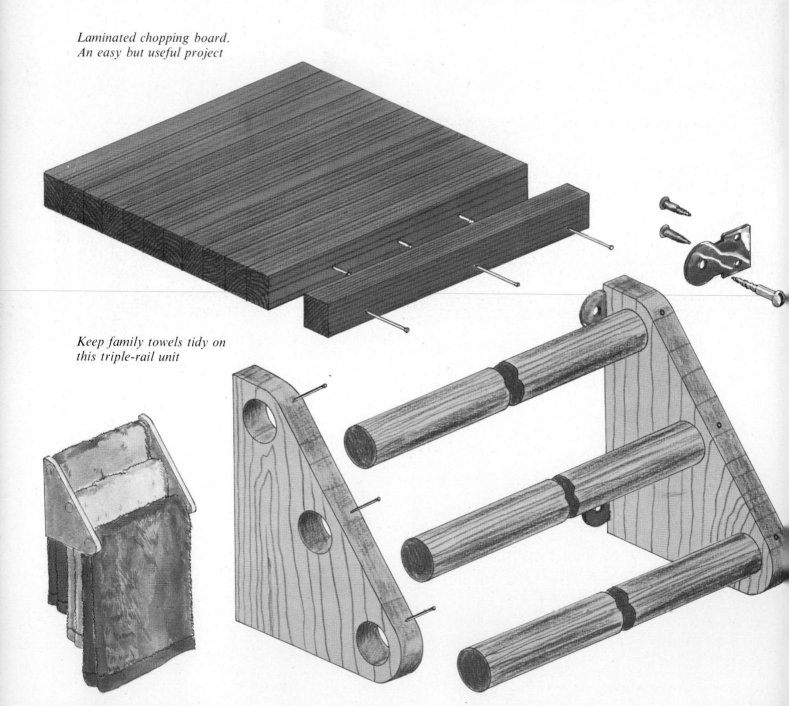

Laminated chopping board.
An easy but useful project

Keep family towels tidy on
this triple-rail unit

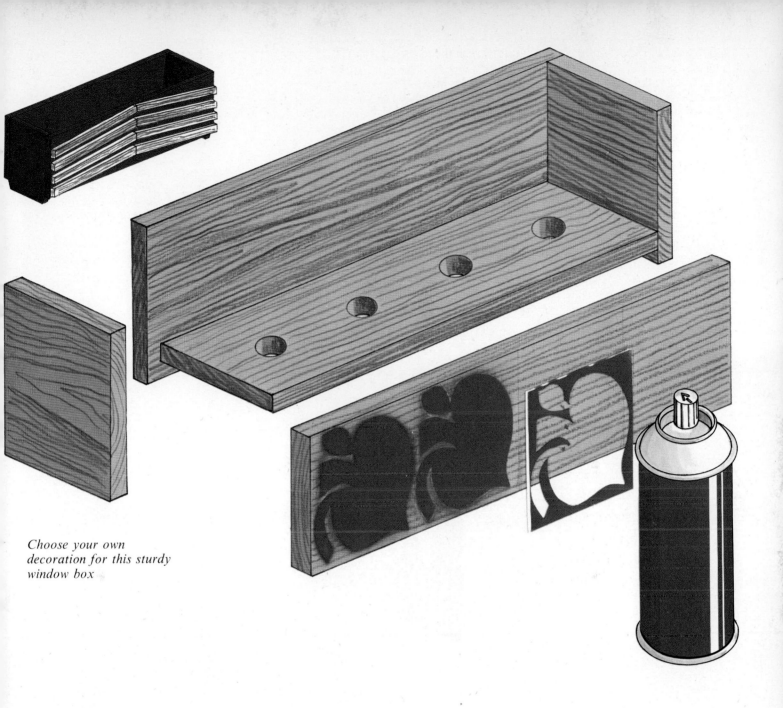

Choose your own decoration for this sturdy window box

indoor use the box may be painted, varnished or covered with self-adhesive decorative plastic sheet.

The box can be further decorated by spray-painting flowers on the sides through home-made stencils. Alternatively glue and nail on a few diagonal wood strips as decoration.

BUILDING FITTED FURNITURE

Planning

Carry out a careful survey of the place where the furniture is to be fitted and make a sketch plan with accurate measurements. The sketch can be used at the design stage to produce a more accurate plan and materials list.

When taking measurements bear in mind that house walls are rarely completely square or upright. Be sure to measure the width of the alcove and the ceiling height at several points. At the design stage, the narrowest width or lowest height will determine the dimensions of the fitted unit. To check whether the building is out of square, use a spirit level in conjunction with a straight edge.

Bear in mind when installing fitted furniture that access to existing plumbing and electricity services is required. Frequently a trap consisting of a short piece of floorboard is left by the builders for access to electrical junction boxes, plumbing and so on, and care must be taken not to create problems by blocking access. Similarly careful note must be made of the location of electricity cables and water pipes to avoid the possibility of these being damaged during the course of the work. A socket outlet, for instance, fitted adjacent to the work will probably have cables running under the floor or up through the wall buried under the plaster. Having established the run of cable or pipe, lightly mark this on the adjacent wall or floor to serve as a reminder during subsequent fitting work.

Then decide whether the work should be carried out completely on site or whether it may be more convenient to prefabricate the main parts in the workshop ready for final assembly. Generally the prefab method is preferred as this avoids moving too many tools to the site and reduces the dust and mess. It is vital to check that access is sufficient to allow any assembled frames or parts to be carried in.

Details and design

After measuring up, draw a sketch of the fittings, making notes of dimensions and any relevant facts. From this sketch work out the details, for example the way the materials will meet at the corner or the way the door will fit inside the opening. Most designers make small sketches of details over and over again until they find the best solution. Keep in mind the standard sizes of sheet materials and of doors. Use the standard hardboard flush door, stocked by most builders' merchants and timber yards in a range of widths. It is far easier to tailor the surrounding framework to accept the ready-made door, than it is to tailor a door to fit the framework.

If possible, prepare a more careful second drawing, preferably to scale, showing planned layout and details of the project.

By doing the thinking and planning before the work begins, you will save a lot of time and expense in avoiding mistakes later.

Finally make a list of materials including sheet materials, hardware and paint so that you have everything on hand during building.

BUILDING AN ALCOVE FITTED CUPBOARD

A fitted cupboard can be used not only for clothes and shoes, but also as a larder to store preserves or an airing cupboard to enclose the hot water tank. It is a simple solution to many difficult storage problems.

In this example a cupboard is built to fit an alcove, but the technique is the same wherever it is placed.

After measuring and drawing up all plans and details start by building the main front from standard 100mm × 30mm softwood. After cutting the various parts accurately to length cut the housing and half-lap joints and test them for fit. Cut a recess in any vertical member which has to clear the skirting board. Assemble the frame by fixing each joint with 50mm gauge 10 steel woodscrews and glue.

Build the frame to accommodate a standard hardboard flush door and position it to allow an adequate ground clearance so that any floorcovering can be run neatly into and over the whole floor of the cupboard.

Using a spirit level and straight edge mark a vertical line on the wall to indicate the position of the front edge of the frame. Offer the assembled frame into position and check for general alignment.

With the frame standing in position, the level of the vertical and horizontal inner door frame members should be checked and packing, in the form of strips of hardboard or plywood, added as necessary to ensure that the door frame is square and level.

After locating the frame, fix the right-hand vertical member to the wall at at least four points either where packing has been added or where the wall and frame come solidly into contact. On no account should fixings be positioned where a gap exists between frame and wall as this will pull the frame out of shape.

With ordinary brick walls, the best method of fixing is to use conventional wall plugs and screws. Drill holes in the vertical member and mark the hole locations on the wall before removing the frame to drill the holes and insert the plugs in the holes. Reposition the frame and packing and fix the screws. At this stage do not fix any other parts of the frame permanently.

To hang the door use the flush fitting Hurlinge which can be fitted directly to the door and frame without the need for recessing. Note that the door must extend beyond the front frame by 3mm to allow for the hardboard which will be used as a cladding to the front of the frame.

After hanging the door make any final adjustments to the frame to ensure that the door closes neatly. Add strips of 30mm × 15mm door stop beading to the inner face of the frame after a suitable door catch has been fixed. Secure the

Beware of untrue surfaces, particularly in old houses. Use a straight-edge and spirit level to find errors. Do not obstruct access to cable and pipe runs

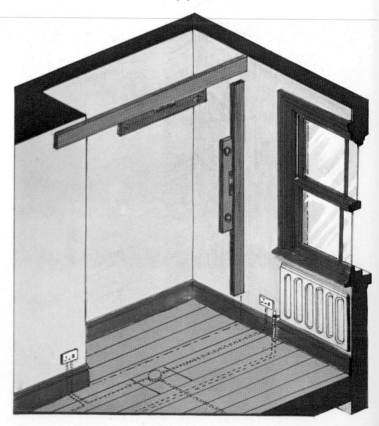

frame to the floor with screws driven through the two lower members. With a solid floor, plugs as used for the wall provide a suitable fixing. Screw the top frame member where possible to the ceiling joists. Where this is not possible use a spring loaded cavity fixing toggle.

In this case the left-hand side panel to the cupboard is cut from a length of 12mm chipboard, trimmed to fit around the skirting board, and then slipped into position as shown. The outer front edge of this panel must be flush to the front edge of the door frame member. Fix it with screws and wall plugs to the wall and with panel pins to the frame member.

After fixing the 12mm chipboard panel, cover the front with the hardboard cladding starting with the top strip. Nail the hardboard with plated pins to prevent rust. Punch the pins below the surface ready for filling.

Finishing

If the cupboard is to be wallpapered, fill any gaps and cupboard joints with a plaster filler. Alternatively fill the gaps and holes, sand smooth and paint the surfaces with two coats of paint.

Nail on matching door architrave and skirting board to make the cupboard blend in as part of the room. Similarly continue any ceiling cove round the ceiling line of the cupboard.

Cut corner joints in the architrave, skirting board and ceiling cove with the aid of a mitre block.

A recess can be enclosed to provide a kitchen cupboard, wardrobe or airing cupboard. Bottom is shown the framework construction for the front of the cupboard

FITTED WARDROBES

Properly planned fitted wardrobes provide a tremendous amount of storage space in the bedroom where it is needed.

There are two ways of building-in wardrobes. You can build individual modular units and add to them as your need grows to eventually make it a completely fitted cupboard. Or you can build the entire cupboard with sliding doors to cover the entire width of a wall.

The basic dimension to keep in mind is the 560mm depth and the 1.4 to 1.7m height required for hanging clothes. Include several shelves or drawers to store away shirts, socks and shoes.

Building the modular unit

Although these units aren't truly fitted, they have several advantages. They can be made one at a time and interchanged from room to room. An important consideration is that they are easily transported when moving to a new house.

White plastic veneered chipboard is the easiest material to use. Use the full 2440mm length and make up the remaining distance to the ceiling by adding a plywood or hardboard pelmet.

The construction is very simple. Screw strips of 25mm square softwood to the insides of the cupboard sides for fixing the shelves. Cut the battens to length and drill three screw holes for each strip.

Build the opening to fit a standard size door, rather than the other way round! Use packing pieces between the frame and the walls. The facing material fills the gaps

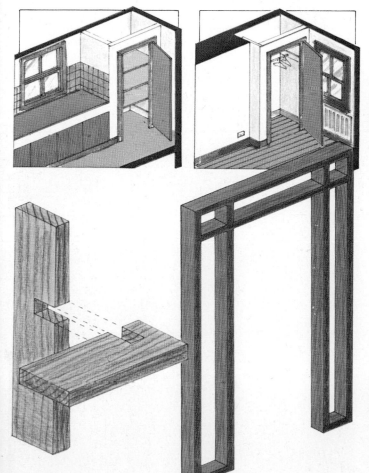

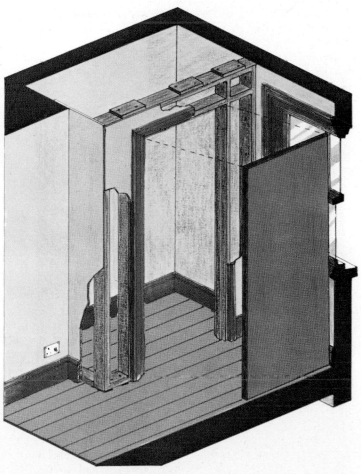

This basic modular unit system can be varied in details to suit kitchen, dining room or bedroom

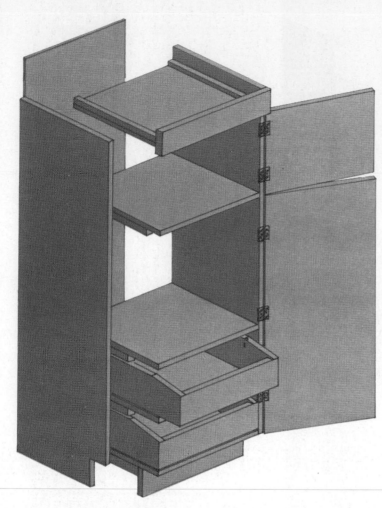

Cutting list (not including doors)

Veneered chipboard
A   two pieces 560 × 2440mm
B   four pieces 560 × 600mm
C   one piece 75 × 600mm
Hardboard
D   one piece 625 × 2440mm

Assembly

Cut the panels to size and mark the location of the horizontal members in soft pencil on the inner faces of the verticals. Screw the shelves through the joint battens, to one side and then add the second side.

The back is cut from either plain or enamelled hardboard and fixed in position with 18mm screws. With the back fixed, the unit will be quite rigid and square. Finally add the top strip cross member and bottom plinth.

Notice that the two additional strips support the simple drawer made from veneered chipboard and a hardboard bottom.

Cut the doors to length from a veneered chipboard panel and cover the cut ends with iron-on trim. Lift-off pivot hinges provide a simple method of hanging the doors. Each part is simply screwed in by hand pressure to the pilot hole drilled in the cupboard and door edges.

After fitting two sets of hinges hook the doors into position ready for use. Where necessary the hinge may be adjusted by lifting off the door and either loosening or tightening the fitting.

Using the same easy construction make several other cupboards and place them together as a fitted wall unit. You may want to provide a space between them for a dressing table with a mirror. Or you may want to place them on either side of the bed for a totally built-in look. For open shelves simple take off one of the doors.

Building the fitted wardrobes

This unit also uses standard veneered chipboard panels to keep sawing to a minimum. And it uses sliding doors which are more flexible since their width is not critical. The entire unit is quite easy to construct. Make the unit 2440mm high, then fit a strip of the same material up to the ceiling. Start by cutting the main components from veneered chipboard.

Cutting list

Veneered chipboard
A   two pieces 150 × 2440mm
B   two pieces 600 × 2440mm

Screw two battens to the insides of each divider, B, one along the back and one to support the top shelf 600mm from the top. Also screw two mirror brackets to each divider as shown. Then fix the dividers to the walls through the batten. Cut away the bottom to fit around the skirting board if necessary. Also fix the ends A to the end walls adding the necessary packing.

Don't fix the bases of the dividers until later. Attach 25 × 50mm battens to the wall to support the top shelf. Use the battens on the dividers as a guide for the level.

Depending on the overall length of the cupboard, the fascia panels will probably need joining in the centre. With the top strip this join can be reinforced with the door track mounting panel. For the lower strip use a short strip of 25mm square batten.

Cut the fascia boards out of veneered chipboard. Screw the 25 × 25mm batten and the 25 × 75mm door support to one, leaving gaps where the divider and ends A will be attached. Fix the fascias in place, then measure, cut and install the shelves by screwing them to the battens on three sides and the fascia on the front side. Screw down the dividers and fix the sliding track according to manufacturer's instructions. Finally cut the doors to size leaving an overlap of about 50mm.

Guides, supplied with the door track, will be required at the bottom of the doors. These normally consist of L-shape brackets about 30mm long, which may be fitted either directly on top of lino or tiled floor. On carpets a small floor mounted chipboard block will be required as a platform to raise the brackets above the carpet.

A bedhead shelf unit can be made as a simple box-like structure, sized to slip between the main central panels and fixed by screws from each cupboard side.

The top pelmet strip, cut from hardboard or veneered chipboard should be trimmed to a neat fit between cupboard and ceiling before being tacked in place with panel pins. Gaps between the end vertical members and the wall can be sealed using suitable size strips of quadrant moulding pinned in position.

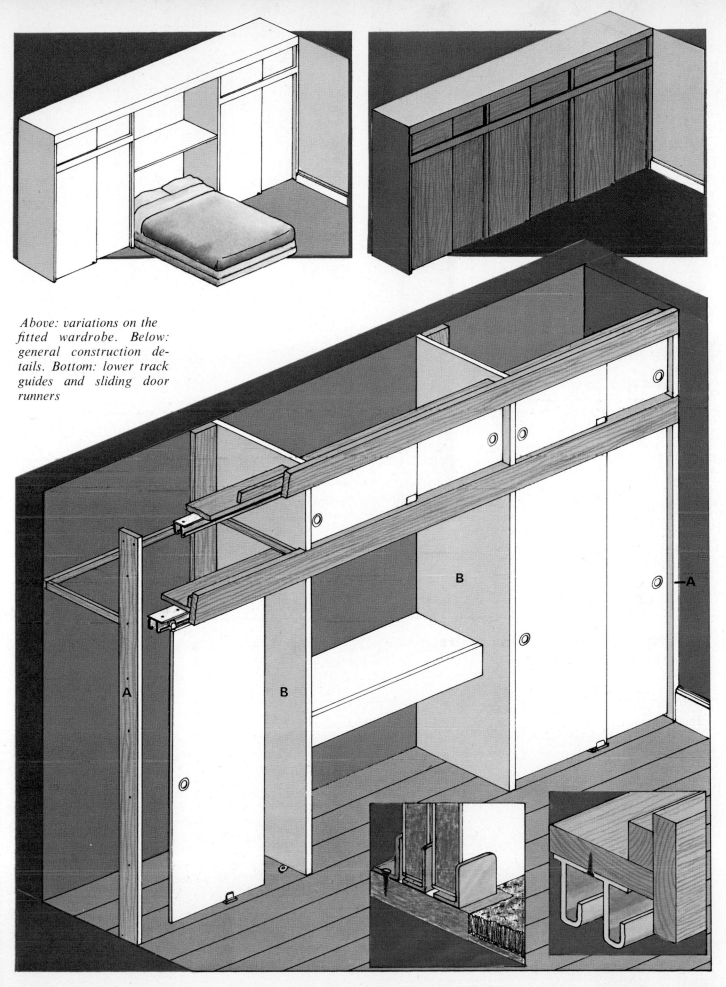

Above: variations on the fitted wardrobe. Below: general construction details. Bottom: lower track guides and sliding door runners

BUILDING A FITTED KITCHEN

Planning the kitchen

The easiest way to lay out the kitchen is to prepare a plan. Draw it out using a scale of say 10cm on the plan for every metre of the room. Cut out shapes to scale for the cooker, sink, refrigerator and any other fixed components. Then try different arrangements to make the layout as convenient as possible. But remember to keep the sink near the waste outlet and the cooker near the power supply. Most kitchen equipment manufacturers supply free catalogues with many planning ideas.

To combat condensation place the cooker against an outside wall in order to facilitate the installation of an extractor fan and ducted collecting hood. Place the washing machine next to the cooker extractor so that this will then serve a dual purpose.

Draw the final layout carefully and use it to plan out the dimensions of the fittings. The working surface height should be 900mm above the floor but can, of course, be varied to suit individual needs. Pay particular attention to the cabinet doors. Decide which way they should open and the type of hinges to be used. This example shows a technique which can be adapted to units of any size. The end and central dividers made from veneered chipboard are the same no matter how long the unit is. The basic framework can then be fitted with cupboards, drawers and other fittings to suit the planned layout.

Location of the central dividers must allow for any fitted sink, cooker hob or other fittings. They should be positioned if possible so that standard panel widths can be used for the main cupboard doors. They should also be positioned so that ready-made drawers will fit snugly in between them.

Design the working surface as a completely independent part of the cupboard unit so that it will simply drop over the unit to cover fixing screws and joints. Avoid joints in the laminate covering wherever possible. Drop-in type sinks are ideal for flush laminate tops since they can be located anywhere. To accommodate the conventional rectangular top consisting of sink and draining board, design the base unit to allow the top to drop neatly into position. Where a working surface abuts this type of sink the joint must be completely water sealed using a flexible purpose-made sealant.

Building the basic unit

After making a drawing of the unit showing the dimensions and locations of shelves and drawers, cut the end and centre dividers from a panel of material of the correct width. Carefully mark and saw out the plinth recess (ends) and batten recesses (divider). Cover the visible cut edges of the plinth recess with an appropriate edge trim material. Cut the two top horizontal cross members from 75mm × 25mm softwood. Then use these to measure out the length for the full length base shelf, cut to the same width as the ends.

It will probably be necessary to cut away the top part of one of the dividers to make room for the sink. Measure the sink depth and mark it on the drawing so that you know where to position the divider and how much to trim off the top.

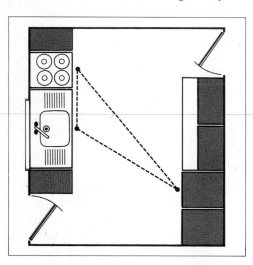

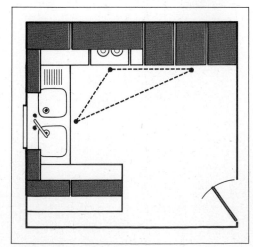

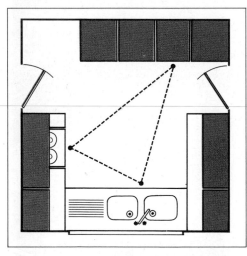

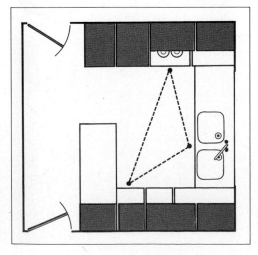

When planning a kitchen layout, make maximum use of storage possibilities including wall units and peninsular units as shown in these layouts. Keep the distances between sink, cooker and fridge as short as possible because these appliances are most used. Here are four typical layouts. Top left: this is not a good arrangement as the pathway between the house and garden crosses the working paths. Top right: this arrangement is a little better but the through route still crosses the work paths

Bottom left: a good arrangement where no through route is needed and storage and cooking areas are closely grouped. Bottom right: the through route here is isolated from the compact food preparation area

This construction system can be extended and modified to suit almost any kitchen base unit required, with or without drawers or other fixtures. In this example, drawers have been constructed from timber and hardboard, but plastic drawer kits can be used. Instead of the all-over sink top, an inset sink can be fitted into a worktop (see overleaf). Drawer and/or false fronts and cupboard doors are surface fixed to hide the divider edges

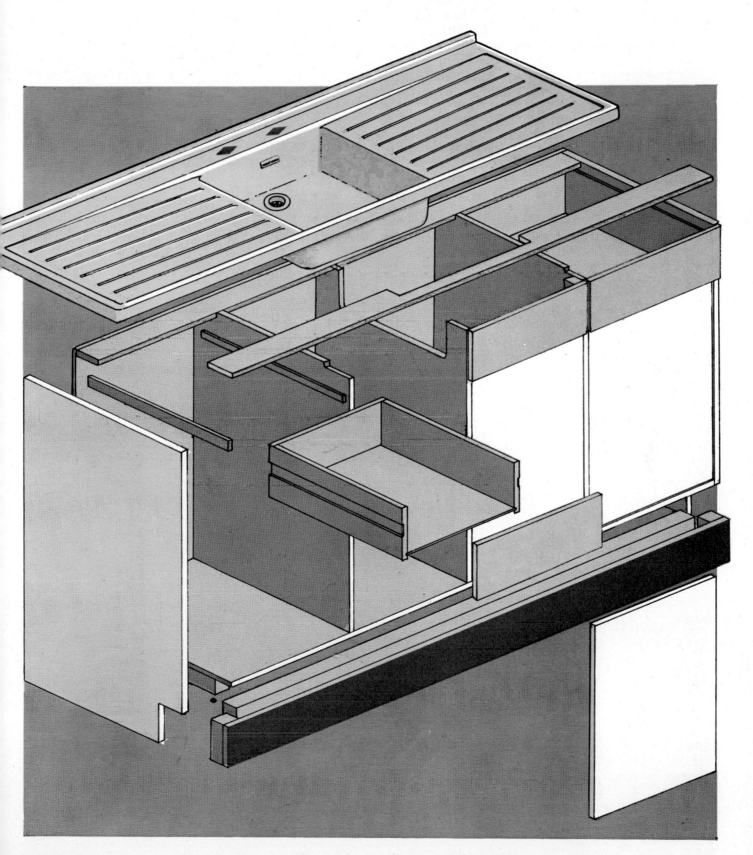

Lay the ends and dividers together on a flat surface, back edge to back edge in pairs and, using a soft pencil, carefully mark the location of the base shelf and any intermediate shelves. Refer to the sketch to locate all battens supporting shelves or drawers. Next mark the location of dividers on both softwood cross-members and on the base shelf.

Drill and fit end battens to the base shelf and then fix the shelf by screws from the underside to all the dividers. Fix the softwood cross-members to the dividers.

To complete the assembly fix the ends by screws to the base shelf through batten and to the cross-members.

Cut the back from enamelled hardboard with dimensions taken direct from the assembled unit. Note that the back panel terminates at the lower edge of the base shelf. The back may be either pinned in position or fixed with screws, after any necessary cut-outs have been made for waste fittings and tap connections. If the back is cut squarely and checked with a large square, the frame will automatically be square if the back edges line up.

For the plinth use a matt black finish which will not show the scuffs from shoes and brooms. Simply paint a piece of plain chipboard with two coats of matt black after assembly. Alternatively fit a strip of black plastic laminate after assembly.

Cut the plinth and screw battens along the top and two sides. Fix it to the ends and base shelf with screws.

Fit a blanking plate opposite the sink to conceal the underside of the bowl.

Now fit cupboard doors and drawers to the unit. Build drawers from purpose-made plastic components faced with plastic veneered chipboard panels to match the main unit. To fit the drawer fronts accurately, first fit the drawer and runners in the unit and then hold up and fit the fronts in turn starting from the top and working down. In this way each front can be levelled with the one above. Full details for fitting the fronts to the assembled drawers are included with the plastic kit parts.

Hang the doors using either the lift-off type hinge or the lay-on type. Fit shelves after main construction using purpose-made removable plastic supports.

On site fixing

Place the unit without its top in its final position. House walls are seldom completely accurate, so some adjustment is often necessary for a neat and level fixing. Check levels in both directions using a spirit level. Generally it is the front to back level that will need some adjustment and this can be carried out by trimming the bottom edge of the ends. Mark any additional holes necessary for plumbing on the unit and cut them before the unit is finally fixed.

Provided the unit is firmly and accurately sited, fix the unit to the wall with four screws, fitted through the back and into wall plugs. The top, including the sink, is the last component to be fixed. In kitchens with more than one unit such as a sink and hob unit, it is best to fit all the units first, then fit the worktop continuously over everything.

Hob unit

This unit is built in much the same way as the sink unit. If your kitchen is arranged in an L-shape it is best to attach one unit to the next. Plan the units so that the end of one fits neatly over one opening of the next unit. Avoid wasting the corner space by cutting a large opening in the divider next to it.

Instructions supplied with the hob unit will probably specify an asbestos lining to the underside housing which should be carefully fitted for safety.

Fitting a sink/drainer top

A combined sink/drainer top fits directly over the unit. The working top is made to fit tight against the stainless steel edge with a sealer between to prevent leaks. Check the fit of the top by holding it against the unit. It may be necessary to trim away part of the softwood cross members to provide clearance for the bowl and to make small notches for the steel edge to seat properly. The drop-in type sinks and hob plates are fixed in a different way by cutting holes in the finished working top.

Working top

With the cupboard units in place, measure for the counter-top.

The core of the working top is cut from 18mm thick blockboard which is much more resistant to warping than chipboard. Plan the main top so that if possible it can be cut from one sheet of blockboard. Where joins are necessary then these should be arranged over the centre of a cupboard area, rather than over a divider, so that a strengthening block may be fixed to the underside. Note that the working top is designed to project approximately 25mm over the top front edge of the cupboard units in the form of a lip consisting of a strip of 25mm square softwood.

With the blockboard cut to shape, fix the edge lip with

A sink/drainer top must fit closely over the base unit. An inset sink gives a central bowl with worktops either side – but draining crockery is a problem. Long worktops can be joined as shown. Cover the join with laminate

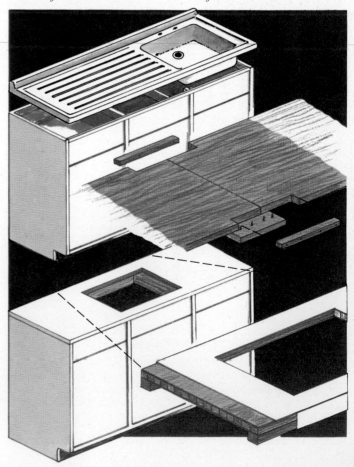

screws from the underside. Make sure that the softwood strip lines up perfectly with the edge of the blockboard. Plane off any parts that are not flush and straight.

Face the visible edges of the top with a strip of plastic laminate. Proceed carefully when applying the trim to keep it from going out of alignment. Take care also so that the trim does not bridge any internal curves. Hold the free end of material well away from the adhesive-coated edge with one hand while pressing the edges together with the other hand. Trim the top and bottom edges using a smoothing plane.

Cut the laminate for the countertop to shape allowing an approximately 3mm overlap all round. Spread contact adhesive on both mating surfaces. Once the adhesive has set, align the laminate before gluing it down. Use strips of timber between the adhesive coated surfaces as the laminate is being manoeuvred into position. Then remove the strips one by one as final contact is made. Finally trim and sand the edges using a plane and glasspaper.

When cutting the aperture for an inset sink, bore holes at the corners and join them with jig-saw or pad-saw cuts. Experience with a jig-saw will enable you to go all around in one go. Bottom: fitting twin sinks

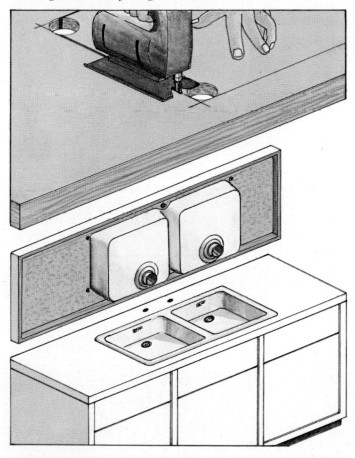

Construction of a hob unit (left) and an eye-level oven enclosure. The latter incorporates ventilation holes to admit cooling air. To use the bottom as a cupboard, the inlet holes can be put at the back or sides

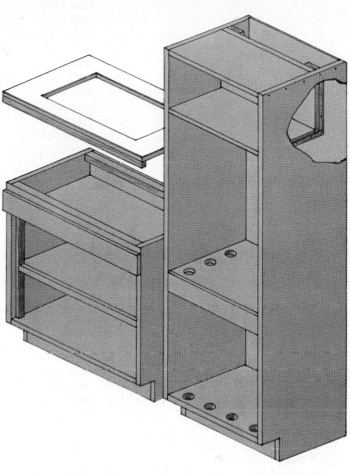

After carefully marking (and checking) the sink and hob plate, cut holes in the top using either a power jig saw or a pad-saw. Start by drilling a hole within the cut-out area to provide a starting point for the saw.

Oven unit

It is important to read the manufacturer's instructions and specifications before planning the oven unit in order to provide adequate clearance and ventilation.

The unit is constructed using the same techniques but different dimensions from the other units. First cut the ends to length. Then cut the plinth recess and face the front edge with edge trim before marking the locations of the various shelves. Cut the shelves to size and make ventilation holes to the oven manufacturer's specification. Use a holesaw to make large diameter holes of this type. Where this is not available drill a small hole and then enlarge it to the required diameter using either a power jig-saw or pad-saw.

Assemble three pieces of veneered chipboard in the form of a three-sided box, as a high level storage cupboard. Make it to allow ventilation through the complete unit. After fitting joint battens to the ends of the shelves screw them to the two sides. Finally fit the back to make sure the unit is stable and square.

Fitting the drop-in sink and hob plate

Manufacturers of the drop-in type sinks and hob plates use differing methods of attachment. Some supply a templet as a guide for cutting out the hole in the working top. It is also necessary to apply a sealer sometimes supplied by the manufacturer between the bowl rim and laminate to prevent water seepage.

stepladders

scaffold board

paint kettle

paste brush

crevice brush

cutting in brush

brushes

wire brush

roller and tray

blow lamp

paint pads

glass paper

sponge

stripping knives and shavehooks

putty knife

136

PAINTING INDOORS

A lot of money can be saved by doing decorating jobs yourself. The cost of having painting, papering and wall-covering jobs done is high and with the proper tools and techniques the home handyman can do excellent work. It is a useful exercise to estimate the cost of materials for a decorating job and to compare this cost with a tradesman's fee. The saving is considerable. And doing your own decorating will give you the satisfaction of having beautified and increased the value of your home.

Two kinds of paint are commonly used indoors; emulsion, which can be thinned with water and oil-base paint which is thinned with white spirit. Both types contain pigments which are held together by various forms of synthetic resins. In oil-base paints, the resin binder is dissolved in solvent which enables a very smooth, even coat to be applied.

The large range of paints available can be confusing. Many of the different names such as alkyds, vinyl, acrylic, co-polymer and polyurethane are simply descriptions of the binders or additives which give each paint its individual quality. These qualities are important in making a selection.

Prices vary according to the quality of paint. The easiest type of paint for the beginner to apply is non-drip jelly paint which contain additives which make it almost gelatinous. Large quantities of this thixotropic paint can be picked up on the brush without dripping. Once applied it spreads easily and often one coat of this paint will cover as well as two coats of ordinary paint. Thixotropic paint does not need to be stirred and it should not be thinned. Both emulsion and oil-base paints are available in this jelly form.

Other oil-base paints can be difficult to apply as drips must be smoothed repeatedly to create an even surface. If possible, position work to be painted with oil-base paint horizontally to minimise dripping. Oil-base paints are available in several finishes; gloss, semi-gloss, which is often called eggshell or lustre, and matt. Surfaces to be painted with oil-base paints must first be primed and, if gloss paint is used, an undercoat is necessary. It is advisable to paint a surface already painted with gloss with oil-base paint.

Emulsion paints are more pleasant to use as spills and drips can be cleaned up with water and there is less odour. But emulsion is not suitable for woodwork except if used as an undercoat for oil-base paint. Emulsion paints are available in matt, satin or sheen finish.

Matt finishes are generally favoured for walls and ceilings. Because of their high pigment content they tend to be better, litre for litre than gloss, for covering over old colours. The high resin content of gloss makes it stronger than emulsion and easier to clean. For these reasons it is ideal for woodwork.

A primer is necessary to cover unpainted surfaces which are either new or have been stripped. The type of primer used depends on the type of material being painted, whether it is wood, plaster or metal. There are all-purpose primers available which can be used on any surface. Undercoats are used to cover previous sound coats of paint before applying the final new coat.

Equipment

To produce really good results it is essential to be thorough with preparation and to use the right equipment.

A stripping knife, with a 75mm wide blade is used to scrape paint off flat surfaces. Triangular or shaped shavehooks are useful for scraping paint around mouldings and in awkward corners. And a paraffin or gas blowlamp is used for melting paint on woodwork so that it can be scraped off easily. Use a glasspaper block for rubbing down paintwork and a filling knife to repair bad cracks in plaster.

Pour the paint into a paint kettle or any container with a handle. Tie an old nylon stocking over the top of the paint kettle and pour the paint through it to strain out dust and paint skin which can mar the finish.

The type of ladder or scaffolding needed will depend on the job. Always be sure to set up a sturdy working platform on which the paint kettle can rest securely.

Besides a good set of overalls to protect clothing and dust sheets to lay over the floor, the only other equipment necessary is applicators. There are three popular methods of applying paint; by brush, roller and paint pad. These all produce a good finished job.

Left: stir paint with a lifting, rotary action. Right: strain paint through a nylon stocking to remove bits

Brushes

There are brushes made of natural or synthetic bristle to suit all requirements. Most indoor jobs can be done with 50, 25 and 12mm brushes; 100 and 150mm brushes are used for walls and ceilings.

There are special brushes with angled tips for painting difficult places like window frames. An old narrow brush snipped off at an angle will make an adequate brush for this purpose. A crevice brush has a long wire handle which can be

Brushes that are well looked after will repay the care with many years of service. Here are tips on cleaning, renovating, and storing between painting sessions

scraping bristles on to newspaper

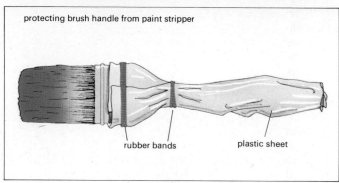
protecting brush handle from paint stripper

rubber bands   plastic sheet

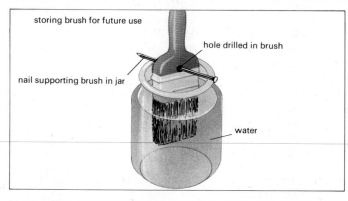
storing brush for future use

hole drilled in brush

nail supporting brush in jar

water

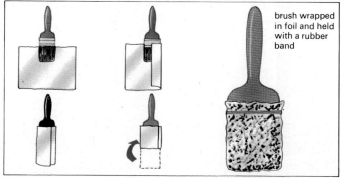
brush wrapped in foil and held with a rubber band

bent to any angle and is used to paint behind pipes and radiators. Good brushes are expensive but if they are well cared for they will last for a long time. All new brushes lose hairs at first, so break them in on undercoat.

It is important to clean and store brushes correctly after using. Lay the brush on newspaper and run a scraper from the handle end of the bristles to the tips to squeeze out excess paint. Do the same on both sides of the brush. Use a solvent or proprietary brush cleaner to remove any paint from the body of the brush and then clean the bristles thoroughly with solvent. Then wash with soap and water, rinse and dry.

Emulsion paint can be cleaned off brushes by simply working the bristles under cold running water. Be careful not to distort the brush by rough handling.

If paint has dried and hardened on a brush it will have to be soaked in paint stripper before cleaning. Wrap the handle in plastic sheet secured with an elastic band to prevent the stripper from removing the varnish.

After the brush has been cleaned and allowed to dry, put an elastic band around the bristles before storing to help retain the shape of the brush. If a painting job is to continue for a few days, save the tedious process involved in cleaning oil-base paints by leaving the brush in a jar of water overnight, with the level covering the bristles. Support the brush so that the bristles do not squash against the bottom of the jar. Before using the brush, shake out the excess water and wipe the bristles on a dry rag or newspaper.

Alternatively, dip the brush into the paint to collect a dollop of paint. Then wrap the bristles in aluminium foil. Use an elastic band over the foil to keep it in place. When the brush is needed again remove the foil and it is ready for use.

Rollers

Paint can be applied more quickly with a roller than by brush and often with a more even finish. They are particularly useful on ceilings and walls where brushwork is tiring. But rollers use more paint than brushes and they cannot be used in very tight corners. Use a 25mm brush to cut in at corners. On a rough surface, rollers will not spread paint evenly.

Rollers can be used with nearly all paints but work best with emulsion. Felt, foam and synthetic fur are used as coverings for rollers and replacement sleeves can be purchased. Foam rollers can distort and splash paint and therefore it is better to use synthetic fur rollers with long pile for a rough surface and short pile for a smooth surface.

When using a roller it is essential to have a step-ladder with a platform at the top, on which the paint tray can be placed when working. Many trays have special feet for hooking on to the working surface.

The biggest disadvantage with rollers is that if work is stopped they must be thoroughly cleaned with solvent for oil-base paint and warm, soapy water for emulsion. Rollers are therefore impractical for painting small areas. Wrap rollers in paper once dry.

Paint pads

A paint pad consists of a fine pile mounted on a foam pad fixed to a handle. Some types have throwaway foam pads which can be easily replaced. There are sets available which contain pads of different shapes and sizes. The sets include a tray from which to load the pads with paint. The trays have built-in scrapers on which to wipe off excess paint. If the pad has a paint wheel the correct quantity of paint is automatically picked up from the tray.

Use a large pad for applying emulsion paints. Paint doors and skirtings with a medium-size pad and use a special small frame pad for window frames, radiators, fluted woodwork and other hard to reach places. The paint pad is probably the fastest type of applicator for painting large, smooth surfaces with emulsion. And they are excellent for painting over textured surfaces.

Before using a new paint pad, rub it over your hand to remove any loose pile. It is a good idea to rinse the new pad in clean water and allow it to dry before using it. Paint hardens quickly on the pile and can ruin the pad. As soon as you have finished using emulsion paints rinse the pad in water, rubbing lightly to ease the paint out of the pile. Remove oil-base paints by washing the pad in white spirit and then in warm soapy water.

Pads are useful for applying glue size to walls when wallpapering or for soaking wallpaper before stripping.

Preparation

The work done at this stage matters almost more than the actual painting itself. No amount of paint will hide bad defects in the surface underneath. Before starting work, remove door fittings and other obstructions, lift fitted carpets and take down curtains.

Preparing woodwork

Paintwork which is sound should be washed down with soapy water if the paint is oil-base. Roughen the surface with abrasive paper to provide a receptive surface for the new paint. Sand damaged areas thoroughly, first filling holes and cracks with wood filler. Emulsion painted surfaces need only be washed down after removing any flaky paint. Any bare woodwork should be primed before painting.

If the paint is damaged and sanding will not achieve a smooth surface, the paint will have to be stripped off using a scraper and a blowlamp or chemical stripper.

Removing paint with just a scraper is hard work and should be restricted to small areas. Scrapers with serrated edges for scoring the surface and a flat blade for scraping off the paint are useful tools. Scrapers are available in various widths for different jobs.

Burning off old paint is a quicker and less difficult method of stripping. The paint is melted by the heat of the blowlamp and comes away from the surface making it easy to scrape off. Be careful not to concentrate the flame on one spot for too long or it will damage the wood. If the wood becomes charred, it will have to be sanded down before painting. Blowlamps are not suitable for removing paint from plaster walls, asbestos surfaces or too close to window glass. After burning off the paint finish the surface with abrasive paper.

Chemical strippers are useful for removing paint around windows. But these chemicals can be dangerous to use and can cause serious burns to skin. Follow the manufacturer's instructions before using and handle with extreme care. Wear rubber gloves when working with chemical strippers. After the chemical has loosened the paint it can be scraped off. The surface is then cleaned with white spirit and sanded smooth. The paint which has been stripped off should be wrapped in paper and burned to prevent it from damaging other surfaces.

If the woodwork is blistered or bubbled, the damaged paint can be cut out and the area refinished. Fill the holes with wood filler, sand smooth, and prime the surface.

Crazing results from applying different types of paint on top of each other which expand and contract at different rates causing cracks. If large areas are damaged by crazing they must be stripped and repainted. Smaller areas can be sanded smooth.

Woodwork in old houses will have been finished with varnish or wood stain. Sand it down to remove as much of the finish as possible. Even then paint may not stick very well. To be certain of a good result, strip off the varnish and treat the woodwork as though it were new.

After stripping woodwork, apply knotting to knots and resinous patches to prevent bleed-through and fill any small holes and cracks with wood filler. When the filler has hardened, sand flush. Prime any surfaces which have been stripped back to bare wood before painting. Oily and resinous woods require special primers.

Preparing metal surfaces

Clean metal window frames with a wire brush wearing goggles to protect the eyes. Sand off unevenness and rust spots and treat with a rust inhibitor. Clean off and renew loose putty. Use a suitable chemical stripper to remove badly damaged paintwork. Treat other metal surfaces such as radiators and pipes similarly. If the paintwork is sound, sand it smooth before applying fresh paint. Prime all surfaces rubbed back to bare metal with metal primer before painting.

Left: remove paint on narrow sections with a shavehook.
Right: use a straight-edge guide when patching corners

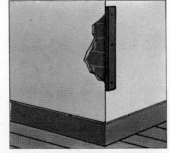
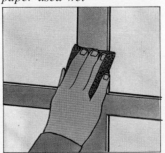

Left: good paintwork is merely keyed before repainting.
Right: keep the blowlamp moving when paintburning

Left: a wire brush deals with rusty window frames. Right: key paintwork with wet-or-dry paper used wet

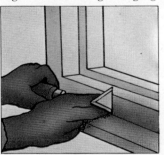

Left: strip paint on mouldings with a shavehook. Right: for large, flat areas, a stripping knife is best

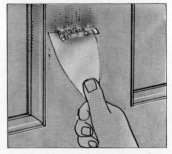

Preparing walls and ceilings

Allow a drying-out period of about one year before using gloss paint on the walls of a new house. Emulsion can be applied from new as it allows the wall to breathe and continue drying out. Sponge down walls with soap and warm water and then rinse clean. Use abrasive paper on gloss finishes to form a receptive surface for the new paint.

If the walls were painted with distemper, this will have to be stripped off if it is loose or flaking. A sound surface can be just washed over and then emulsion painted. Some distemper will wash off with warm water and a detergent. Use a sponge and stripping knife and be careful not to scratch the plaster. If an oil-base distemper does not respond to prolonged soaking, use a steam stripper to remove it.

Make good any defects in plaster surfaces. Fill them with cellulose filler and then sand down.

If a plaster surface has large cracks, hack away loose or damaged material and apply fresh plaster with a trowel. Allow to harden and continue adding layers until the new plaster is not quite level with the surrounding plaster. Scratch lines to make a receptive surface for the top layer of plaster and leave to harden. Apply the top layer with a trowel and finish by smoothing with a wet trowel.

If large areas are damaged, new plaster must be applied to repair the surface. When an external corner is damaged, line up a batten on one edge of the corner and nail it to the wall. Plaster up to it and carefully remove the batten when the plaster has hardened. Then hold the batten along the finished edge and plaster the other edge of the corner. When dry, smooth off sharp edges with abrasive paper.

If walls are mouldy, the surface must be treated with a fungicide before repainting with a special mould resistant paint. Find the cause of the mould before repainting. (See page 42.)

Walls may be affected by efflorescence, a white deposit which forms on the surface. The area must be stripped, allowed to dry and finished with an alkali-resistant primer before painting.

Painting over wallpaper can cause problems as the paint may cause bubbles or even pull the paper off the wall. The inks in the paper may bleed through the paint, ruining the job. If painting over wallpaper, test a small area for bleeding and check the entire surface of the wall to see that the paper is well stuck down. Bleeding can be prevented by using a suitable primer.

Start painting a ceiling above a window and work towards the opposite wall in strips to keep a wet edge

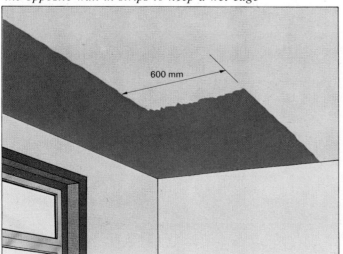

PAINTING

Allow any dust from the preparation stage to settle overnight before beginning to paint. Remove as much furniture from the room as possible. Cover the floor and remaining pieces of furniture with dust sheets.

The correct order for painting is ceiling, walls and finally woodwork. Always work so that an entire section is finished in one session. A half-finished wall will leave a line which will be visible through the finished surface. Always paint methodically. With a ceiling, start at one end of the room above a window. Start painting at the point where the ceiling meets the wall and continue by painting in 600mm strips from wall to wall across the ceiling to the opposite end of the room. If using a roller, or pad brush, paint in corners where they cannot reach with a brush and then join up to the brush marks with the pad or roller. A pair of step-ladders and a scaffold board make an excellent platform from which to paint the ceiling.

When painting walls with oil-base paint, divide them into manageable squares. Start in a top corner and apply the paint evenly in vertical strokes. Then join the vertical strokes with cross-strokes and lay-off, smoothing gently back into the painted area. Top coat and undercoat should be brushed on in the same direction to avoid a pattern showing through. Apply only a single coat of paint at a time and do not overload the brush. Work in squares small enough not to dry before adjacent squares are started. Emulsion is applied in bands across the wall working from top to bottom.

A spray gun can be used to apply paint to walls or ceilings. The area to be sprayed is masked off to confine the paint to the desired area. Follow manufacturer's instructions concerning thinning paint and using the spray gun. It is important to spray from the correct distance and to work parallel with the surface. Wear a face mask when spray painting and be sure the room is well ventilated. It will take a little practice to be able to apply the paint evenly. In general, spraying is not suitable for domestic work.

Paint on woodwork should be applied in the direction of the grain. Apply a primer if the wood is bare and both an undercoat and top coat. Complete a whole door or other section without stopping for any length of time. With panelled doors, start at the top and paint the panels first. Work from both ends of a panel towards the middle. Do not apply too much paint to mouldings, or the paint will drip and collect in the grooves.

Deal with walls in convenient areas, taking trouble to keep the paint edge wet—easier with paint pads

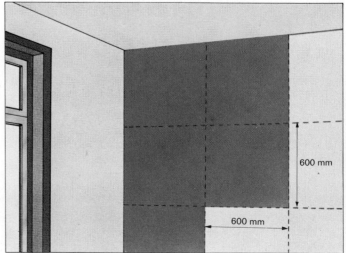

With sash and casement windows work inside out, painting the woodwork closest to the glass first and then working outward to the window frame painting this last. Take care on narrow sections where paint is the most likely to run. Smooth any drips before they harden.

If the surface of the paint is grainy, this is usually a result of dust settling while it is still wet. The dry surface can be smoothed with fine glass paper and a fresh coat applied. Drips on the paint must be allowed to dry before sanding smooth and applying a final coat. Should the old paint be visible, another layer of new paint will be needed to cover it. If the coat of paint fails to stick to the surface, it must be sanded smooth when it has dried and another undercoat and top coat should be applied. Paint which does not dry may be the result of painting on grease or wet primer. The paint may have to be stripped off and the surface repainted. As the paint is still wet, this can be done with a scraper.

To avoid having to scrape paint off glass after painting window frames, use masking tape around the edges of the glass, or hold a thin metal shield tight up against the frame while painting. The tape should be removed as soon as possible or it may be extremely difficult to remove.

DECORATING TIMBER FLOORS

Timber floors can be wax polished, sealed with a polyurethane varnish or stained. Wax polish is the easiest of the finishes to apply and should be used over an existing finish. Polyurethane varnish and stain should be applied to bare timber.

Before sanding down and smoothing the floor, scrape off any existing varnish and sweep over the floor. If a large surface has to be sanded down it may be wise to hire a special floor sanding machine. If linseed oil has previously been used on the floor, it may not be possible to remove it completely as it will have soaked well into the wood.

Stains

There are water, oil and spirit stains and all must be sealed after application. Oil stains are quick-drying and can be bought ready for use. Spirit stains are also quick-drying. They are made by dissolving powder in methylated spirits and are available ready-mixed in bright colours and natural wood shades.

The cheapest and easiest to use are water stains, made by dissolving crystals or powder in water. Water stains can be lightened with a wet cloth if the stain turns out too dark. Before applying any stain it is advisable to test it on a similar piece of wood so that you can be sure of what to expect.

Apply water stain with a non-fluffy cloth, working along the grain of the wood. To achieve an even finish work quickly over the whole area, ensuring that wet edges are joined before they dry. Try not to go over the same area twice. Once dry, rub down the surface and brush it clean before applying a sealer.

Proprietary sealers, which bring out the grain of the wood, will provide a durable finish and are easy to apply. They are worked into the timber with a brush or clean rag. After each coat rub down with fine wire wool and wipe clean before applying a further coat.

Cellulose lacquers, available clear and in colours, will dry quickly to a hard finish. These should be applied with a good quality soft bristle brush, always brushing in the direction of the wood grain. Coats should be allowed to dry before rubbing down and applying further coats.

numbers show order in which to paint.

Mask (left) or shield glass when painting windows

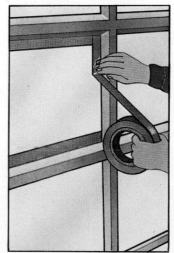

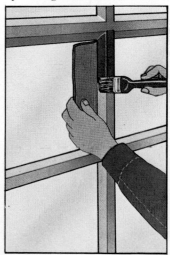

Polyurethane varnish

One-pack and two-pack types are available in both matt and high gloss finishes. They give a hard finish which is resistant to heat, water and abrasion. They can be used on bare wood or as a protective coating over a wood stain. There are also colour polyurethanes which stain and polish the wood in a single operation.

One-pack is sufficient for normal use and can be applied immediately. Two-pack, which gives a slightly harder finish, has to be mixed first. Polyurethane varnishes should be applied with a good quality brush along the grain of the wood. Rub down and wipe each coat before applying further coats.

PAINTING OUTDOORS

Most houses will need to be redecorated outside every five years. This is a big job and one which requires great care. There is always a temptation to skimp on preparation but then the overall finish will look noticeably less attractive. If the surface is not properly prepared, the paint may peel or crack and the surface will have to be repainted.

Damp, heat and frost affect exterior paintwork. Dampness will cause the paint to peel, heat may cause it to blister and frost may cause the gloss paint to look flat. Ideally, weather conditions for exterior painting should be warm and dry, and windless, preferably after a dry period. The best time to paint is usually in late summer or early autumn, when exposed timber has had a good chance to dry out.

Start painting in the morning as soon as the dew has dried and stop in good time for the paint to be able to dry before the evening dew falls.

Applicators

Choose a 100mm to 150mm brush which will hold plenty of paint for exterior painting. It is as well to use an old brush if possible, as the roughness of exterior surfaces soon wears down bristles. If using a roller, use an old one if possible or buy an exterior grade shaggy nylon roller which will last longer on rough surfaces than the softer type used for interior work.

For woodwork and metal window frames, use the same brushes as for interior woodwork or use a pad brush which deals more easily with narrow edges than a conventional brush and produces a very smooth finish. Clean and care for applicators as described for interior painting.

Cover wall surfaces in the area not to be decorated with canvas or polythene. Tie back any wall plants and wrap them in plastic sheet for protection. If paint gets on to glass, remove with a razor blade or commercial paint scraper. Any other spattered surfaces should be cleaned with thinner before the paint dries.

Equipment

Safety is very important with exterior decorating as much of the work is carried out on ladders or scaffolding. For this reason it is essential to work with good equipment of the correct type.

To reach ground floor windows it is sufficient to work on a scaffold board, supported between two step-ladders. Make sure that the step-ladders are both fully open so that they are balanced. Working above ground floor level requires the use of extension ladders or scaffold towers. Never over-reach when working at height or to improvise with equipment.

Ladder safety is essential. Bear these points in mind

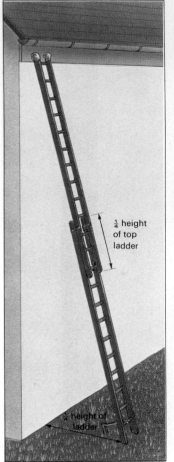

Ladder tied to eye-hook
pads made from rags

wooden blocks on uneven ground

large board on soft ground

sandbag on solid ground

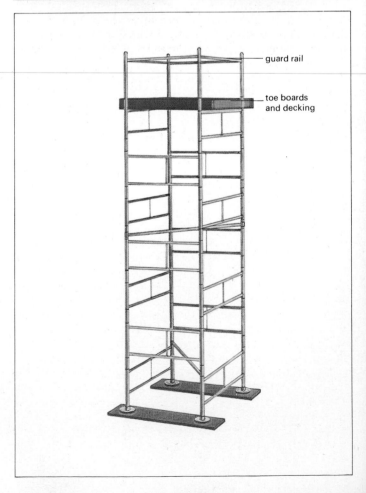
guard rail
toe boards and decking

The best type of ladders to use are extension ladders because they are easy to adjust to the height of work. Examine the ladder carefully for cracked and rotten rungs or loose joints. Never work from a ladder which has been painted as it is impossible to spot structural defects. Choose a ladder which is at least as tall as the highest point to be reached. Rope-operated ladders are best if extension is to be more than about 5 metres and they are much easier for one person to handle.

Wrap rags around the top of the ladder stiles to prevent damage to the paintwork. Never rest the ladder on glass, plastic guttering or glazing bars. Use an S-shape hook to hang a paint kettle to a rung allowing you to paint with one hand and hold on with the other.

Erect the ladder by pushing the foot of it against the base of the wall and walking towards the wall, raising the ladder gradually into the vertical position. Extend the ladder as required, then pull out the bottom of the ladder from the wall to a distance of about one quarter of the ladder height.

If the ground is uneven, place wood blocks under the ladder to form a firm base and tie the bottom rung to a peg, knocked into the ground. On soft ground, stand the ladder on a wide board, with a batten screwed across the board to act as a backstop to prevent the ladder from slipping. Drive stakes into the ground and tie the sides of the ladder to them for support. On a hard surface place a sandbag or other heavy object against the foot of the ladder to prevent it from slipping. Tie the top of the ladder to a ring bolt, screwed into the fascia. Don't over-extend the ladder and make sure that at least three rungs of the top ladder overlap the section below. To paint a wide overhang, fix a stay to the ladder which will position it farther out from the wall. Remember to adjust the distance at the base accordingly. If the ladder is to be moved along, first lift it clear of the house. Dragging it along gutters or over brickwork and rendering can cause serious damage. If work is being done on the roof or over an asbestos garage roof, work from a crawling board, which can be hooked securely over the roof ridge.

Sectional scaffold towers are the easiest and safest type from which to work. The large working platforms allow work to be done more quickly and a greater area to be covered before the scaffolding has to be moved. The main disadvantages with towers is that they take longer to erect than ladders and they cannot be used in narrow passages or where the ground is not firm and smooth. The height of a free-standing tower should not exceed more than three times the minimum base dimension. Scaffold towers can be fitted with castor wheels, each with its own locking device. Make certain that all four wheels are securely locked before climbing the frame. The decking boards, guard rails and posts and the toe boards can be fixed at different heights on the tower.

Order of work

The basic rule with exterior decorating is to start at the top of the house and work down, cleaning, repairing and then painting. While the equipment is on site, make any necessary roof repairs. Cure any damp problems before painting.

Divide the job into easily workable sections. Do one side of the house at a time as long spells on a ladder can become strenuous.

Gutters and downpipes

Clean out the gutters and brush and wash them down. Repair any cracks with a bituminous mastic and smooth the surface with a wire brush. If joints between metal sections leak, separate the sections, chip out the old putty joint and renew with metal casement putty. Areas of gutters and pipes affected by rust must first be treated with a rust remover and then primed before being painted. It is a good idea to replace old and badly rusted metal parts with modern plastic ones. (See page 72.)

Paint asbestos gutters with exterior grade emulsion. If metal gutters and pipes were not previously painted with bituminous paint, the interiors of gutters and the outsides of gutters and downpipes can be painted with two coats of good quality exterior gloss paint. Where bituminous paint has been used, apply another coat of it or seal the old surface with an aluminium sealer and apply gloss. If gloss is applied directly to a bituminous surface, the old colour will bleed through.

Plastic pipes and gutters need only be wiped over with a damp cloth and detergent. To paint them a different colour, it is best to wait for about one year after fitting, to ensure that the paint sticks satisfactorily to the plastic. This period allows the rain to wash out any release agent used in the manufacturer's mould. Thoroughly clean the plastic and apply two coats of gloss paint. Primers are too oily and undercoat is too highly pigmented for this purpose.

When painting downpipes it is a good idea to hold a piece of card behind the pipe to protect the wall.

Exterior woodwork

Preparation is much the same as for interior woodwork. Make any necessary repairs to doors and windows and replace any cracked putty. Before working on doors remove all metal fittings except hinges. Rub down all surfaces where paintwork is sound with glasspaper to form a receptive surface for the new paint. If the paintwork has deteriorated and is flaking or peeling, strip it back to bare wood using a blowtorch and scraper. Use a chemical stripper around the glass in doors and windows. Coat all bare wood with a lead-base primer before painting. Primed surfaces can be left for about a week before undercoating becomes necessary. Brush the primer in well, especially into nail holes, crevices and the end grain of wood to provide good adhesion for fillers or putty. When the primer has dried, sand over it lightly and fill holes with putty or wood filler. Use knotting over knots before priming and sand smooth before applying paint.

Window sills are often badly decayed. Scrape out any rotten wood, prime and fill with water resistant filler. Use this filler on other badly damaged surfaces or where the wood grain is irregular. It is best applied with a flat scraper held slightly askew so that surplus filler is forced out to one side. Allow the surface to dry and sand smooth before painting.

Apply an undercoat to all prepared surfaces and two coats of gloss for added protection. Lightly rub down the surface between coats. Gloss coats should follow the undercoat as soon as it is dry. Avoid painting over the edges of doors and windows as the build-up of paint may make it difficult to close them.

It is better to use a good quality varnish on hardwood surfaces rather than paint. If they were painted previously, rub down as much of the old paint as possible and fill the grain with a hardwood filler. When the filler is dry, apply a thinned coat of primer, undercoat and two top coats.

If the house has timber cladding, scrape and rub it down to remove old sealer. Then apply two coats of a suitable wood preservative. Cladding can also be cleaned with dry wire wool and treated with a liquid to restore the colour.

When painting down pipes, protect the wall with a shield

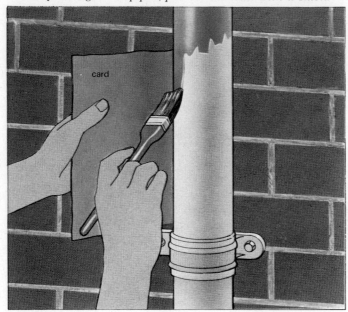

Use a wire brush and weak acid to clean a dirty wall

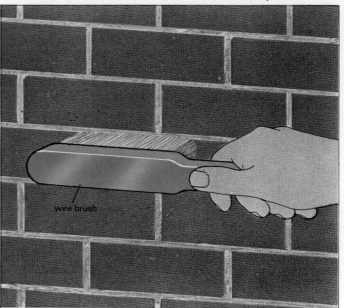

Fill cracks in timber sills with epoxy resin filler

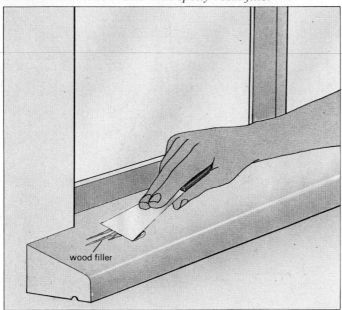

Metal windows

Use a wire brush to clean and remove flaking paint from metal window frames. Coat bare metal with the appropriate metal primer before applying undercoat and top coats.

Exterior walls

Inspect walls carefully for damage. Repoint brickwork where necessary (and replace badly damaged bricks. If facing bricks are in good condition clean them by either brushing them down with a stiff wire brush or rubbing over them with a brick of similar type and colour. Brush on a silicone water-repellent, a colourless liquid which seals the brickwork and prevents efflorescence.

Clean dirty brickwork with a solution of water and 10% spirits of salts which is brushed on, rinsed and brushed down with a wire brush. Remove any moss growth and then sterilise the area with a solution of ordinary household bleach. Always wear goggles when using spirits of salts and keep a supply of fresh, clean water alongside as you work. If the acid is splashed on to bare skin wash immediately with clean water.

Apply two coats of a cement or stone-base paint which is decorative and offers good protection. Alternatively, use an exterior grade emulsion. First seal the surface with a thinned coat of emulsion or a special liquid masonry covering, containing a fungicide to prevent moss or mould growth. This requires only one coat and no sealer and undercoat. Gloss paints are expensive and do not look as attractive on exterior walls.

Decorative finishes such as rendering, pebbledash and roughcast can also be painted with cement paint or exterior grade emulsion. Repair any defects in the surface with mortar before painting. Leave the repairs to set hard before brushing down the walls and painting. Cement paints tend to be the best for filling hairline cracks in rendering. Apply a coat of paint over patched rendering as soon as the repair has dried. Then, starting in a top corner of the wall, apply two full coats over the whole surface. Remember to paint in small sections so as not to allow edges to dry before adjoining sections are painted.

Decorating
Wallpapering

The thickness and weight of a wallpaper is usually an indication of its quality. The thicker, heavier papers are the easiest to handle and are useful for concealing blemishes and minor defects in a wall. Thinner and cheaper papers stretch, fade and tear more easily than good quality ones, so always buy the best that you can afford. It will be cheaper in the long term.

Most wallpaper is machine-printed. Cheaper papers have the design printed directly on to the paper, but with better quality paper the surface is first covered with a solid colour before the pattern is overprinted.

Hand-printed papers produced by block, screen or stencil printing are more expensive, but the quality of printing is superior and the design likely to be exclusive. There are also textured papers with a pattern embossed into the paper during manufacture, flock papers which have a velvety pile and woodchip paper which has bits of sawdust and wood applied to the pulp during manufacture. These papers are hung over lining paper using heavy duty paste. Be careful not to flatten the texture while hanging and do not roll the seams.

Basic wallpapering kit. An extra step-ladder and a scaffold board are useful, particularly when doing ceilings. Shown here is an ordinary large paintbrush for pasting, but a purpose-made paste brush is preferable. Instead of the pasting table, an ordinary flush door, laid on, say, a kitchen table, is an excellent substitute

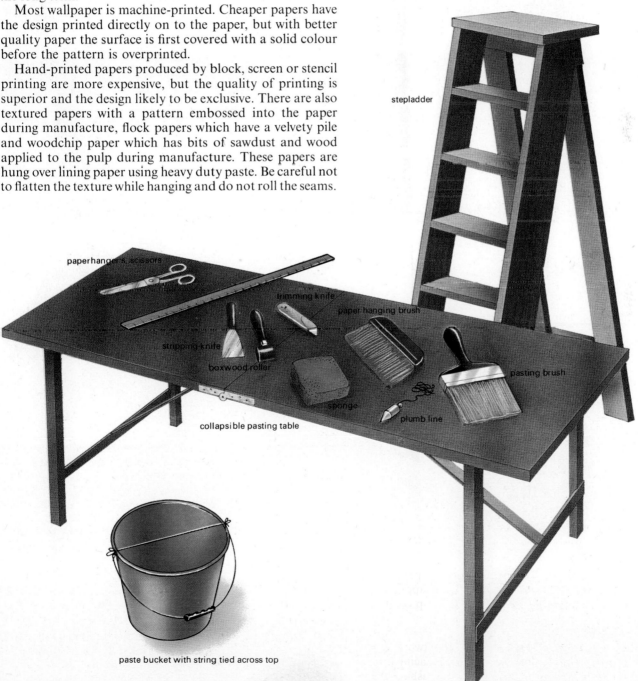

stepladder

paperhanger's scissors

trimming knife

paper hanging brush

stripping-knife

boxwood roller

sponge

pasting brush

plumb line

collapsible pasting table

paste bucket with string tied across top

Soak the paper and remove with a stripping knife

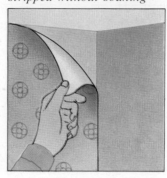
Score washable papers to allow water to penetrate

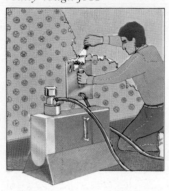
Hire a steam stripper for really tough jobs

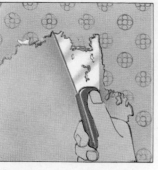
Vinyl wallcoverings can be stripped without soaking

There are special washable papers which are ideal for use in kitchens and bathrooms, where condensation levels are high. They are coated with clear resin which protects the paper from water penetration. Washable papers should be hung using a fungicidal paste.

Estimating

The majority of wallpapers are sold in rolls 10.5m long by 530mm wide. Continental papers are sometimes narrower and custom made papers are available in different sizes. A standard size roll of wallpaper will cover an area of 5 square metres.

Always allow extra when calculating the number of rolls needed for a job, to ensure that there is enough paper to complete the whole job. There is always the danger that the line has been discontinued or that another batch varies slightly in colour.

There are several methods of calculating the number of rolls of wallpaper required, the easiest and probably most accurate is to refer to a manufacturer's chart for average rooms. Alternatively calculate the number of rolls for a job by measuring the height of the room, from skirting boards to ceiling, and dividing this distance into the length of one roll of wallpaper. After taking into account pattern matching, this gives the number of lengths which can be cut from one roll.

Multiply the number of lengths by the trimmed width of the wallpaper roll and divide the answer into the perimeter of the room. This will give the total number of rolls necessary. Round up the figure to the next whole number as it is better to have too many rolls than too few. The extra paper for windows and doors is usually sufficient to compensate for the wastage of paper due to pattern matching.

Tools and equipment

A number of basic tools are required for papering. A large distemper brush is ideal as a paste brush. A pure bristle hanging brush is needed for smoothing the paper on the walls. A paste bucket with a string tied across on which to rest the brush and wipe off excess paste is essential. A pair of paperhanger's scissors, plumb line and a boxwood roller are also needed as well as a trimming knife, sponge or squeegee, stripping knife and abrasive paper.

A sturdy working surface is important for a good job. Ideally the pasting table can be folded away when not in use. Folding metal tables specially made for papering are available or a kitchen table can be used for the job.

Adhesives

Always use the paste recommended by the manufacturer. It should be mixed following instructions and used while fresh. A paste which is too thick is better than one which is too thin and generally the thicker the paper the thicker the paste should be.

There are two main types of paste: starch paste and cellulose paste.

Cellulose pastes are in powder form and are mixed with water. Cellulose pastes are easier to use than starch flour pastes and do not stain the paper badly if spilled but they do hold a lot of water and can cause excessive stretching in some circumstances.

Preparation for papering

Clear the room of as much furniture as possible and cover the remainder with dust sheets. It is best to place furniture which cannot be removed in the middle of the room where it will be out of the way. Take down curtains and roll up non-fitted carpets. Lift fitted carpets or cover with polythene sheet which is also suitable for covering the floor. Before stripping begins, lay newspaper over the floor so that the wet and soggy stripped paper can be rolled up in the newspaper and thrown away. Never attempt to paper over old wallcoverings as the result will probably be disastrous. The new adhesive will probably cause the old surface to lift, unless it has been

Make good with filler

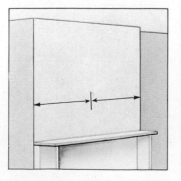
Measure the chimney breast

Mark the central vertical

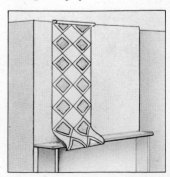
Hang the paper to the line

painted. In any case it is advisable to strip off the old covering.

Conventional wallcoverings can be removed by soaking with warm water and using a wide blade stripping knife. Hold the stripping knife at a slight angle to the wall to avoid digging into the plaster. Strip areas of about 2 square metres at a time. Then dampen the area again and scrape off any small patches of lining paper which may remain on the wall. Start work at the base of the wall and work upwards, soaking the paper with a brush so that the water penetrates through to the paste. Score painted or varnished papers with a wire brush or scraper to allow the water to penetrate. There are various strippers which can be used as an aid, or try adding a few drops of household detergent or some cellulose paste powder to the water. If the wallpaper is exceptionally difficult to remove, or if very large areas are to be stripped, a commercial steam stripper should be used and can easily be hired. This concentrates hot steam on a small area to soften the paste holding the old paper on the wall. However, use with care, following the instructions.

To strip washable wallcoverings it is usually necessary to score the impervious coating to allow water to soak through to the backing paper. It can then be stripped by conventional methods. Modern vinyl wallcoverings are much easier and quicker to strip and can be removed, leaving a base paper in place. Just loosen one corner and peel off the decorative coat without soaking with water or using a chemical stripper.

Wallpaper can be hung over surfaces which have been painted with oil-base paints, provided they are properly prepared. Rub down the surface with abrasive paper and wipe with a damp cloth to remove surface deposits. Emulsioned surfaces need only to be washed down before applying size.

For the best results, surfaces must be as flat and smooth as possible. Scrape away and replace flaking and crumbling plaster. Then wash the walls down and rub over with abrasive paper. Fill any cracks in plaster with a cellulose filler, allow to dry and rub down lightly with abrasive paper. Do not paper over new plaster until it has dried out completely. This usually takes six months but in damp weather it can take even longer. If the walls are papered too soon, moisture in the plaster weakens the adhesive and the alkali salts in the plaster may stain the decorative surface. Apply an emulsion paint in the meanwhile to give an attractive finish and at the same time allow the wall to dry out properly.

Sizing

Applying size to a wall seals the surface so that it does not absorb water too quickly from the paste. If the wall is too absorbent, it will reduce the time in which the paper can be repositioned easily, once on the wall. If size is not applied, it is likely that when the paper dries out, the edges will not stick.

Glue size powder is mixed with water following the manufacturer's instructions. Size which is too strong makes a wall too slippery and makes hanging paper difficult.

When using cellulose pastes, a thinned coat of paste will serve as a size. Add a handful of whiting to the size if the surface being prepared has been painted with oil-base paint. Allow the sized wall to dry before hanging lining paper.

Lining

Lining paper is available in different weights and qualities and provides an even surface of the correct porosity so that maximum adhesion can be obtained when the wallpaper is hung over it. Always use lining paper underneath wallpapers if a high quality surface finish is desired. Good surfaces require only a lightweight lining paper, whereas surfaces with minor blemishes or irregularities can be made more even by applying a thicker lining paper. When a heavy wallpaper is to be used, a thick lining paper should also be used. Try to choose a lining paper as near to the colour of the wallpaper as possible. On surfaces which are likely to move, such as battened wallboards or tongued and grooved woodwork, a cotton-backed lining paper should be used.

Hanging lining paper around a room horizontally ensures that no joins will align with the joins of the decorative paper which is hung vertically. If walls are covered with hair-line cracks or are very uneven, lay a double lining, the first horizontally and the second vertically.

Start hanging the lining paper in the top corner at one end of the room. Cut off strips which will cover the length of the wall and continue for about 12mm around the corner on to the next wall. Hang the next strip of paper butted up to the first.

When working with long lengths, lay the end of the paper on the pasting table with the rest hanging over one edge. Paste the length on the table, then fold back about 400mm over the table, paste to paste. Continue in the same way for the remainder of the cut length, pasting and folding, to make an easy to handle concertina shape. Hold the folded length in one hand and release the paper, one fold at a time, smoothing it out with a brush or roller. Trim off excess paper at ceiling and skirting board levels. Hang vertical lengths using the same method as for hanging decorative paper on walls.

Papering walls

With a plain or slight overall pattern wallpaper, start work always at a window which offers good light and work away from it in both directions continuously to meet and finish in the darkest corner of the room. It will first be necessary to mark off a true vertical line so that the first length of paper, which acts as a guide for the following lengths, is hung

Measure offset of pattern

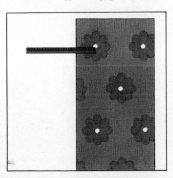

Mark offset from centreline

Hang paper to new line

Clean off paste as you go

correctly. Hang a plumb line about one wallpaper strip width from the starting point and mark off several points along the line. Connect these marks using a pencil and straight-edge. Start work from this side of the window and continue around the room. Take a vertical on the other side of the window, then work around the walls to meet in the same corner.

When using large patterned papers, it is essential that the middle of the main design falls down the vertical centre line of the chimney breast or other main feature of the room for the room to be balanced. The middle of the main pattern will either be on the paper edge or farther in. If it is on the paper edge, hang the first strip of paper on the chimney breast flush with the centre line of the chimney breast. Butt join the next strip the other side of the centre line to complete the main pattern. Establish the centre line by measuring and marking the centre of the wall, then hanging a plumb line through the mark to draw a vertical line.

Order of work for wallpaper pasting. You can work from the left-hand side if you find it easier

centre of wallpaper strip pasted

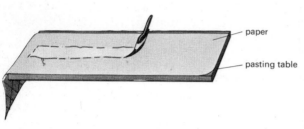

paper

pasting table

pasting edges of paper

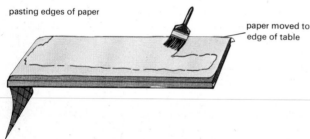

paper moved to edge of table

completed section folded over on to itself

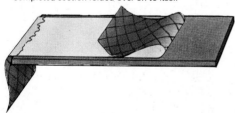

remainder of strip pasted

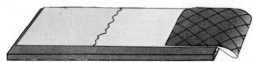

completed strip ready for hanging

148

Cutting paper

Basically, there are two types of pattern in wallpaper; a set pattern in which the pattern repeats horizontally across the width and a drop pattern in which the design is repeated diagonally across the width. Large pattern sequences account for the greatest paper wastage and designs which repeat diagonally across the width are usually more extravagant than horizontal designs.

It is essential to work in good light when pattern matching. Check the colour shades of each roll before starting work. If there are any noticeable variations in shade from one roll to another, the effect can be minimised or even eliminated by using alternate strips when hanging. The sheets are butted against each other when they are hung so the patterns must be matched carefully while the paper is being cut into lengths.

There are no problems when cutting plain, striped or textured wallpapers. It is as well to cut the required number

The type of pattern on a wallcovering can dictate the amount of waste caused by matching

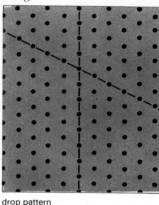

set pattern

drop pattern

wallpaper pattern types

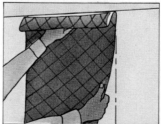

method of carrying pasted strip for hanging

strip positioned at junction of ceiling and wall with 50mm overlap

edge of strip positioned against vertical line on wall

brush paper down on to wall and repeat above process at bottom

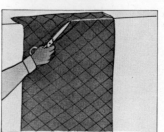

using back edge of scissors to mark trim line.

of strips of paper for the entire room before starting hanging. Before doing so, however, do make absolutely sure you have measured up correctly. Use either a pair of scissors or a metal straight-edge and sharp knife for cutting the paper. Allow a minimum of 50mm at either end of each length for trimming and fitting when hung. Remnants from rolls may come in useful for small areas over doors and windows.

Cutting a paper which has a definite pattern requires much greater skill and care. Lay a length of paper on the pasting table with its patterned side uppermost and locate the main pattern or motif. Cut along a line about 75mm above the main pattern, measure off the required length from this line and add on 75mm to allow for the standard drop pattern. If the pattern has a big drop, there may be quite a lot of wastage. Less wastage may be incurred by using another roll and cutting alternate lengths from the two rolls. Manufacturers usually offer guidance on the length the pattern drops for their designs.

Pasting

Set up the pasting table as near to a light source as possible. Stand the paste bucket nearby in a safe place. Place a length of paper, decorative side down, on the pasting table. Position the paper so that it lines up with both the opposite side and one end of the table. Allow excess paper to fall on the floor. Dip the brush into the paste and wipe off the excess against the string tied across the top of the bucket.

Always paste from the middle of the paper out towards the edges. Never brush in from the edges or paste may get under the paper on to the decorative surface. First coat the paper along the middle section towards the end edge, then paste out towards the opposite edge. Pull the paper back towards you so that the edge of the section still to be pasted is level with the nearside of the table. Paste this section towards the front edge of the table.

The first half of the strip is then complete. Loop the pasted end over to the middle of the length, paste to paste, but do not crease. Then move the folded loop along the table so that it overhangs the end. Paste the second half in the same way as the first and fold it over so that the ends meet in the middle of the strip.

Hanging

Carry the pasted paper over one arm to the wall. Separate the top half of the length and position it on the wall. Slide the paper into position allowing about 50mm at the ceiling line for trimming. Brush down the middle of the paper, working out towards the edges to remove any air bubbles. Repeat at the bottom, leaving a similar trim margin.

Mark where the paper needs to be trimmed along the ceiling and skirting edges by running the back of the scissors along the edge. Gently pull the paper away from the wall and cut along the marked line. Brush the paper back into position and smooth it down. Position the next length of paper on the wall close to the first and slide it into position so that it butts up to the first piece. Smooth down and trim the overlap as for the first strip.

Wrinkles in the paper indicate that there are still air bubbles trapped under the paper. Gently peel back the paper, reposition it then brush out.

Wipe excess paste from skirting boards, ceiling and woodwork as you work. About ten minutes after hanging, gently roll the seams where the sheets meet with the boxwood roller. Do not roll seams of embossed papers because this will flatten the pattern.

Corners

Never attempt to hang a complete width of paper around corners as these are usually out of true and the paper will crease. For inner corners, add on 10mm from the last sheet to the farthest distance into the corner. Cut the sheet to this size and hang it so that it overlaps the corner. Trim and fit at top and bottom. Hang the offcut from the sheet on the adjoining wall, so that it overlaps into the corner. Use the plumb line to check that it is vertical.

When papering from a side wall around a projecting corner on to a facing wall, measure up to the corner from the last sheet of paper and subtract 10mm. Cut the paper and hang it, butt joined to the last sheet. This leaves a 10mm gap from the edge of the paper to the corner. Measure from the paper around the corner on to the next wall, a distance equal to the width of the offcut, minus 3mm. Use the plumb line and mark a true vertical on the wall at this point. Hang the offcut up to it and fold the paper around the corner to overlap its mating piece.

When papering from a facing wall around a projecting corner on to a side wall, butt join from the last sheet of paper up to the corner a sheet which overhangs the corner by 10mm. Mark a true vertical line on the side wall using the plumb line and hang a sheet of paper up to the corner. Fold the 10mm overhang around the corner and paste it to the sheet on the side wall.

Take special care when large pieces of paper have to be trimmed. The weight of the paper could easily cause it to tear. Cut off as much of the waste as possible before papering areas of this sort.

To make a neat fit around a door or window frame, hang the full sheet so that it overlaps the door. Trim roughly, leaving an overlap of about 25mm at the top and sides of the frame. Make a diagonal cut in the paper at the top corner of the door and brush the paper into the angle between the wall and frame along both edges. Crease along these lines with the back of the scissors, peel back the paper, trim and press it back in place.

Before papering around electrical fittings, turn off the electricity supply at the mains. Projecting light switches can be papered around by making a series of cuts in the paper and fitting it around the fixture.

Alternatively remove the cover of a flush switch, make a hole in the paper over the centre of the switch area. Cut diagonal lines to beyond each corner of the switch area and trim to fit the paper just inside this area. Refit the cover and turn on the electricity supply.

Paper inside window recesses leaving a gap on the wall which is then concealed by a separate patch piece, as shown on page 151.

Stairwells

Arrange a system of ladders and planks or scaffold tower components to allow easy access to all parts of the wall. Hang the first piece of paper on the side wall adjacent to the end wall with about 50mm of paper overlapping the end wall. Allow about 50mm at both the top and bottom of the length for trimming. Establish a true vertical on the side wall with a plumb line before hanging the first length.

It may be necessary for a helper to stand below and give extra support to long pieces of paper. The weight of the paste can stretch or even tear the paper if it is not adequately supported. Continue papering along the side wall, then complete the end wall.

Measure the gap and cut a piece of paper 10mm wider

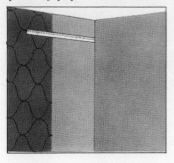

Hang the paper so that 10mm turns on to the next wall

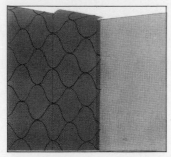

Use the paper offcut so that the pattern matches

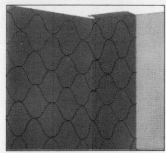

Check with a plumb line that the paper is vertical

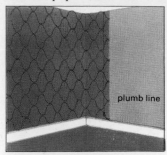

Turning corners, both internal and external, must be mastered, but there are tricky situations. Walls are rarely true and corners hardly ever dead square, so there are techniques for overcoming these obstacles. A chimney breast, being the focal point of a room, must be correct, so be careful to follow the right sequence

On a chimney breast stop 10mm short of the corner

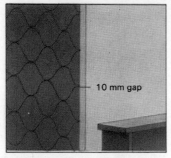

Measure around the corner and draw a vertical line

The offcut is pasted in place truly vertical

Going off the face of the chimney breast, add 10mm

Hang the piece on the next wall. Ensure pattern match

Turn the 10mm overlap on to the next piece of paper

At openings, overlap and cut roughly to shape

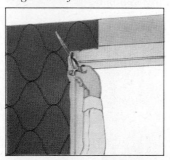

Cut at 45° into the corner to give the frame clearance

Brush into the frame angles leaving surplus projecting

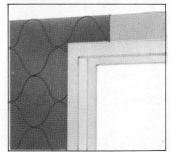

Finally trim accurately and brush well into the corners

When a bubble is found, cut a cross with a sharp knife

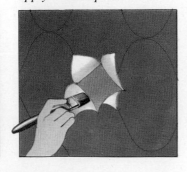

Peel open the flaps and apply a little paste

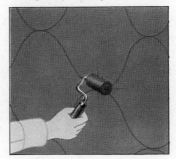

Fit the flaps back and roll gently until flat

Edges that lift should be restuck with clear adhesive

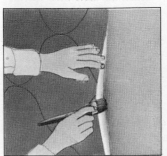

Ceilings

It is essential when papering a ceiling to use access equipment which is safe and which enables the width of the room to be covered without having to step down. Two sturdy step-ladders spanned by a plank will be sufficient.

Start working above a window at the lightest end of a room. Chalk a line on to the ceiling from which to start work so that the first strip is accurately positioned. Cut enough strips of paper to cover the ceiling before beginning hanging. Make reasonable allowance for trimming the ends of strips. Paste each strip as for papering walls, but fold them concertina fashion.

Unfold a strip one fold at a time supporting the paper from underneath with a spare roll of paper. Smooth down with a brush as it is unfolded. Trim the ends leaving a 10mm overlap on to the wall. Butt the next strip of paper to the first and continue in this way down the length of the ceiling. Fit the paper around light fittings by making cuts as for light switches.

Wallpaper repairs

If a small area of wallpaper becomes damaged or badly marked, it is possible to repair it by inserting a patch. Cut a piece of matching paper larger than the damaged area and roughen its edges to soften them so that once pasted on to the wall the joins will be barely detectable.

After checking that the patch exactly matches the surrounding pattern, remove the damaged area and paste the patch into position. As the paste begins to dry, smooth out the patch from its centre to its edges with a boxwood roller.

To remove any trapped air under paper which is fixed in place, make horizontal and vertical cuts across the bubble with a sharp knife. Pull back the paper flaps, apply new paste and allow it to soak in. Refix the paper and roll lightly.

Stairwell access is difficult. Here is one method

well wall   head wall

first strip hung to a plumb line on well wall   50 mm overlap

bannisters removed
for clarity

Where joins along strips have not stuck evenly, peel back the paper and apply a thin film of clear adhesive. Stick down the edge and roll lightly.

Ready-pasted papers

No special technique is required to hang ready-pasted wall-coverings. All that is needed to activate the paste is water applied from a trough. Cut the paper leaving some at each end for trimming, roll it up very loosely with the pattern outwards and immerse it in the water trough for no longer than one minute. Make sure that no air is trapped in the roll. The trough should be positioned at the base of the wall.

Slowly pull up the top end of the length, letting the roll gradually unwind in the water, allowing excess water to drain

Cut towards the corners of switches, fold back and trim

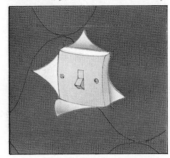

Make star-shape cuts around ceiling roses and trim

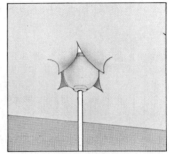

Mark where the paper will reach on the wall

Electrical fittings can be papered around by turning off the supply at the main switch, loosening the fitting screws and tucking a narrow edge under the cover plate before retightening. Window reveals can be done by following the sequence shown

The 6mm cut-back gives an overlap in the reveal

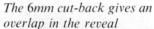
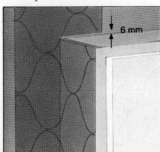

6 mm

Above the window and the reveal top is done next

The small square is now covered, plus an overlap

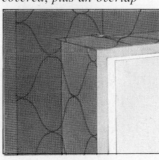

The overlap is torn so it will blend in at the front

151

back into the trough. Position the length on the wall and slide it into place. Use a sponge to smooth from the middle of the length towards the edges. Trim off the surplus at each end, then repeat the process with the remainder of the roll.

Make sure that all joins are butted. Where overlapping is absolutely unavoidable, use a latex adhesive. For papering angles in the wall where material less than full width is needed, cut the paper to shape before it is wetted.

The adhesive contains a fungicide to prevent mould growth so wash your hands after hanging ready-pasted paper and store it away from children and animals.

One of the more recent wallpapering techniques is to paste the wall and hang the paper straight on to it. This type of paper is easy to handle and quick to hang.

Other wallcoverings

There is a variety of other materials which make excellent decorative wallcoverings.

Hessian for walls is made from jute and is available both backed and unbacked. The backing prevents stretching and wrinkling. Hang unbacked hessian on a lining paper similar in colour to the hessian or paint the wall a similar shade first. Use a heavy-duty paste, applied with a foam roller to both the wall and the hessian. Smooth out the hessian with a felt roller, working from the middle of each length out towards its edges.

Felt is available in widths of up to 1830mm in a wide range of colours. Its size and weight make it very difficult to handle, so roll cut lengths on to a batten and support the batten between two step-ladders.

Press the felt to the wall starting at skirting level and smooth it with a paint roller working from the middle of each length outwards. Hang using a latex or PVA adhesive and overlap the edges of the lengths so that both pieces can be cut through with a sharp knife to make a straight butt join. Brush the nap of the felt to make the joins less obvious.

Linen wallcoverings are also available either backed or unbacked. Backed linen is laid as for felt. Unbacked linen is hung on a wall pasted with latex or PVA adhesive.

Silk wallcovering is finely woven silk cloth, glued to a backing paper. It is very expensive. Hang using a heavy-duty adhesive, but take extra care as silk stains easily.

Grasscloth is a textured wallcovering made of grass and bark, held together with thread on a paper backing. Colours may vary widely, so be sure to match the paper carefully before hanging. To prevent edges from fraying, trim with a sharp, curved blade.

Anaglypta is a durable material which is highly resistant to cracking. It is made from embossed cotton fibre and is available in standard length rolls. It is made in many patterns of either high or low relief. Hang low-relief, lightweight Anaglypta on a lining paper, using starch paste. The very strong and heavier high-relief grades are hung using a special paste applied with a stripping knife or a small trowel to the parts of the panel which contact the wall. Before pasting, soak the backs of the panels until they are supple and less springy. Position with panel pins until the adhesive has dried. Paint Anaglypta after it has been hung with matt or silk finish emulsion. It can then be washed without coming away from the wall.

Lincrusta, made from linseed oil and fillers, is bonded to a flat backing paper and is available in rolls or as tiles. It is made to look like wrought iron, wood panelling, stonework tiles or fabrics. Lincrusta is hung on lining paper, but the back must first be sponged with warm water and allowed to soak for about 20 minutes. After wiping off excess moisture, paste is applied and the length is hung on the wall and smoothed into place with a rubber roller.

Cork wallcoverings are either sheets of thin cork or cork shavings bonded to a paper backing. Hang these by applying a PVA adhesive to both the material and the wall.

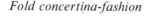

Pasting ceiling paper

Fold concertina-fashion

Use a spare roll as support

Score, but cut 10mm longer

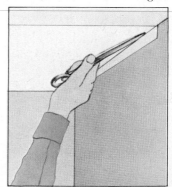

Remove the damaged piece

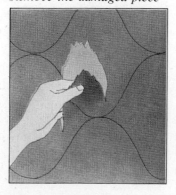

Match with a new section

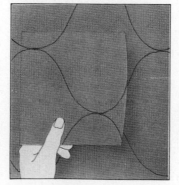

Tear to blend with surround

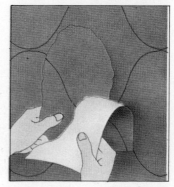

Roll lightly to make flat

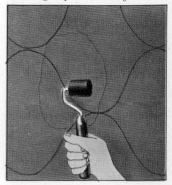

Lift and hang ready-pasted wallpapers   *Felt is heavy and awkward to handle. This arrangement will make the job easier*

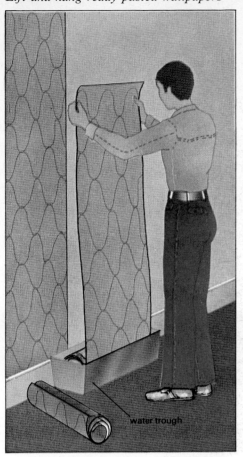

water trough

hanging wall felt

length of felt

Right: ceiling tiles and cove add the finishing touches

Fixing ceiling cove

Cracks along the angle of the ceiling are difficult to repair, so a permanent solution is to cover the angle with ceiling cove. When fixed in position, it forms a rounded joint between the wall and ceiling. Instructions follow for fixing a plaster cove. Expanded polystyrene is cheaper and easier to fix, but the result is not so effective or permanent. Special adhesive is supplied for plaster cove, but if there is a timber background, small-head galvanised wallboard nails or brass screws are preferred.

Hold a length of cove in position and mark the area it will cover on the wall and ceiling. Remove any wallcovering, soft distemper or flaking paint from within the lines. Scratch the area to provide a key for the adhesive. Brush away any loose material.

Cut lengths of cove to suit the lengths of the walls. Mitre the ends of the cove at the corners using the templet supplied by the manufacturers. Cut the cove with a fine-tooth saw. Smooth the sawn edges with glasspaper and place the sections in sequence around the skirting. Damp the area where the cove will be fixed to the walls.

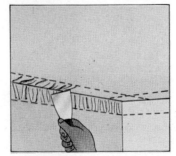

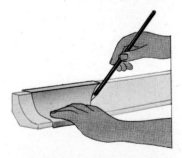

Mix the adhesive to a creamy paste, butter it on to the back of the cove and press it into position. With long lengths, it is useful to have an assistant for this job. A full length of cove is fairly heavy, but the adhesive should hold it in place immediately. If it doesn't drive some nails into the wall to support the lower edge while the adhesive sets. Use the adhesive which squeezes out from behind the cove to fill the joints and make good the mitres.

153

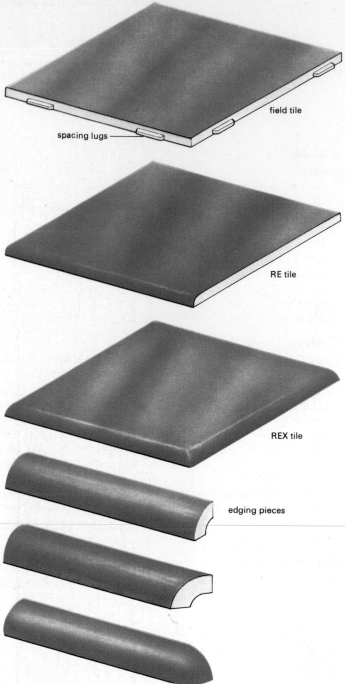

field tile

spacing lugs

RE tile

REX tile

edging pieces

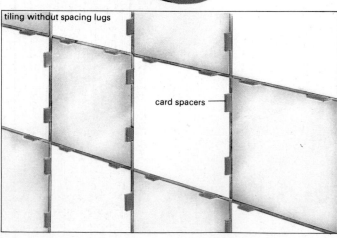

tiling without spacing lugs

card spacers

DECORATING WITH TILES

Tiling was once restricted to using 152mm square, plain white tiles perhaps with a border colour. Today the range of tiles available is staggering. There are plain, patterned and textured finishes. Plain tiles are usually available in eight colours which match the most popular bathroom suite colours.

Textured tiles are usually made in the same colours in a choice of textures. Textured tiles can be used either on their own or as accents set among plain tiles. Patterned tiles are made in a large variety of standard patterns. They are usually available only to order. Transfer tiles decorated with images of birds, fish and cars are also available.

Besides these tiles there is a large range of more expensive tiles, produced for the building industry which offer an even greater variety of colours, patterns and embossed effects. For details of these, enquire at a builders' merchant or write directly to the manufacturer.

Ceramic tiles are one of the most popular surface treatments for walls and floors and can be used to brighten the appearance of a room and give it a personal touch. Half room height tiling is most often installed though interesting results can be achieved by covering complete walls. New tiles can even be laid over old ones which have cracked and dulled.

Tiles are laid mainly in kitchens and bathrooms where they provide an attractive water-resistant, wipe-clean surface. They are particularly useful for covering cracked walls and for splashbacks around sinks and wash basins. Special outdoor tiles are useful for porchways, patios and feature walls. They have been treated to withstand cold temperatures. Choice of tiles is not restricted, however, as any tile can be treated to withstand the lower temperatures, but the process can be done only at the factory and this makes the tiles more expensive.

When tiling around areas exposed to intense heat such as fireplaces and areas adjacent to solid fuel cookers, heat resistant tiles must be used. Special thick tiles are necessary if they are to withstand cracking. These special tiles are made without spacer lugs.

Types and sizes

Most ranges of ceramic tiles are made in two basic sizes: 108mm square by 4mm thick and 152mm square by 6.4mm thick. The smaller tiles are the most popular and easiest to work with. Most types have spacer lugs on the edges which enable them to be spaced accurately and evenly with the minimum of effort and skill.

For most household projects only three tile sections are required; field tiles, one round edge tiles called RE tiles and two round edge tiles known as REX tiles.

Most of the surface area on walls or floors is covered with field tiles. These have square edges and usually have spacer lugs which provide 2mm gaps between laid tiles, which are later filled with grout. Some field tiles which do not have spacer lugs must be spaced accurately using pieces of cardboard or special pegs in the joints. RE tiles are made without spacer lugs and are used for finishing the edges of tiled areas. REX tiles, also without spacer lugs, are used for finishing off the corners of tiled areas.

Accessories

Tile manufacturers usually offer a range of accessories such as soap dishes, toilet roll holders, toothbrush racks and towel holders to match their tiles. These are fixed in the same way as tiles.

To seal the gap between the bath and the wall use either ceramic edge strip or a silicone rubber sealant which can be applied from a tube. Edge strip is sold in packs which include ready-cut mitres for corners and shaped finishing pieces for the ends. Another edging is made of moulded plastic in a Y-shape section, which is held in place by the edge of the bath or sink.

A flexible rubber-base adhesive is supplied with ceramic edge packs. It will stick to tiles, porcelain and enamel surfaces but it may peel off paint.

Estimating

Calculate the area of wall to be covered and allow some extra tiles to cover breakages and waste. A simple way to calculate the number of tiles required is to mark off a long batten into tile widths and then hold it horizontally and vertically against all surfaces to be covered and multiply the totals together. Count the corners and hence the number of REX tiles needed. Note that a projecting corner needs one REX, one RE and one field tile.

Tools

Essential tools for tiling are a metal or plastic spreader, a tile cutter, a tile nipper, sponge, spirit level and plumb line. A carborundum stone is useful for smoothing off rough edges after cutting. Use a masonry drill for making small holes in tiles and a radius cutter for making larger holes.

For tiling a large area, a notched trowel is the best tool to use. For smaller areas a plastic or metal spreader is adequate. Cut the tiles with a tungsten carbide tipped scriber. To cut tiles into shape, ordinary pincers can be used effectively, though special tile nippers are available. Use a sponge to apply grout between the tile joints.

Adhesives and grout

Tile adhesive can be bought ready to use or in powder form to mix with water. Mix only small quantities of adhesive at a time as it has a limited life.

There are thin bed, thick bed, waterproof, flexible and heat resistant adhesives available for use on different surfaces. Use thin bed adhesives on smooth and level surfaces. Thick bed adhesives are designed for use on rough and uneven surfaces and are more difficult to apply. Use other adhesives for fixing tiles in the areas their names suggest.

Grout is a cement-base fine white powder which is mixed with water and used for sealing gaps between the tiles. Where tiles are to be exposed to running water, use a waterproof grout.

Surface preparation

Surfaces to be tiled must be clean, flat and dry. Remove screws and other projections, fill cracks and smooth down

Tools likely to be needed for tiling work, although all are not essential

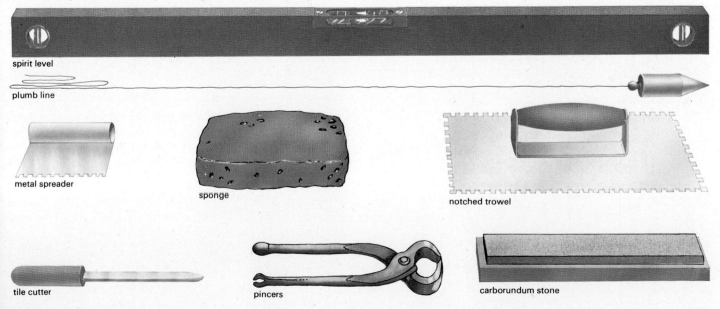

spirit level

plumb line

metal spreader

sponge

notched trowel

tile cutter

pincers

carborundum stone

any irregularities. Painted surfaces which are sound provide a good base for tiling. If the paint is damaged, it is best to strip it off. Score gloss painted surfaces to give better adhesion.

Leave newly plastered surfaces to dry for at least a month before tiling. Hack away loose areas of plaster on old walls and repair with new plaster. To prevent the tile adhesive from being absorbed too quckly, seal porous or dusty plaster with a primer. Concrete is not a good surface to tile. It should be attempted only if the surface is in very good condition. Rough and uneven concrete must first be screeded. Do not lay tiles on new concrete for at least a month.

Building boards such as plasterboard, blockboard, chipboard, insulating board, hardboard and plywood are excellent surfaces to tile. Should you want to tile up to ceiling height it is best to first line the walls with some type of building boards unless the plaster is perfectly level. The boards must be well supported on a latticework of timber battens on the wall. Fix sheet material to the timbers with the

smooth side facing inwards with either large head galvanised nails or countersunk screws. Condition the boards before fixing (see page 26) and coat the backs and sides with an undercoat to prevent moisture penetration.

Walls

First thoroughly clean the surfaces to be tiled. To establish a surface from which to work, fix a batten to the wall with its upper edge a tile width above floor. Use a spirit level to set the batten horizontally. Continue the batten around the room.

Use a spare batten for a measuring staff and use two tiles to mark off a number of tile widths along the batten. Position the staff on the batten fixed to the wall and transfer the marks. Tiling should be arranged centrally so that spaces at the ends of each row will be equal. Tile symmetrically around openings to avoid unattractive narrow cuts.

At one end of the fixed batten draw a vertical line on the

Use two field tiles to mark the measuring staff

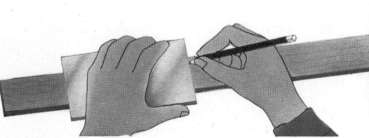

Mark the tile spacing on the horizontal batten

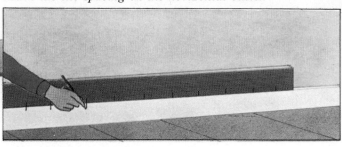

Position and check, with three tiles, the vertical batten

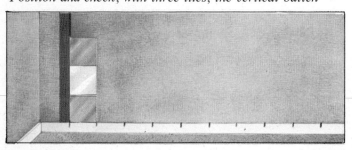

Spread adhesive over a convenient area

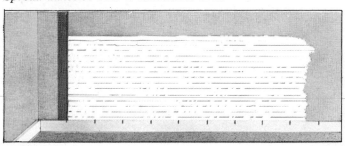

Position the first tile firmly on the adhesive

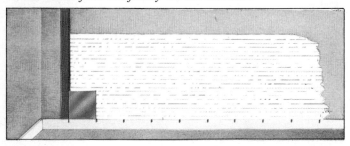

Continue until the area is full – check with a level

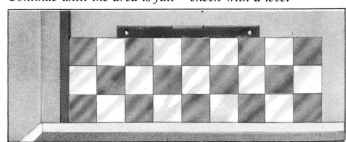

Around openings, deal with the cut tiles last

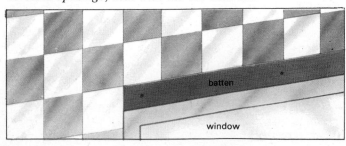

At window reveals, the cut tiles are next to the window

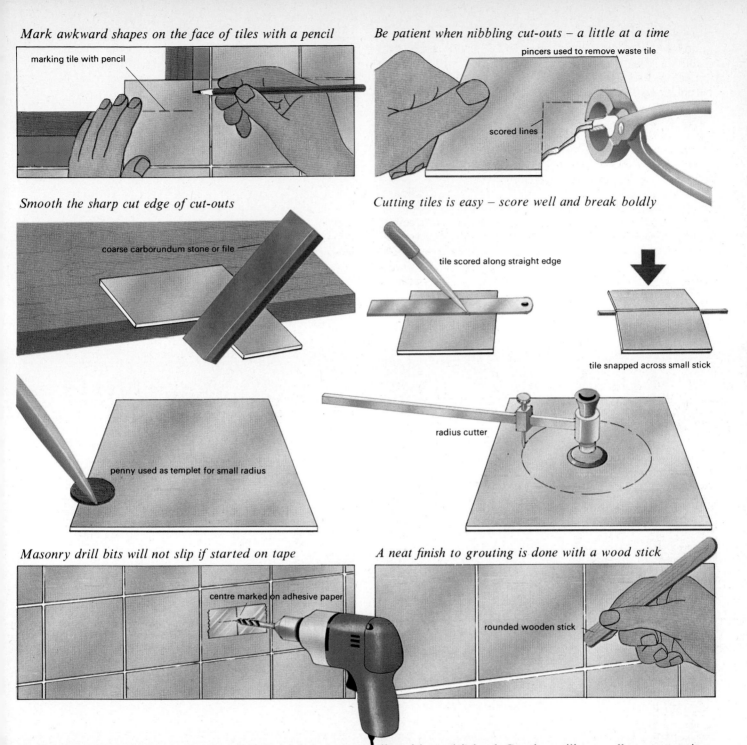

Mark awkward shapes on the face of tiles with a pencil

marking tile with pencil

Be patient when nibbling cut-outs – a little at a time

pincers used to remove waste tile

scored lines

Smooth the sharp cut edge of cut-outs

coarse carborundum stone or file

Cutting tiles is easy – score well and break boldly

tile scored along straight edge

tile snapped across small stick

penny used as templet for small radius

radius cutter

Masonry drill bits will not slip if started on tape

centre marked on adhesive paper

A neat finish to grouting is done with a wood stick

rounded wooden stick

wall and fix a batten along it. Be sure that the angle between battens is 90°.

Some adhesives are supplied in tins ready for use. If the adhesive must be mixed, follow the manufacturer's instructions. Apply the adhesive to the wall over an area of about 1 square metre and use the spreader to form even ridges in the adhesive the depth of the notches on the spreader.

Lay the first tile in the corner where the horizontal and vertical battens meet and press firmly into the adhesive without sliding it. Lay the next tile on the horizontal batten touching the spacer lugs of the first tile. Continue working along the horizontal. Then lay rows above the first working in the same way.

Before going on to spread another area of adhesive, check that the tiles are firmly embedded and check the level of the

tiles with a spirit level. Continue tiling small areas at a time until the main area has been finished. Before the spaces at the ends of the rows can be filled let the tiles set for several hours and remove the battens.

With the battens removed, individual tiles can be cut and fitted in the spaces around the main area of tiling. Wipe off any adhesive which gets on to the face of tiles before it dries.

When tiling above window frames, baths, sinks, wash basins, and other fittings it may be necessary to fit cut tiles. Tile alongside the fitting first and leave the area above it until last. Fix a batten at the height of the nearest line of adjacent tiles above the fitting to act as a guide. Tile above the batten in the same way as before and when the adhesive has set, remove the batten and cut tiles to fill the remaining space. Take the thickness of the tile and the adhesive into account when fixing round edge tiles at external corners.

Where an accessory such as a soap dish is to be fitted, fit a field tile temporarily in the intended position. Remove it after completing the main area of tiling. Spread adhesive to a depth of about 2mm over the back of the accessory and press it into place. Stick tape across it and on to the tiles on either side to give it extra support until the adhesive has set.

Cutting and shaping

To cut L-shape tiles to fit the corners of doors and windows and to go around square or rectangular light fittings, hold a full tile up to the wall and mark off the waste. Score the glazed surface and cut the waste from the tile with pincers. Clean and smooth the cut edges of the tile using a carborundum stone or special file. For a round shape, the pincers can be used in conjunction with a curved stone or file. To fit tiles in the spaces around the edges of the main tiled area, place a tile over the space it is to fill and mark the tile at two points where it is to be cut allowing for the grout space. Join the two points and score the glazed surface along the line. Place a small piece of wood like a matchstick under the tile and along the scored line. Press down gently on the corners of the tile and the tile should break cleanly. When cutting tiles to fill the space along the bottom of the wall under the main tiled area, you may find that each tile has to be trimmed individually.

To cut a circular hole at the edge of a tile, place a templet such as a coin on the tile and score around it. Score the glazed surface within the area to be cut and nibble it away. Clean rough edges with a file or abrasive stone.

To cut a fairly large hole in the middle of a tile, use a radius cutter. Small holes can be made in tiles using a masonry bit in a hand drill or electric drill running at a slow speed. Support the tile firmly or it may break.

Grouting

Before grouting, tiles should be allowed to dry for a day to allow the adhesive to set. Using a sponge or squeegee rub the grout well into the joins. Once it has started to dry, remove excess grout with a damp cloth. When the grout is thoroughly dry, dust off the grout from the tiled surface and go over the joints with a piece of wood with a smooth rounded point. Finally, polish the tiles with a ball of newspaper.

Over old tiles

If old tiles are sound it is possible to tile over them in the same way as if tiling a plain wall. If any of the tiles are loose, refix them with tile adhesive. To ensure that they are flush with the surrounding tiles, it may be necessary to chip away the old fixing mortar from the wall and the back of the tile. If the old tiles are in very bad condition, they will have to be removed before the wall is retiled. The best way to do this is to hire an electric hammer with a combing attachment.

Where new tiles are hung full height over a previously half-tiled wall, disguise the step by creating a mini-shelf using a strip of hardwood.

Floors can be covered with an all-over layer such as sheet vinyl or carpet or with various types of tile.

Carpets

Carpets are a versatile floorcovering and there are types for every room in the house. Carpeting is a large part of the expense of decorating so it is important to pick a type that will be hardwearing and practical in the room where it is to be laid.

Because any all-over floorcovering can dominate the decoration in a room, it is best to avoid over-bold patterns and use more traditional patterns and quiet colours that will blend more with other decorations. An expanse of neutral colour can make a room appear more spacious. Rich, dark colours and bold patterns have the opposite effect. They make rooms feel smaller and cosier. A high ceiling will appear lower if the carpet and ceiling are dark and the walls are light. A low ceiling can seem higher if it is a slightly lighter shade than a carpet of the same colour.

Plain carpets, especially in light colours show stains far more than patterned carpets. A patterned carpet is therefore a good choice for a hallway and for a much used living room. An easily cleaned floorcovering is essential in these areas.

Types of carpet

Carpets are manufactured in two types; woven and non-woven. Wiltons and Axminsters are the best known woven carpets. In these, each tuft is woven with the backing and the carpet has selvedges to prevent fraying.

With a non-woven carpet, the tufts are inserted into a woven backing and then secured with a coating of latex. Many tufted carpets have a backing of latex foam which makes a separate underlay unnecessary. Some non-woven carpets have a flat, non-pile surface, some have a looped pile and others a brushed directional pile.

Carpet fibres are either natural or man-made, but often a carpet is made from a blend of fibres.

Wool is the most often used natural fibre because it is long-lasting, resilient and warm. It keeps its appearance well and is resistant to soiling and cigarette burns. The major drawback is its cost. For this reason wool is often blended with other fibres. A blend of 80% wool and 20% nylon produces a cheaper but not quite as soft carpet which retains most of the advantages of wool, while adding the strength of nylon.

An all man-made blend of 80% Evlan and 20% nylon produces an inexpensive, hardwearing carpet with fair resistance to flattening but it tends to show stains. They are comparatively cheap, although rather harsh to the touch. Other man-made fibres, like acrylics, polyesters and polypropylenes are tough and durable and are available in blends with other fibres.

Carpet can be laid as broadloom in a single piece or in strips which are sewed together called body carpet or strip carpet. Body carpet is usually sold in 2 widths of 69cm and

Carpet stretching

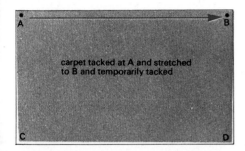

carpet tacked at A and stretched to B and temporarily tacked

using a carpet stretcher

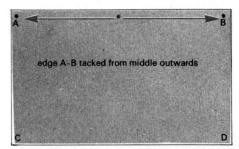

edge A-B tacked from middle outwards

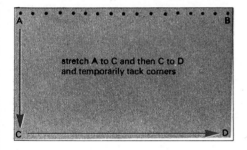

stretch A to C and then C to D and temporarily tack corners

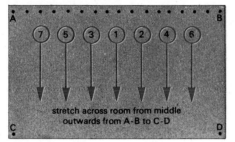

stretch across room from middle outwards from A-B to C-D

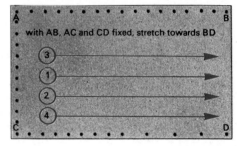

with AB, AC and CD fixed, stretch towards BD

Fitting pointers

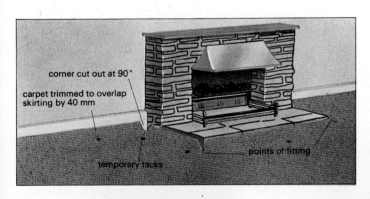

corner cut out at 90°

carpet trimmed to overlap skirting by 40 mm

temporary tacks

points of fitting

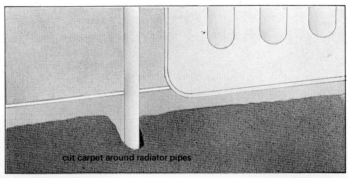

cut carpet around radiator pipes

hem tacked at 125 mm intervals

temporary tacks removed

underlay trimmed 50 mm from wall

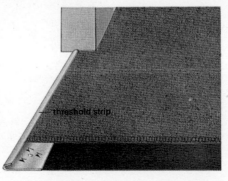

threshold strip

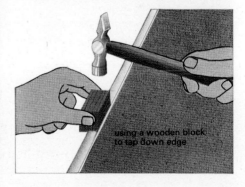

using a wooden block to tap down edge

Using tackless fittings

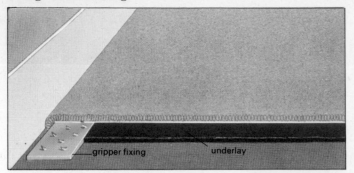

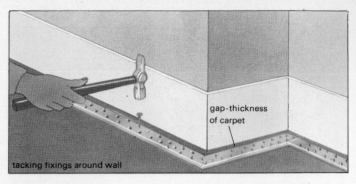

gap-thickness of carpet

tacking fixings around wall

gripper fixing   underlay

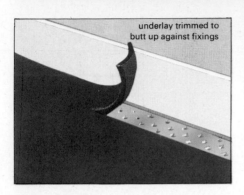

underlay trimmed to butt up against fixings

carpet hooked over fixings

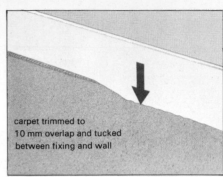

carpet trimmed to 10 mm overlap and tucked between fixing and wall

91cm. Broadloom widths are 1.83m, 2.74m, 3.66m, 4.57m and rarely 5.49m. It is best to consult the carpet salesman as to the best method of fitting your rooms.

Underlay

Underlay is required for all types of carpet unless it is rubber backed. A layer of brown paper, or even newspaper, laid on the bare floor will prevent dust from blowing up from beneath the floorboards and prevent the underlay from sticking to the floor surface.

Underlay provides heat and sound insulation, cushions the carpet against wear and eliminates slight unevenness in the floor. It is made from paper felt, hair or wool felt or natural or foam rubber. Rubber underlays should not be used in rooms with underfloor heating. Felt underlay is the best type to use with strip carpet as it allows the seams to lie flat. Felt paper should be used only under carpets with built-in underlays or as an underlay in light traffic areas.

For awkward rooms get the carpet fitted by an experienced carpet fitter, especially if fitting stairs is involved. However, if you are prepared to take a little care there is no reason why you can't do a good job yourself.

Methods

First be sure the floor is firm, level and dry. Remove protruding nails or knock them below the surface. Fix loose floorboards, fill wide gaps and smooth the floor if necessary. If it is a solid floor, use a floor-levelling substance to smooth it if necessary. (See page 21.)

The simplest way of fitting a carpet is loose laying. The carpet is cut to fit around the walls and is tacked down only to stop the edges from lifting at doorways. It may be necessary to tape the exposed edge of woven carpet to prevent fraying.

The turn and tack method is ideal for fitting patterned carpets which camouflage the tack heads. Cut the underlay 50mm smaller all round than the room size. Turn under a 40mm hem around the edge of the carpet and tack down at 75 to 100mm intervals.

To fit a carpet so that tacks do not show, tackless fittings are used. These are wood battens with many projecting angled nails on one side or metal strips with projecting teeth. Nail the fixing strips all around the room about 6mm from the skirting board with the spikes angled towards the wall. With solid floors the strips are glued in place. Cut the underlay to butt up against the strip. The spikes grip the carpet backing and hold the carpet in place. With carpets which have built-in underlays, the backing must be trimmed away around the edge.

Another method of invisible carpet fitting is called ring and pin. It takes more skill to lay a carpet by this method but it is easier to lift the carpet for cleaning or decorating. Sew special rings to the carpet backing all around the edge. Hook the rings over screws positioned at equal distances close to the skirting.

Laying a carpet

Clear the room and take off doors that open into the room. Roll out and roughly position the carpet, then fold back half and lay the underlay. Carefully replace the carpet and repeat the procedure with the other half making sure that the underlay does not become wrinkled during positioning.

If tacks are used, the carpet should turn 40mm up the skirting boards to leave enough material to turn under. Drive in tacks in one corner 150mm from the skirting to about half their length to hold this corner in place. The tacks should protrude so they can be removed easily later. Stretch the carpet lengthwise and temporarily tack the adjacent corner. This long side can now be tensioned properly using a hired tool called a knee-kicker. If one is not available, shuffle along the carpet in rubber-sole shoes. Start in the middle of the wall and stretch alternately towards both corners. Fasten with temporary tacks as you go.

Then stretch the carpet widthwise from the corner where it was first fixed. It can then be stretched and temporarily fixed along the other long wall and the last corner temporarily fixed. By stretching several times across the width of the room, the second long wall can be temporarily fixed.

After allowing time for shrinkage, trim sheet vinyl this   way

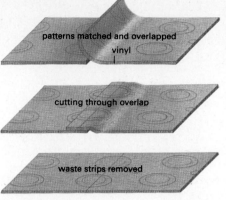

patterns matched and overlapped

vinyl

cutting through overlap

waste strips removed

Multi-blade trimming knives can be fitted with this special blade for easy cutting of vinyl floorcoverings

A nail-and-batten scriber. The batten slides along the wall, the nail marks

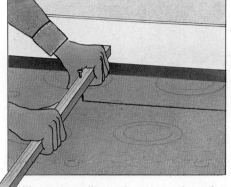

Trim butt joins first. Overlap pieces, matching the pattern carefully

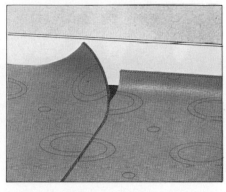

Using a knife and straight-edge, cut through both layers of vinyl

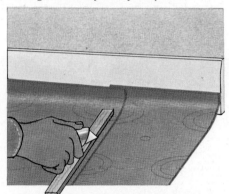

The join made, make a pencil mark on the vinyl, 200mm from the skirting

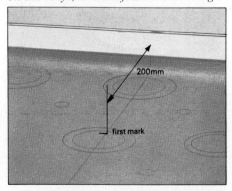

200mm

first mark

Lay the vinyl flat and make another mark 200mm nearer to the skirting

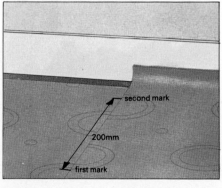

second mark

200mm

first mark

Adjust   the vinyl so that, starting at the second mark, scribing can be done

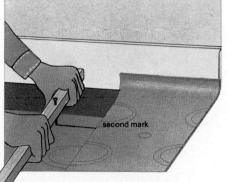

second mark

When dealing with awkward shapes, tear a rough shape and mark, using a spacer, a slightly larger outline

paper

hole roughly cut in paper pattern

Put the pattern in   place on the vinyl and, using the spacer, mark   the true outline on the vinyl

Then stretch the carpet lengthwise, and fix across one end at a time. When you have finished, the carpet should be perfectly flat and temporarily tacked all around about 150mm from the skirting.

Cut slots for radiator pipes and make 90 degree cut-outs at the corners of obstacles such as fireplaces. Trim the underlay about 50mm from the wall to allow the carpet hem to turn under. Trim the carpet, fold the hem under and tack down all around the edge at 75 to 100mm intervals. The carpet should be finished off in doorways with carpet threshold strip. Slip the edge of the carpet under the lip of the strip which is tapped down to grip the carpet. Use a block of wood to protect the strips from direct hammer blows.

If tackless fixings are used, tack the underlay down and trim it so its edge just butts against the fixings. Tack the carpet temporarily and stretch as before. When satisfied with the positioning, bend the nose of the knee-kicker downwards all around the edge to hook the carpet on to the spikes. Trim the carpet about 10mm oversize and push it down into the gap between the gripper fixing and the wall.

Sheet vinyls

Sheet vinyl is cheaper, easier to lay and more hard-wearing than linoleum. It is suitable for solid floors which have been damp-proofed and properly ventilated timber floors. Be sure the floor is smooth and dry before installing vinyl.

Vinyl is easy to cut, but the size of sheets makes them harder to lay than vinyl tiles. But sheet vinyls are available in a far wider range of patterns than tiles and sheets can be laid with very few joins. Many rooms can be covered with no joins at all. Vinyl sheet is usually available in 1220mm, 1830mm and 3660mm widths.

Conventional vinyl has a smooth finish but many styles of cushioned vinyl have a slightly embossed finish. Cushioned vinyls are available in several qualities depending on the type and thickness of the backing. They are softer and quieter to walk on than plain vinyl.

Laying sheet vinyl

Loosen the rolls, stand them on end and keep them in a warm room for 48 hours before laying.

Create your own design with carpet, vinyl, cork or ceramic floor tiles. With carpet tiles, you can change the design to suit your mood, as they are loose laid

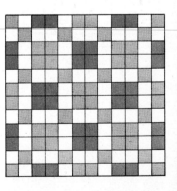

162

Some vinyls may shrink slightly after laying unless they are stuck down all over. If this is a possibility, overlap the seams by about 15mm and allow about 25mm to turn up the skirting boards. Trim to allow the door to open then leave for two to three weeks before fitting properly.

Very flexible vinyls can be fitted to the walls by knifing-in. Make a diagonal cut in one corner and take slices off until the cut edge fits snugly into the corners. Then, holding the knife as upright as possible and pressing in against the wall, cut the vinyl.

Less flexible coverings can be fitted by the scribing method. A scriber can be made by knocking a nail through a scrap of wood. Pull the floorcovering away from the wall so the nail is close to the edge. Keeping the wood at right angles to the wall run the scriber along the skirting so the nail scratches a line.

Trim the sheet to the scratch line and push the vinyl to fit up against the wall. If there is a centre join in the covering, the opposite wall can be fitted in the same way and the overlap in the middle trimmed by cutting through the two thicknesses with a sharp blade held against a straight-edge.

Fit the vinyl with the ends extending about 25mm up the skirting. Make a pencil mark on the vinyl at any convenient distance from the skirting, say 200mm. Pull the sheet back so that it lies flat and mark a spot towards the end of the sheet, 200mm from the first mark. Hold the scriber on the skirting and slide the sheet until the nail is touching the second mark. Hold the sheet steady and run the scriber along the skirting. Trim to this line. The vinyl will fit exactly. Use this method to cut around corners and angles and repeat for the opposite end of the sheet.

To cut intricate shapes out of the flooring material, use a paper pattern or an adjustable templet former which consists of a row of movable needles which take the shape of an object. If there are many intricate shapes, in a toilet for example, it is a good idea to make a paper pattern for the whole room.

Vinyl tends to curl at the edges if it is not stuck to the floor. Ideally the vinyl should be bonded all over, but on a timber floor it is often best to stick it down only on the edges as it may be necessary to lift the floorboards.

For all-over bonding, work on areas of about a square metre at a time. Use a vinyl flooring adhesive following the manufacturer's instructions. After positioning the vinyl, use a soft broom to expel air pockets and ensure good contact with the adhesive. An unheated domestic iron is useful for pressing down seams and along walls and corners.

When only the edges are bonded, either flooring adhesive or special double-sided tape can be used. Fix the tape under each joint close to the walls. Some adhesives are flammable – extinguish all naked lights while using them.

Tile and strip floorcoverings

Tile and strip floorcoverings are popular because a wide variety is available. They are easy to lay and will cover odd-shape floors with very little waste. They are light and easy to handle. Only the tiles around the perimeter of the room need to be cut. A mistake in trimming will spoil only one tile. With a tile floorcovering, worn or stained areas can be replaced easily without disturbing the entire floor. And by carefully combining tiles of different colours it is possible to build up exclusive and interesting patterns.

Vinyl tiles

Vinyl tiles have all the advantages of sheet vinyls but the range of patterns is more limited. Cushioned tiles are not

Laying tiles

A taut chalked string makes a straight line on a floor

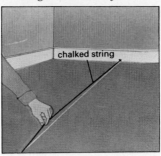

chalked string

Two tiles can be used to draw a right angle

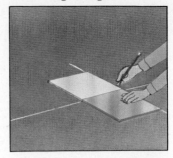

Loose lay a row of tiles to see what the border gap is

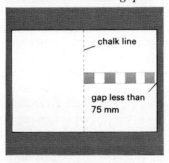

chalk line

gap less than 75 mm

When the border is less than half a tile, move the line

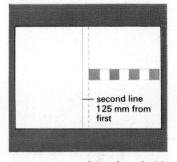

second line 125 mm from first

Loose laid tiles are placed at right-angles to the first

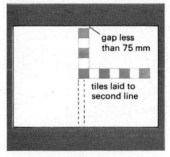

gap less than 75 mm

tiles laid to second line

Again, a gap less than half a tile means moving the line

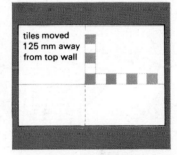

tiles moved 125 mm away from top wall

To keep all square, tiles are laid in this order

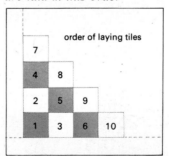

order of laying tiles

7
4 8
2 5 9
1 3 6 10

A spare tile is used to mark out a border piece

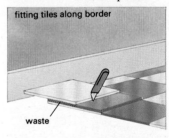

fitting tiles along border

waste

To cut around mouldings first make a paper pattern

paper pattern

A template former makes awkward shaping easier

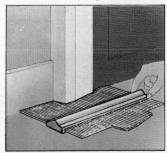

available. Some tiles have smooth surfaces, others are deeply embossed to recreate various textures.

Ordinary vinyl tiles can be laid on wood or solid floors as long as there is no trace of dampness. Vinyl asbestos tiles, which are more brittle will tolerate some damp and should be used for a solid floor if the damp-proof membrane is suspect.

Most vinyl tiles are fixed with special adhesive although some are made with a self-adhesive backing and need only to be pressed into place on a clean, dry sub-floor. The standard tile sizes available are 229mm, 250mm and 300mm square.

Cork tiles

Cork tiles are becoming very popular because of their attractive texture and warmth. They are softer and quieter to walk on than wood, vinyl or lino. Finished tiles require only an occasional application of floor polish to keep them in good condition. Vinyl-coated cork tiles are more expensive, but require only washing to keep them in good condition. Because they are impervious to water, these cork tiles should not be laid on a solid floor. Unfinished cork tiles are the least expensive but they require sanding and sealing after laying. Cork tiles are usually 300mm square.

Laying plastic and cork tiles

As with sheet vinyl, the sub-floor must be clean, dry and smooth. Mark a centre line down the room using a chalked string tightly stretched between two nails. Pluck the string to leave a chalk line. Lay a row of tiles without using adhesive, from the centre line towards the wall.

If the space between the end tile and the wall is less than half a tile, move the chalk line half a tile width to left or right. Find the mid-point of this line and use a carpenter's square or two tiles accurately placed to draw a pencil line at right angles to the chalk line. Extend this line to the skirtings to quarter the room. Once again, check the border width.

Spread the adhesive according to manufacturer's instructions. Work from the centre of the room in a pyramid-shape area. Lay all the whole tiles, leaving the border tiles to be cut and laid last.

Fit border tiles by placing each one exactly over an adjacent fixed tile. Another tile is then placed over the two and held against the wall while the overlap is marked on the tile below. Cut the tile along this line. The piece removed will exactly fit the border. Use a paper pattern or an adjustable templet former to mark intricate shapes.

Carpet tiles

Carpet tiles are easy to lay. They can be rotated to even out wear and are easily lifted for cleaning or redecorating. They are available mainly in plain colours in 300mm or 500mm squares. Nearly all have built-in underlay which cushions the tread and prevents the tiles from moving about in use. Carpet tiles have a conventional tufted pile, a high quality twist pile, a special loop pile or a bonded felt-type pile. In the last case, the fibres from adjacent tiles tend to work together after laying thereby hiding the joins between tiles. Tiles are made from various types of animal hair and fibres similar to those used for sheet carpets. Some are made from tough man-made fibres on a strong PVC backing, so cleaning is simply a matter of picking them up and washing them under the tap.

Laying carpet tiles

Prepare the floor as for sheet carpet and mark the floor as described for vinyl tiles. Carpet tiles are simply laid in place butting up against one another. The tiles around the border

are cut to fit with a sharp knife. In some cases the pile is directional and the tile should be laid according to the arrow on the reverse side. It is best to use carpet threshold strip at doorways to prevent the edges of the tiles from being kicked up. Most tiles are just laid in place so by careful choice of colours it is possible to make up a square or striped pattern which can be altered at will.

Ceramic tiles and quarry tiles

These types of tile are very hardwearing, easy to clean and waterproof. They are also noisy, hard on the feet and tend to be cold to walk on.

Quarry tiles are usually from 75mm to 150mm square, although a wide range of sizes and types is available. They are made in shades of reds, yellows and browns. They are usually plain and unglazed, although some are lightly embossed with a pattern. There is also a range of glazed quarry tiles.

All ceramic tiles are glazed and are available in a large range of colours, patterns and shapes. The most common size is 150mm square. Many ceramic floor tiles are imported and prices vary greatly but generally they are very much more expensive than quarry tiles.

When buying ceramic tiles, check that they are suitable for flooring as wall tiles are too brittle for the purpose. Floor tiles can, however, be fixed to the walls to give a unified look to the floor/wall area. Matching cove skirting tiles with internal and external angles are sometimes available.

Laying ceramic and quarry tiles

Ceramic floor tiles need a flat and firm sub-floor. Cover uneven wood floors with 9mm plywood or 13mm chipboard. Mark out the room as for plastic tiles. Ceramic tiles are fixed

Timber floors

Marking the floor lines

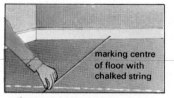

marking centre of floor with chalked string

Special threshold strip

Fixing to a solid floor

spreading adhesive

Room for expansion

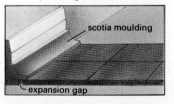

scotia moulding

expansion gap

Fixing on a timber base

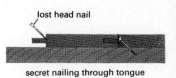

lost head nail

secret nailing through tongue

One design for easy laying

pushing in panel pins

Underlay comes in strips

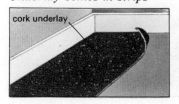

cork underlay

Tapping tongues into slots

Ceramic and quarry tiles

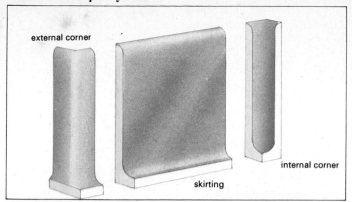

external corner

internal corner

skirting

Start work in one corner

Making grouting spaces

wood spacer

Mark cuts with a pencil

Oporto makes a clean break

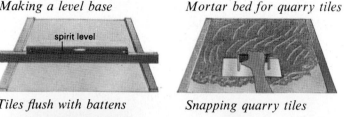
Making a level base

spirit level

Mortar bed for quarry tiles

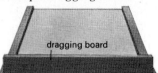
T-shape dragging board

dragging board

Using the dragging board

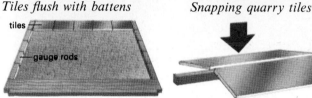
Tiles flush with battens

tiles

gauge rods

Snapping quarry tiles

Grouting with a squeegee

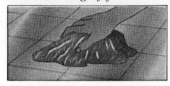
Final cleaning of floor

with a thin layer of cement-base tile adhesive. Space the tiles about 2mm apart by using wooden spacers or thick cardboard.

To cut ceramic tiles, make a score line with a tile cutter. Support the tile along the line and press down evenly on each side of the line. The tile should break along the line. A tile cutter makes this job a lot easier. Try to plan the work to avoid narrow strips.

Before laying a quarry tile floor, check with an expert to make sure that a timber floor can take the additional weight. Fix quarry tiles with a mix of one part cement to three parts sand to which a PVA agent has been added. More care is required in laying a quarry tiled floor to make sure the mortar bedding is smooth and level. It is best to fix battens to the floor an exact distance apart corresponding to, say, six tiles plus 3mm joints. The battens can then be levelled and used as formwork for the mortar in the same way as a tamping board is used with side boards to lay concrete paths (see page 30).

Make a tamping board with a notch at either end to about half the depth of the batten. Fill the space between the battens with mortar and smooth down by dragging the board back and forth. Then bed the quarry tiles flush with the top of the battens, while the mortar is still wet. Remove the battens and use a rubber squeegee to force a cement grout into the joints. Finally smooth the mortar joints and clean off the tiles.

Quarry tiles are cut in a similar fashion to ceramic tiles. To score a line, support the tile on a brick and tap along the line with a sharp cold chisel. Place the score over the edge of a brick or batten and strike sharply downwards.

Wood floorcoverings

Wood is both a decorative and hardwearing floorcovering and is available in strips or parquet blocks. These are made from various solid hardwoods or from plywood blocks faced with hardwood veneers. Parquet blocks are available in a variety of thicknesses and sizes. A popular size is five strips on a felt backing forming a 230mm square. Mosaic blocks consist of a number of hardwood strips glued together to form different patterns and made up into 457mm square panels with felt backing. Wood strips are usually 75mm wide and are available in various lengths.

Laying wood floors

A smooth and dry sub-floor is essential for a wood floor. Parquet blocks are usually laid in a herringbone or chequer-board pattern from the centre line of the room. They are stuck down with a bitumen-base adhesive which allows the blocks to expand and contract slightly. Leave a 10mm expansion gap around the skirting. Cover this gap neatly with a scotia moulding nailed to the skirting board.

Strip flooring can be laid across the floor from one skirting to another, but it is best to work outwards from the centre line. Leave expansion gaps all around. Strips may be stuck down on solid floors. On timber floors it is usual to secret-nail them by inserting panel pins diagonally through the tongued lip of each strip or through the interlocking ears that protrude from the sides of the strips.

To soften the tread and reduce noise, some slot-together wood blocks are laid on special bitumen and cork underlay. The underlay is laid in strips over the sub-floor leaving a 10mm expansion gap between each strip and at the skirtings. The interlocking panels are laid without fastenings of any kind starting at the corner with the longest uninterrupted run of wall. The panels are tapped together. The last few must be glued to those already laid and cut to size if need be.

Some parquets are sold sanded and gloss finished. Others must be carefully levelled with a belt sander after laying, then wax polished or coated with polyurethane varnish.

Glossary

Acrylic sheet: a rigid plastic sheet, usually about 3 mm thick in clear, coloured or opal. ICI Perspex is an example.

Aggregate: broken stone and/or gravel which makes up the bulk of concrete.

Alkyd resins: synthetic resins used in paint manufacture.

Arris rails: the horizontal rails of a fence to which the upright boards are fixed. Arris rails are usually triangular in cross-section.

Ballast: mixture of stones, sand and grit of fairly small size.

Barge boards: sloping boards fixed to the gable end of a roof to protect the ends of the roof timbers.

Blockboard: sheet material consisting of a core of wood strips, less than 25 mm wide, sandwiched between veneers. Made in various thicknesses and board sizes.

Btu: British Thermal Unit. The quantity of heat required to raise the temperature of 1 lb. of water through 1 °F from 39 °F to 40 °F 1 Therm = 100,000 Btus.

Cap and lining joint: a type of joint for making a connection to a tap.

Chipboard: man-made board comprising wood chips bonded under pressure with synthetic resins. Sometimes veneered.

Cladding: a top surface, usually decorative, applied to a wall or ceiling.

Coarse stuff: mixture for first and second coats of plaster, usually consisting of lime, sand and cement.

Compression joint: a brass plumbing fitting for joining copper pipes. The watertight joint is made using only spanners.

Consumer unit: an electrical distribution unit in a domestic premises. It contains the main switch and fuses.

Copolymer: a technical term used to distinguish varnishes used in the manufacture of certain paints.

Crazing: hair-line cracks in a rendered or painted surface.

DPC: damp-proof course between brick courses, usually about 150 mm above ground level.

DPM: damp-proof membrane, either under a floor screed or between outer and inner leaves of a cavity wall at openings.

Dry lining: an internal finish to walls composed of sheets of plasterboard rather than wet plaster.

Dynamic head: the driving force generated by the central heating pump.

Efflorescence: powdery white marks on the surface of brickwork, caused by salts left after moisture dries out.

Epoxy resins: synthetic resins used in high-strength adhesives.

Fascia board: the vertical board fixed to the rafter ends. It carries the gutters around the eaves.

Fibreboard: a lightweight, low-density board, usually with a high heat insulation value.

Flashing: a strip of material, such as zinc, lead or plastic, which prevents water entering a junction such as that between a roof and a wall.

Flaunching: a curved mortar fillet around a chimney pot and on the top of the stack to throw water off.

Float: a wood plastering or rendering tool.

Foam plastic: a plastic material containing many air bubbles, like a sponge.

Frenchman: a tool for neatly trimming the mortar when using the weathered type of pointing.

Frog: the indentation in one side of a house brick.

Gauge rod: a rod, marked in courses, to ensure accuracy when building a wall.

Glass fibre: glass strands bonded together into a mat or cloth. When impregnated with a chemically setting resin, it forms a rigid structure.

Grasscloth: hessian, interwoven with strips of grass to form a sheet wallcovering material.

Grout: the filling material between ceramic tiles to give a neat finish.

Gravity circuit: a heating circuit which utilises the natural circulation properties of hot and cold water in pipework.

Hardboard: a board made of fibre and formed under pressure. Offered in various thicknesses, finishes and grades.

Hardwood: timber from broad-leaf, usually deciduous, trees. Not always hard.

Integral ring fitting: a plumbing fitting with the solder already incorporated in the form of a ring.

Knee-kicker: a tool for carpet fitting. Spikes grip the carpet and the tool is bumped with the knee to stretch it.

Mycelium: the thin strands of growth of a fungus.

O-ring joint: a plumbing joint where the seal relies on a rubber or plastic O-ring between two surfaces.

Pantile: a roof tile which has a double curve and interlocks with its neighbours.

Polyester: a technical term used to distinguish varnishes used in the manufacture of certain paints.

Polyurethane: a synthetic resin used in paint manufacture.

Polypropylene: a plastic material with good resistance to heat and solvents.

Polystyrene: a plastic compound, usually in the expanded form, for heat insulation and decorative purposes.

PVA: polyvinyl acetate. A chemical compound commonly used in adhesives.

PVC: polyvinyl chloride. A plastic material with many applications, including electric cable sheaths.

Rag-and-putty joint: an old-fashioned, unhygienic joint between a toilet flush pipe and the lavatory bowl.

Rendering: a coat, usually of cement mortar, applied to a surface for protection and/or decoration.

Scale: the deposit left when water is heated to the point where dissolved hard-water salts are deposited.

Scriber: a pointed instrument for marking a workpiece by scratching.

Silicones: chemical substances used in lubricants, polishes and other commercial products.

Slow bend: a type of plumbing elbow which has a gradual bend.

Soakaway: a hole, usually about 1·5 m cube, filled with rubble to accept non-foul waste water.

Swan-neck bend: a double bend commonly found in rainwater down pipes.

Thixotropic paint: a paint which does not drip – often called a jelly paint.

Traps, P, S, U: water-filled devices which keep drain smells and draughts out of the house.

Two-pipe system: central heating system where the hot water is fed through one pipe and the cooled water from each radiator is returned by another.

U-value: the figure given to a material to indicate its resistance to the passage of heat.

Urea formaldehyde: heat-setting resins used in certain adhesives.

Vermiculite: a lightweight, granular material used domestically for insulating lofts.

Watt: a unit of power. There are 746 watts in one horsepower.

Metric and Imperial measurements

Note: Conversion is not always straightforward. For example, the metric equivalent of ½in copper tube is not 12.7mm, but 15mm, because metric tube is measured by outside diameter while Imperial tube is measured by the bore.

Length

1 in	= 25.4mm
1 ft	= 30.48cm
1 yd	= 0.9144m

1mm	= 0.03937 in
1cm	= 0.3937 in
1m	= 39.37 in
10mm	= 1cm
100cm	= 1m

Volume

1 cu in	= 16.39cc
1 cu ft	= 0.02832 cu m
1 cu yd	= 0.7646 cu m

1cc	= 0.061 cu in
1 cu m	= 35.315 cu ft
	= 1.308 cu yd

Area

1 sq in	= 6.452 sq cm
1 sq ft	= 0.0929 sq m
1 sq yd	= 0.836 sq m

1 sq cm	= 0.155 sq in
1 sq m	= 10.764 sq ft
	= 1.196 sq yd

Weight

1 oz	= 28.35g
1 lb	= 453.6g
1 cwt	= 50.802kg
1 ton	= 1016kg
	= 1.016 tonnes

1g	= 0.03527 oz
1kg	= 2.2046 lb
	= 35.274 oz
1 tonne	= 2204.6 lb
	= 0.9842 ton

Capacity

1 pt	= 0.568 litre
1 gal	= 4.546 litres

1 litre	= 61.025 cu in
	= 0.22 gal
	= 1.76 pints

Temperature

$1\,°C = 1\frac{4}{5}\,°F$

To convert: temperature T:
$(T+40) \times F-40$
Centigrade to Fahrenheit $F=\frac{9}{5}$
Fahrenheit to Centigrade $F=\frac{5}{9}$

Heat

1 watt	= 3.413 Btu/h
1 kW	= 3413 Btu/h

Index